THE *Ultimate*
CONTAINER
GARDEN

THE *Ultimate* CONTAINER GARDEN

DAVID JOYCE

FRANCES LINCOLN

To Anna

Frances Lincoln Limited
4 Torriano Mews,
Torriano Avenue,
London NW5 2RZ

The Ultimate Container Garden
Copyright © Frances Lincoln
Limited 1996
Text copyright © David Joyce
1996
Planting plans © Frances
Lincoln Limited 1996
First Frances Lincoln edition:
1996

**British Library Cataloguing-
in-Publication Data**
A catalogue record for this
book is available from the
British Library

ISBN 0 7112 1009 8

Printed in Hong Kong

9 8 7 6 5 4

HALF TITLE PAGE *Blue marguerites in
a patterned bowl.*

FRONTISPIECE *A collection of pots
containing abutilon, agapanthus,
petunias, heliotropes and trailing
Scaevola aemula.*

RIGHT *A large pot of hostas provides
a focal point in a formal garden.*

CONTENTS

VERSATILE CONTAINERS

In its long history, reaching back even into antiquity, container gardening has never been as popular as it is today. This is partly because it fits in with so many aspects of modern life. In city centres and other areas where space is at a premium, for many the garden is no more than a small yard, terrace, balcony or rooftop, even a simple window sill. In these settings plants take on a special value and often the only way to grow them successfully is in containers. Householders who have more space increasingly enjoy a relaxed lifestyle in which the distinction between indoor and outdoor living is often blurred. Container-grown plants provide an ideal way of softening a hard-surfaced area, bringing the garden right to the very door of the house.

Whether we choose strong or subtle colours, lavish or simple planting schemes, container-grown plants provide a versatile way of making the places where we live more beautiful. Container gardening is also rewarding in offering both the proficient gardener and the beginner an enjoyable challenge that leaves ample opportunity for individual creativity.

In a small city garden, planting in containers is often the best way to capture the full richness of the passing seasons. This little garden is full of interesting detail, with containers of different materials, shapes, textures and colours placed at strategic points. Large terracotta pots planted with petunias frame a view to a spectacular raised container brimming with plants. Pots of daturas (Brugmansia) and regal lilies (Lilium regale) add to the interest of the foreground planting.

STRONG AND BRIGHT COLOURS

In the wild, it is mainly tropical plants that have flowers of brilliant and intense colour. Thanks to centuries of plant selection and breeding, in temperate regions too we can now choose pelargoniums of vivid pinks or reds, nasturtiums (*Tropaeolum majus*), or African and French marigolds (*Tagetes*) of smouldering and sometimes incandescent oranges, impatiens of polychrome fluorescence and violas and petunias in vibrant, startling colours. Such exotically coloured flowers bring an adventurous glamour to container gardening.

Many of the most colourful flowers are sun-lovers, but there are strong colours, too, for containers in shade. In spring, the gold of daffodils radiates cheerfully from a dark corner. Many camellias have vivid pink or red flowers and rhododendrons and azaleas cover a broader range of colour, from cool blues to burning oranges and reds. For long summer displays, among the most useful of brightly coloured, shade-tolerant plants are tuberous begonias, fuchsias, impatiens, lilies, monkey flowers (*Mimulus*) and pansies (*Viola*). Plants that need strong light to thrive but put up with short periods of shade are also available. Capitalize on this by regularly rotating your displays,

ABOVE *The thickly clustered flowers of the fuchsia 'Thalia' are orange-red and their colour is intensified by the velvety maroon depths of the foliage. Here the pairing with a bright Ivy-leaved pelargonium is calmed by the feathery grey leaves of* Senecio viravira.

LEFT *Of all spring bulbs, tulips provide the widest range of bright colours. They are exceptionally strong in glowing, satiny reds, like those used here with tall Lily-flowered white tulips, rusty wallflowers and blue winter-flowering pansies.*

returning plants such as verbenas and petunias for a rejuvenating spell in full sun after they have served a few days in a shady position.

Dense clusters of clashing bright colours can be jarring. But it is possible to combine clashing colours artfully so that an arrangement makes an impact without overpowering. Modify the effect of clashing colours by using smaller flowers. Introduce a calming influence in the form of a grey-leaved *Helichrysum petiolare* or other foliage plant.

Avoid random mixes of strong colours. Harmonies based on colours close to one another are generally more pleasing. Try orange or brick-red with shades of yellow and lemon, purple-red and bright pink with mauve, purple and violet with blue. Designs based on contrasting colours can also be successful. Associating red with complementary green or pairing yellow and violet will almost always create a pleasant effect.

In the end, whether strong colours appeal is a matter of personal taste, but they will transform a dull setting into a cheerful and eye-catching one. Always use them with discrimination. Vibrant colours that work well in a single pot may seem overwhelming when repeated in several containers. Brilliant colours that sizzle agreeably under a tropical sky can shock where the sunlight is less intense. In soft, moisture-filtered light, the quieter colours, pallid under a blazing sun, reveal their full subtlety.

ABOVE *Many of the summer-flowering Ivy-leaved pelargoniums have flame-red flowers, but the lustrous rich green of their leaves is cooling.* Bidens ferulifolia *produces airy sprays of golden stars.*

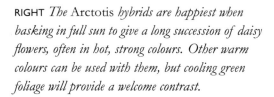

RIGHT *The* Arctotis *hybrids are happiest when basking in full sun to give a long succession of daisy flowers, often in hot, strong colours. Other warm colours can be used with them, but cooling green foliage will provide a welcome contrast.*

LEFT *A flight of steps leading into a garden provides a dramatic staging for a cool colour scheme. The matched plain terracotta pots are planted with the white-flowered marguerite* (Argyranthemum), *a plant that gives an unflagging summer display of neat flowers over feathery leaves.*

BELOW *Two matched plantings provide a cool study in mauve and purple. The larger container is dominated by verbenas combined with the lilac hibiscus* (Alyogyne huegelii) *and the blue marguerite* (Felicia amelloides). *In the smaller pot grey-leaved* Plecostachys serpyllifolia *trails beneath mauve* Nemesia caerulea.

SOFT AND COOL COLOURS

Soft flower colours range through pastel shades of pink, mauve, yellow and blue to pale tints of blush, cream and lavender. White and pale blue are the coolest of these colours. Pale flower colours can be successfully allied with the many shades of foliage green, which, with their contrasts of texture, provide some of the loveliest and most restful components of the container garden.

These subtle colours show well in diffused and subdued light. They are also the easiest to live with on intimate terms, making them especially valuable in the confined space of a small patio. Soft colours blend readily with many building materials and look pleasing against stonework

or weathered brick. Pale colours and white inspire a buoyant mood in large and small gardens and can give a sense of space where buildings, trees and shrubs seem to crowd in. Their luminosity in the failing light of evening lends a garden or courtyard a ghostly beauty that continues long after the sun has set.

The dramatic confrontations that make vibrant colours difficult to combine do not occur with the softer range in the gardener's palette. Random mixtures of soft colours can be very appealing, although more sophisticated designs are best based on harmonious associations of closely related colours or on subtle contrasts. Among the most

successful contrasts are those using pale yellows and soft blues. Pinks, mauves and pale blues also work well together and complement pots of weathered grey stone.

Another design option is a single-colour scheme, a device which can be used as a unifying theme in a garden. The repetition of a single colour in a collection of planted containers strikes a formal note. White, especially, gives a clean and precise finish and there are innumerable white flowers to fill containers. Window boxes and pots of white spring bulbs – snowdrops, crocuses, daffodils and tulips – can be replaced in summer by lavish plantings of white marguerites (*Argyranthemum*), petunias, flowering tobacco plants (*Nicotiana*) and verbenas, as well as foliage plants with cool variegation.

ABOVE *Pastel shades of pink, blue and yellow mingle easily but another component is needed to give drama. In this country garden a dramatic effect has been created by planting creamy yellow* Anthemis tinctoria *'E. C. Buxton' in a dark ceramic pot placed at the intersection of two paths.*

Alternatively, consider a sequence of colour schemes, starting with a mixed theme in spring, moving on to white and then perhaps to yellow for late summer and autumn. Or add light touches of another colour to a mainly monochrome scheme. For example, hints of cream, blue or blushing pink will relieve the starkness of a white scheme without detracting from the overall impression of white. Silver foliage will set off a predominantly pink scheme.

11

THEATRICAL IMPACT

Any planting that makes a strong and immediate visual impact will heighten the drama of a garden. Use such a planting to provide an eye-catching individual feature within a large garden, or to turn a city plot or a small courtyard into an extravagant outdoor room set. Placing a theatrical planting in a container allows it to be positioned exactly where it will attract the most attention.

Often, the most dramatic effect is created by a single plant of shapely form, such as a Japanese aralia (*Fatsia japonica*), or one that is exotic in character, like the slightly tender daturas (*Brugmansia*), positioned to make an impression. Alternatively, groups of pots, tubs and planters can be brought together in a collection in which the role of individual pots is subordinated to the overall scheme. Yet another way to create theatrical extravagance is by mixing plants in a layered arrangement in a single container so that they combine the lax charm of a sumptuous border with the artful flourish of a lavish flower arrange-

ment. Although mixed plantings on a grand scale offer the stiffest challenges – and the most satisfying rewards – of container gardening, they are within the competence of even novice gardeners. The most important ingredient is a dash of creative flair.

Any large or medium-sized container can be used for an extravagant planting, provided that it is stable and holds sufficient potting compost to anchor and sustain the plants. Avoid light or narrow-based containers, which, when densely planted, are vulnerable in high winds. Wooden half-barrels, Versailles tubs, large terracotta pots and stone jars or urns all lend themselves to extravagant planting.

A lavishly planted container will fail to make its full dramatic effect unless well placed. In a formal layout, choose a prime location such as the endpoint of a major vista. In a courtyard, make it the focus of an informal cluster of pots. Use a plinth or improvised base to raise a handsomely planted container to the commanding position it deserves.

LEFT *The converging bars of a metal arbour focus attention on a magnificent display of plants imaginatively assembled in a huge terracotta pot. Off centre but dominating is* Melianthus major, *with jagged grey-green leaves. Beneath it are New Zealand flaxes* (Phormium), *marguerites* (Argyranthemum foeniculaceum) *and pelargoniums, all woven together by the trailing stems of a grey-leaved helichrysum.*

RIGHT *Layered arrangements feature prominently in this garden, where formal elements contrast with loose planting. In the centre background a topiary sweet bay with a twisted stem is underplanted with gold-laced polyanthus and black violas. In the foreground, mophead boxes are ringed by dwarf butterfly flowers* (Schizanthus), *matching a candy-pink ranunculus.*

EFFECTIVE SIMPLICITY

There are often practical reasons for restricting the range of plants grown in a container. Cultivation is simplified and it is easier to maintain displays that change with the seasons. However, the prime reason for growing plants or groups of the same kind of plants in individual containers is aesthetic. Seen in isolation, the character of a plant's flowers, the architecture of its branches and the subtlety or boldness of its foliage can be fully appreciated.

Many plants of distinctive character need to be displayed alone to be seen to best advantage. This is true for certain shrubs as well as for good foliage perennials – including grasses, hostas and ferns – and some bulbs. The beautifully irregular Japanese maples (*Acer palmatum*) make magnificent solitary container shrubs for sheltered gardens. The sword-like leaves of the evergreen New Zealand flaxes (*Phormium*) make bold clumps for sunny positions and can be equally effective when used as focal points or as components of a container grouping.

Plants, such as box (*Buxus sempervirens*), that are trimmed into topiary shapes, usually look best without the clutter of additional plants. Box can be pruned into fanciful shapes, but for a smart, tailored look just trim it into simple cones, pyramids and balls. Specimens of topiary can be distributed at regular intervals along a path or clustered into groups, but the plants themselves need to be grown in individual pots.

The dwarf bulbs of late winter or early spring have a season that is quite brief but so special that they are worth growing on their own in shallow pots. The refined detail of snowdrops (*Galanthus*) and of the various forms of *Crocus chrysanthus*, as well as the exquisite beauty of autumn-flowering *Cyclamen hederifolium*, stand up well in isolation.

Lilies are some of the loveliest of all summer flowers and they always look best grown alone. To maximize their visual impact, grow them in a nursery area and move them into position in the garden only as they come into flower.

ABOVE *In the eighteenth and nineteenth centuries, when auriculas and other old-fashioned flowers were shown competitively, they were displayed growing individually in plain pots that allowed the plant to speak for itself. Repetition enhances the charm of these small-flowered violas in hand-thrown terracotta pots.*

LEFT *The pale pink buds of the lily 'Mont Blanc' open to radiant white blooms lightly speckled with maroon. This display, standing in isolation, makes a sumptuous effect in an old copper with a rich, sea-green patina.*

OPPOSITE *Few perennials can match the magnificence of large hostas such as* H. sieboldiana *var.* elegans. *The restrained dignity of a bold clump planted in a handsome container makes an effective contrast to a border mixture.*

EYE-CATCHING CONTAINERS

Many containers fulfil their practical role satisfactorily while remaining inconspicuous. A successful planting will obscure the frame of a hanging basket in a miraculously suspended cloud of flowers and foliage. Plastic pots often remain unnoticed when placed among a cluster of other containers, hidden by leaves, flowers and more glamorous pots.

Ornamental containers allow more room for originality. Pots and troughs made of traditional materials such as terracotta, plain wood and stone are perennial favourites, because of their colour and texture. While being quietly decorative, they make an appealing setting for plants. Terracotta containers are often ribbed, fluted, or crisscrossed with a basketweave pattern. These surface decorations or even more elaborate bas reliefs can relieve the severity of a formal planting.

Oversized containers and urns and jars of distinctive shapes and proportions are often best left unplanted, playing a sculptural role in the garden. But if you are filling them with plants, choose those that show off the shape of the container. A cascading clematis creates a flattering

BELOW LEFT *Fanciful colouring and shape can give a container the charm of eccentricity. Although nestling deeply among plants, this pot signals for attention by the muted glow of its mosaic pattern. It is planted with* Lavandula stoechas *subsp.* pedunculata, *which has curious ear-like bracts.*

BELOW RIGHT *A high-shouldered, dark ceramic pot retains its sombre dignity beneath the jagged leaves and airy flower sprays of* Heuchera micrantha *var.* diversifolia *'Palace Purple'.*

off-the-shoulder effect in a tall vase, while a mixture of bushy and spreading plants such as diascias, pelargoniums and fuchsias gives a satisfying fullness to a wide urn. Place shapely containers carefully so that their form is seen to best advantage, or isolate a large pot or urn, giving it additional height and importance by setting it on a plinth or an upturned pot.

Strongly coloured containers can be deliberately used to give a planting scheme more depth or dash. Capitalize on the green patina of an old copper by planting it with amber and gold tulips and wallflowers (*Erysimum*). Containers can be painted to match a specific colour scheme. This is often done with wooden window boxes, so they echo the colours of the exterior paintwork of a building. Large tubs painted black and white make fine bases for formally shaped trees such as the Portugal laurel (*Prunus lusitanica*). Abstract or representational decoration is usually most successful when the shape of the pot is stronger than the colour or the decoration – for example, in large jars ornamented with oriental motifs. Boldly coloured and decorated containers can be used as structural components in the garden. Try placing a single, vividly coloured pot, perhaps filled with a plain foliage plant such as the bamboo *Fargesia murieliae*, at a focal point.

BELOW LEFT *The basketweave pattern and minimal planting of dwarf box* (Buxus sempervirens '*Suffruticosa*') *relieves the severe form of this impressive weathered stone container on its matching plinth and paving stones.*

BELOW RIGHT *A lively pattern of arches makes a buoyant motif around the wide basin of a terracotta urn planted with the variegated ground elder* Aegopodium podagraria '*Variegatum*' *and framed by a hop* (Humulus lupulus '*Aureus*').

17

CONTAINERS IN FORMAL GARDENS

Formal gardens are generally based on a symmetrical geometric ground plan, often with a generous use of hard surfaces. Planted containers may be positioned to emphasize the geometry and at the same time to relieve the severity of the layout. In small formal gardens they are especially useful, since they overcome the difficulty of planting where there is no soil. Position containers wherever they are most effective, keeping in mind the amount of light available. Placed at focal points they draw the eye; paired, they form a frame; repeated at regular intervals, they establish a rhythm.

Using paired containers is a simple device that works in gardens of any period. Flanking a garden feature with matching containers gives it importance in the overall design. Position paired containers as sentries at gateways and doorways, adding to their significance, or give visual weight to a simple garden bench by placing planted pots on either side of it.

Paired containers can also be used to frame a view, provided they and their plants are large enough to draw the eye. Place a pair of urns outside a window to create a channelled vista along a chosen axis. The scale must be in keeping with the feature that terminates the view. Use paired containers to mark a change of level, setting them on either side at the bottom and top of a flight of steps. In a garden that is almost entirely flat, they will add drama to even a single step.

LEFT *You can focus attention on a garden feature by positioning matched planted containers on either side of it. Here, a pair of pots planted with tall* Lilium regale *is reinforced with* Hosta sieboldiana *var.* elegans. *Although the hostas are out of scale with the arbour they flank, the piles of overlapping blue-green leaves make a strong formal statement.*

RIGHT *These planted containers are arranged with fastidious symmetry. The components are centred on a wall fountain that is almost concealed by the vigorous growth of a large golden hop.*

LEFT *This formal walkway shows how, even on a small scale, a rhythm can be created by repeating paired plantings at regular intervals. Running alongside a brick path are miniature beds planted with evergreen box. Placed between them and echoing their rhythm are terracotta pots filled with white petunias. The petunia flowers and the loose shapes of the box – more often seen tightly clipped – introduce an unruly element, but the restricted colour scheme underscores the formality.*

A formal garden's geometric plan generally dictates where decorative elements should be placed. In flat gardens, where there is little opportunity to take advantage of views, a single planted container of suitable scale makes an ideal eye-catcher to close a vista. An old lead cistern or a modern replica set against a wall might work well in a small garden. Where a more dramatic effect is desired, place a large urn on a plinth (which can be as simple as a stack of unmortared bricks). This platform will help to show off the shape of the urn and the planting, making a strong focal point. Such a planted urn needs the uniform background of a hedge or wall to block out the distracting detail of the landscape beyond.

Single containers, especially when mounted on a base, make impressive centrepieces for the round, square or rectangular beds that are the main components of formal gardens and for the intersection of paths. The repetition of matching containers reinforces the geometry of a formal garden, especially when the planting is also repeated, whether it is loose and flowing or more severely tailored.

A single line of evenly spaced containers can make an emphatic statement. An ideal position for a matched collection of beautiful urns or latticework terracotta pots is a low wall or balustrade that creates an internal division. To make a stately procession along one side of a walkway, set large pots with restrained planting at regular intervals.

Even spacing is the key to other groupings of containers in formal gardens. Instead of placing an urn or a large pot as a centrepiece in an open space where paths meet, arrange matching containers at points of the compass

around the periphery of the area. Embellish a formal ornamental pool with containers at its four corners. As moveable ornaments, containers also offer the best solution for relieving the blank rectangle of a swimming pool.

A variety of containers can be used successfully in formal gardens. Traditional shapes and materials are most appropriate when trying to reflect a particular historical style. The clean-cut wooden planters known as Versailles tubs suggest classical French formality. In an Italianate garden it is better to use large terracotta pots of simple form. Where an opulent effect is required, stemmed urns with broad basins allow lavish planting.

To complete the pleasing proportions of a formal garden, choose containers of an appropriate size and also keep the planting in scale. Plants of regular shape are often the

ABOVE *Large containers, planted on a grand scale, are needed to match grand architecture. The plantings in these terracotta pots, evenly spaced across a courtyard, have a cordyline making a jagged crown, exotic purple-leaved and red-flowered cannas and a full skirt of pelargoniums and tobacco flowers (Nicotiana).*

first choice for containers in formal gardens. The most regimented of all are topiary specimens clipped geometrically, the simple evergreen forms giving the garden a parade-ground precision year-round. For more colourful flowering uprights in summer, use standards of familiar plants such as fuchsias and less common plants such as the yellow-flowered *Lantana camara*, which lend themselves to layered arrangements. On a smaller scale, some bulbs, especially hyacinths and tulips, have a decidedly military air.

INFORMAL EFFECTS

In informal gardens, straight lines are replaced by curves and symmetry gives way to a more fluid, but still balanced, distribution of space. Not all informally arranged spaces are large, rambling gardens with meandering paths. Decked and paved areas also often have asymmetrical and informal layouts, when containers can be moved around to suit changing needs.

To create an informal effect, the plants are more important than the pots and tubs containing them. Draw on all the variations available among the wealth of container plants to make lively and informal planting combinations. Contrast plants that differ in scale and character, for example, tall bamboos such as *Fargesia nitida* with the much laxer low-growing grass *Hakonechloa macra* 'Aureola'. Put upright plants together with those of spreading or bushy growth: lilies, say, with petunias and verbenas. Mix good foliage plants, such as the glossy-leaved and evergreen *Choisya ternata*, with tireless flowerers such as marguerites (*Argyranthemum*).

Introduce variety in the shape and size of containers. A large container surrounded by a flock of small ones creates a pleasing hen-and-chickens effect. Differences in height can be emphasized by the way containers are staged. Use plant stands with an overspill of pots clustered around their base. A similar effect can be created with containers arranged on a flight of steps, but the pots and tubs must be carefully grouped so as not to present a hazard. Where several hanging baskets are suspended from a pergola or

LEFT *Interlocking shapes and blending colours give this informal cluster of containers .coherence. The shades of blue, mauve and pink in Swan River daisies* (Brachyscome iberidifolia), *diascias, salvias and verbenas make a pleasing harmony.*

ABOVE RIGHT *Tulips, so often regimented for spring displays, can also help to create a relaxed and casual mood in the garden, especially when they come in this soft shade of apricot. Here, late tulips and a hosta are tucked into the base of an arching bamboo.*

RIGHT *The best informal arrangements look as though they have happened quite by chance. This calm assembly of simple pots is based on an uncomplicated colour theme of white, in cosmos, grey, in the elegantly cut leaves of* Senecio viravira, *and violet, in lobelia.*

porch, vary their height to avoid any monotony. At ground level, grouping containers of different colour and texture can add to the charm of a cluster. Set a glazed ceramic jar among plain terracotta pots, or mix wicker baskets with wooden tubs.

While it is appealing to have potted plants distributed throughout a large garden, in a courtyard, patio or decked area where space is relatively restricted, containers cannot be distributed with such abandon. Room must be left for people to move about and for garden furniture. Stray containers are likely to get in the way. For practical reasons, it is a good idea to place pots together and there is much to be said aesthetically for an almost random collection of pots and tubs. Use such a grouping to form a narrow border of fluctuating depth along one side of a courtyard, or to create an eddy in a corner of a terrace.

CONTAINERS TO DRESS BUILDINGS

The embellishment of architectural details by container-grown plants offers many exciting possibilities and well-planted containers can also relieve the dullness of blank walls and mask commonplace or unsightly domestic buildings such as sheds.

Container-grown plants can be placed at ground level, by windows and on balconies, hung from fixtures on walls or from porticoes, or suspended above doorways. Simple forms of dressing might use only one kind of container – a window box or a set of window boxes, for example. More ambitious schemes might coordinate plantings in a range of containers – including troughs, pots, window boxes and hanging baskets – at every level of a façade.

At ground level, a simple but effective way of enhancing the front of a building is to position paired containers with matching planting on either side of a door or window. The geometric shapes of topiary specimens can reflect the regularity of a symmetrical façade. Softer planting, using trained standards, shrubs such as the mophead hydrangeas and tubs of spring bulbs or summer annuals, will spruce up a rambling or characterless building.

The rigid lines of a building surrounded by hard surfaces can be softened by a narrow border of container-grown plants. At its simplest, the border might be a row of potted pelargoniums along a street front, but it can be elaborated to include containers of varying sizes arranged two or three deep and stacked at different levels.

The classic way of dressing buildings is with window boxes and balconies filled with containers. The most suitable plants are those that are tolerant of wind, such as short-stemmed daffodils, dwarf tulips and compact cultivars of popular bedding plants. A window box filled with exquisite beauties such as dwarf bulbs will give intense pleasure when viewed from inside. Balconies can also provide the setting for intimate gardens seen at their best from inside, but they really come into their own for impressive hanging gardens using elegant trailing plants such as the grey-leaved foliage plant *Helichrysum petiolare* and nasturtiums (*Tropaeolum majus*). Grow plants in troughs or in pots attached to the surround of a balcony.

ABOVE *In this hanging basket, a welcoming touch at a doorway, soft yellow trailing begonias and* Cuphea ignea *spill over speckled leaves of* Tolmiea menziesii *'Taff's Gold' and pale lobelia.*

OPPOSITE *Clipped standards and white to cream flowers – roses, lilies, pansies and hippeastrums – are grouped around shuttered windows to make a pleasing display from inside and out.*

ABOVE *In some settings the simpler the touch the better. Here a tiny shutter fastened back leaves a simple rustic frame as a perfect border to a single potted pelargonium.*

SUCCESSFUL GARDENING IN CONTAINERS

Foliage and flowering plants that range in size from ground-hugging miniatures to large shrubs and even trees can be grown easily in the vast range of containers available. Even novice gardeners will be rewarded with success if they follow the few simple guidelines that ensure the right conditions for vigorous and healthy plant growth, especially in terms of good drainage, water and food.

The following chapter brings together all the practical information essential to satisfy the demands of plants grown in confined containers. It includes advice on the containers themselves, with suggestions for improvisations as well as decorative finishes. It gives illustrated guides to all the main techniques for planting a wide range of containers with different types of plants. There is guidance, too, on general maintenance, including pruning and training, and how best to deal with problems caused by pests and diseases. For the many gardeners who take pleasure in raising their own plants and increasing stocks, it explains the main methods of propagation. In short, this chapter provides all the background information needed to make a successful container garden.

This garden path is lined with a wonderful collection of terracotta containers, some planted, some waiting to be filled. Apart from skill in marrying plant shapes with the right pot or planter, what distinguishes container gardening is the critical role of the gardener in satisfying the needs of plants at every stage of the growing season.

CONTAINER CHOICE

Garden containers are manufactured from various materials – at one extreme of the price range cheap plastic and at the other end marble and bronze – and all are available in a wide range of shapes and sizes. The essential requirements of containers are simple: they must hold enough potting compost for plants to root securely and to supply sufficient moisture and nutrients to sustain growth; they must have drainage holes to allow excess moisture to escape, so that the mix does not become stagnant; and they must be reasonably stable. Cost, appearance and a few additional practical considerations will therefore influence your choice.

All planted containers must be either watered by hand or linked to an irrigation system. Plastic and fibreglass are impermeable materials and planters made of them require less frequent watering than those made of porous terracotta. However, terracotta pots can be lined with sheet plastic to conserve moisture.

Heavy containers are more stable than those made from lightweight materials such as plastic and fibreglass. In many cases their extra weight is an advantage, unless the planter needs to be moved about. Choose lightweight containers for rooftops and balconies, or anywhere else where the load-bearing capacity is limited.

Durability matters when containers are expensive. Frost can damage earthenware containers, cracking and lifting glazes and shattering terracotta that has been fired at low temperatures. In frost-prone areas, such pots should always be brought under cover in winter. Corrosion of metal containers can to some extent be halted by chemical treatment, and preservatives can extend the life of wooden containers. Synthetic materials, especially plastics, are easily scrubbed and cleaned to reduce the risk of diseases and pests being carried from one season to the next. Garden hygiene is more difficult to maintain when materials are porous or have rough surfaces.

TERRACOTTA AND GLAZED CONTAINERS

The use of terracotta (literally 'baked earth') to make pots stretches back into antiquity. This material is porous so plants need frequent watering, its surface is difficult to clean, and containers, which shatter easily, are frost-proof only if fired at high temperatures. However, terracotta is visually so appropriate to plants that its shortcomings are easily overlooked. Variations in colour result from different clays or firing temperatures. Pots of glazed earthenware, which are non-porous and easier to clean, rarely tolerate frosts, so their planting and siting require specially careful consideration.

WOOD

Versatile wood is an ideal choice when containers have to be made to measure and is durable if treated with a preservative. It can be used for formal containers, such as classic window boxes and Versailles tubs, as well as for rustic troughs and rugged half-barrels (right).

TERRACOTTA WALL CONTAINERS

Small wall-mounted terracotta containers (below) are suitable for displaying a range of trailing plants. They need to be securely fixed to a support.

STONE AND SUBSTITUTES

Containers made from composition stone and concrete (right) are both more moderately priced and readily available than those of marble and sandstone. They quickly assume a weathered appearance that suggests the patina of natural stone. All these materials are heavy and durable.

PLASTIC AND WIRE-FRAME CONTAINERS

Various wire and plastic frames (above) that hold pots can be attached to walls and railings as well as to drainpipes. Traditional hanging baskets have a galvanized or plastic-coated wire frame, and are used with a liner — as are many wall-mounted metal containers.

PLASTIC

Plastic (left) is now the most widely used material for containers, although there is a strong aesthetic prejudice against it when displaying plants. As well as being cheap, plastic is lightweight and easily cleaned, and the heavy-duty kinds are strong and long-lasting. Rigid plastic containers come in many shapes and sizes; sheet plastic, used in growing bags, can make a liner in other containers such as window boxes.

FIBREGLASS

This light, man-made material can be moulded into a wide variety of shapes (below). It is often used to imitate traditional but expensive materials such as lead and bronze and is very effective when formed in plain, clean-lined shapes. Although somewhat brittle, it is quite durable.

LEAD

Containers of wrought or cast metal — lead, copper, bronze and iron — were extensively used in the past and now help to give a period flavour to a garden. Old lead cisterns and urns have proved remarkably durable but they are expensive and hard to find. Modern pieces (above) usually have a traditional design. Even when new, the subdued silver-grey of the metal tones subtly with foliage and flowers.

MAKING A WOODEN WINDOW BOX

Wood is the most versatile material for made-to-measure containers, and a simple window box or trough can be assembled from precut lengths, even by a gardener who has only basic skills in handling tools. The simple method of construction demonstrated here could easily be adapted to window boxes of different dimensions, although it is unlikely that it would be necessary to alter height and width. The front and back each consist of two lengths simply because narrow widths are easier to obtain than broader ones. The base also consists of two lengths, with a narrow gap in between to allow for drainage. If you are making a window box of a length different from the one illustrated, remember that the base is the same length as the front and back, minus the thickness of the end pieces.

The softwood timber used here provides a practical alternative to expensive seasoned hardwood, such as oak. It is easy to work and its life can be extended if it is treated with a preservative. Have it cut to these dimensions:

Front and back: four lengths of $50 \times 9.5 \times 1.5$cm
($20 \times 3\frac{3}{4} \times \frac{5}{8}$in)
Ends: 2 lengths of $17 \times 19 \times 2.5$cm ($7 \times 7\frac{1}{2} \times 1$in)
Base: 1 length of $45 \times 9.5 \times 1.5$cm ($18 \times 3\frac{3}{4} \times \frac{5}{8}$in)
and 1 length of $45 \times 8 \times 1.5$cm ($18 \times 3 \times \frac{5}{8}$in)
Feet: 3 lengths of $21 \times 5 \times 2.5$cm ($8\frac{3}{8} \times 2 \times 1$in)

ASSEMBLING AND DECORATING A WOODEN WINDOW BOX

1 *Assemble the precut lengths of wood on a suitable surface such as a workbench, together with a hammer and three dozen 4cm (1½in) oval nails.*

2 *Without nailing the wood together, place the base pieces over the feet, allowing a 5mm (¼in) gap between the two lengths, and mark their positions. Check the fit of the end pieces.*

3 *Set front, back and end pieces to one side, then nail the base to the feet, driving in two nails at converging angles where each base piece lies over a foot.*

4 *Put together the main framework, hammering two nails at converging angles through both ends of the front and back to join them to the end pieces.*

5 *When the main framework has been assembled, turn the box upside down and tap into place the base, which you have already put together (stage 3).*

6 *Place the container on its back and at three points nail through the front into the base. Then repeat the same operation for the back of the window box.*

7 *After priming or treating the container with a wood preservative that is non-toxic to plants, apply an undercoat. Allow this to dry.*

8 *Apply an exterior emulsion paint that tones with any adjacent architectural features of the house. A stencil or freehand-painted decoration could be added if wished.*

9 *The finished wooden container is suitable either as a window box or as a trough at ground level. Here it is planted with a combination of French marigolds, zinnias and rudbeckias to create a warm, bright focus on a patio.*

DECORATING POTS

One way to give the container garden an individual stamp is to apply your own decoration to pots, window boxes and tubs. The simplest way of personalizing containers is to paint them, and a painted finish is suitable for a wide range of materials, including wood, terracotta, concrete, plastic and metal. Paint is often applied to make the container fit into an overall architectural colour scheme, but the use of colour and decoration can be much more ambitious than this. A light colour wash can be introduced to make a container tone in with a subtle colour scheme. More assertive decoration can be painted on, either as a single colour or in a mixture of colours, as stripes or borders for example. It is easier to paint stripes if the parts of the pot to be left unpainted are protected with masking tape, as in the three-colour terracotta pot shown on these pages. Paint can easily be reapplied to rectify mistakes.

Using stencils – whether commercially produced or designed by yourself and cut out of sturdy stencil card – provides another way of applying a bold and simple design motif, with one or several different colours. A wide range of other effects can be achieved by introducing spongeware techniques, stippling, gilding or freehand decoration, which can be either representational or abstract. The various methods of decoration can be applied on their own or may be used in combination with one another to produce a more intricate result.

Paint finishes can also be used to imitate the effects of metal, in particular the wonderful patina that weathering produces on old copper or bronze containers, such as the copper shown on page 109. The rich complexity of the patina is suggested by applying several layers of paint of different colours (*see pages 36–7*).

A simple planting is often the most successful choice for a boldly patterned or coloured pot. This compact, purple-flowered lavender (Lavandula angustifolia 'Hidcote') fits well with the striped decoration of its container.

STRIPED DECORATION FOR A TERRACOTTA POT

1 *Ensure that the pot is clean and dry, then apply an even coat of blue emulsion paint on the outside and continue over the top 2.5–5cm (1–2in) of the inside of the container.*

2 *When the paint is dry, fix masking tape around the rim and radiate strips of tape from the base, starting with strips about 5mm (¼in) apart at the bottom of the pot.*

3 *Apply a coat of reddish-brown mat emulsion on the exposed surface of the pot. Leave the masking tape in place until the paint is completely dry.*

4 *If you want to add narrow bands beside the blue stripes, place further strips of masking tape parallel to and just to the right of the strips of tape already in position.*

5 *Apply a coat of cream mat emulsion over the narrow bands of reddish-brown paint that are exposed between the strips of masking tape. Remove the tape gently when the paint is dry.*

6 *The simple pattern on this striped pot is only one of many decorative effects that can be achieved with a variety of techniques using either mat or glossy paints.*

1 *Ensure that the pot is clean and dry before applying dark green mat emulsion on the outside. On the inside, paint to just below the expected potting compost level.*

2 *When the first coat is dry, use a short-haired, dense stippling brush, lightly loaded with paint, to apply blue-green mat emulsion. Define the relief decoration first.*

3 *Allow the blue-green paint to dry. To achieve a rich, shadowed patina, stipple more dark green paint lightly in selected areas. The blue-green colour should show through.*

4 *Apply a thin coat of white mat emulsion. Work quickly and preferably paint a section at a time, so that the next step can be carried out while the paint is wet.*

5 *Using a damp, clean cloth, wipe off excess white paint, leaving only enough to subdue the blue-green colouring and to soften the underlying dark green.*

6 *When assessing the painted pot, keep in mind that you are aiming for an impressionistic effect, and remember that you can always reapply paint if you find the results disappointing.*

It is easier to imitate the rich patina of old copper or bronze on a moulded surface, such as that of this handsome terracotta planter, than on a smooth one. Layers of paint are applied in a way that accentuates highlights and shadows. The stems of a lacecap hydrangea have been individually staked to keep them erect and to ensure a balanced display of the flower heads.

37

UNUSUAL AND RECYCLED CONTAINERS

Decorating purpose-made pots, planters and window boxes in a personal style is one way to give the container garden an individual character. Another is to plant in containers that are themselves highly distinctive or original. This generally means looking outside the vast range of purpose-made containers, although even here items of unusual shape and colouring can be found. Old ceramic jars and bowls, metal colanders, pots and buckets, and baskets of various shapes and sizes are among the many domestic items that can be recycled at negligible expense. Some antique pieces make impressive containers but these items inevitably fetch high prices and in a garden that is not secure they are vulnerable to theft. Examples include wellheads, fonts, sarcophagi, tubs and sinks in marble or lesser stone, as well as copper vats and lead water cisterns or hoppers. Chimney pots are more modest architectural features that make useful focal points in small gardens.

The essential requirement of all containers is that they hold enough potting compost to sustain plants and also have sufficient drainage holes so that the mix never becomes waterlogged. Even when containers already have holes, these often need enlarging so that excess moisture can drain away quickly without the compost becoming soggy. Some materials, including glazed ceramic, are difficult to drill. When drilling might risk damaging a piece, use the vessel simply as a holder; plant up a close-fitting, lightweight pot of a suitable depth and lower it gently inside the more decorative container.

Containers with an open structure, including baskets, are best lined with sheet plastic before planting. Pierce holes in the base to provide drainage. Lining will also help to extend the life of some materials, but it is a good idea to treat basketwork with a preservative or to varnish it with a coat of clear polyurethane as an extra precaution.

The imaginative gardener can give many old household items – including discarded cooking pots, galvanized buckets, milk crates and wicker vegetable baskets – a new lease of life by recycling them as plant containers. Salvaged architectural fragments such as chimney pots can also make distinctive planters. Most recycled containers will need to have drainage holes drilled in the base.

RIGHT *A wooden wheelbarrow is ideal for displaying a movable display of summer flowers.*

BELOW LEFT *Line chimney pots for use as plant containers with sheet plastic, or drop a close-fitting light container into the top. Trailing plants, such as the* Helichrysum petiolare *'Limelight' used here, go well with the tall chimney pot.*

BELOW RIGHT *The texture of basketwork, often imitated in terracotta pots, makes a good contrast to foliage and flowers. Petunias and ivies spill out of this basket.*

LEFT *Zonal pelargoniums play the leading role in an attractive mixture of foliage and flowers planted in an old metal container. Its mat slate-blue band, toning with the silver-grey of an old tree stump, makes an inconspicuous but pleasing base for the plants.*

RIGHT *An old copper makes a substantial yet delightful container for a key position in the garden, by virtue of its size and shape, its regular riveting and the richness of its patina.*

BELOW *Old stone sinks are frequently used as containers for small collections of rock-garden plants. Their beauty is more easily appreciated when sinks are raised well above ground level. This old sink, set high against a wall, contains a less conventional planting, of bright gazanias.*

ABOVE *A lead water cistern, bearing an eighteenth-century date, makes a splendid container for a planting of pelargoniums, argyranthemums and a mixture of foliage plants. Authentic examples of these cisterns – and also nineteenth- and twentieth-century imitations, which often carry bogus dates – are among the most handsome of large containers. They need to be set in position before being filled with potting compost and planted.*

LEFT *Double daisies* (Bellis perennis) *and blue* Scilla siberica *jostle together in a wire basket designed to hold fruit.*

MOVING CONTAINERS

Large containers filled with soil and plants are heavy and unwieldy, so window boxes and planters should be planted in their final positions. If they do need to be moved after planting, allow water to drain from them first.

When containers, compost and plants have to be transported around the garden, mechanical aids will greatly reduce the effort involved. A wheelbarrow is useful for transporting all but very heavy objects, which have to be lifted over the sides. A hand truck is more appropriate but, as it may be needed only infrequently, is best rented. A simple trolley mounted on castors is extremely useful for moving planted containers on a flat surface. Some models are intended to provide a permanent base for pots. Simple rollers, consisting of lengths of pipe or pole about 4–5cm (1½–2in) in diameter, with planks laid on top, provide another way of moving large pots.

A simpler method of moving a heavy item is to drag it, for example on a sheet of heavy-duty plastic sheeting. To negotiate steps, make a short ramp with planks. Move pots with a circular base by rolling, rather than lifting. Enlist the help of a strong person when lifting heavy items; keep your back straight and bend your legs to take the strain.

MOVING PLANTS AND POTS BY WHEELBARROW

LEFT *A wheelbarrow is most useful in a medium-sized or large garden for moving empty containers, bags of potting compost and large numbers of plants. The disadvantage when moving heavy objects is that they need to be lifted over the sides.*

ROLLING A CONTAINER

A PURPOSE-MADE TROLLEY

FAR LEFT *Rolling is the easiest way to move a large pot with a circular base.*

LEFT *A purpose-built or home-made trolley mounted on castors is convenient for moving containers along flat surfaces.*

SECURING CONTAINERS

Containers that are not stable and securely positioned risk being blown or knocked over and, in their fall, may be broken or cause damage and injury. Particular care must be taken with hanging baskets, window boxes and containers on roof gardens.

A freshly watered hanging basket is a heavy item that needs a stout support, strong chains or rope to suspend it and a securely fitted attachment, preferably incorporating a swivel. Wall brackets should have an arm that is long enough for the basket to hang well clear of the wall. A pulley system allows you to lower baskets for watering.

The weight of full window boxes makes them quite stable, but safety provisions must be made for those above ground-floor level. A tailor-made safety rail can be inconspicuous. If window boxes need to be set below the window, support them on metal brackets with the ends turned up at right angles. This kind of support, firmly fixed to the wall, can be combined with safety chains.

Load-bearing limitations on roof gardens and balconies often dictate the use of light containers and composts. Choose broad-based pots and group them together near walls or screens for maximum shelter.

WINDOW BOX SAFETY

RAISING POTS ON SUPPORTS

SUPPORTING A HANGING BASKET

ABOVE LEFT *Safety must be a priority with a window box such as this one, unusually positioned above a door. Brackets hold it firmly in position.*

ABOVE RIGHT *All containers that do not have built-in feet or ridged bottoms should be set on low supports, either purpose made or improvised from bricks, stones or wood, so that water can drain away freely.*

LEFT *A sturdy bracket is needed to take the weight of a freshly watered hanging basket. The bracket used to support this basket is a substantial ornamental feature in its own right. The arm is long enough to hold the hanging basket well clear of the wall.*

43

PLANTING EQUIPMENT

Very little equipment is needed for container gardening. It is worth buying tools of good quality, selecting well-made containers and using a planting medium formulated for containers and the range of plants you want to grow.

GARDEN TOOLS

Although it may be handy to have a range of tools, only a few are essential. The two most useful items are a trowel and a hand fork. Secateurs are needed for pruning woody plants; both those with a scissor-like action and anvil models are suitable. The blades must be kept sharp. Hedge shears are necessary only if you have to clip topiary. Kitchen scissors are ideal for clipping the stems of most annuals and perennials.

Many gardeners feel lost without a folding knife, either straight-bladed or with a curved blade for pruning, but a small kitchen knife is a useful substitute. The gardener also needs a watering can and a simple trigger-pump sprayer. Additional useful items include labels, a selection of bamboo and split canes, garden twine and ties. Old kitchen spoons and forks make handy supplementary tools. When large, heavy containers are planted up, some equipment to facilitate moving is desirable (see page 42).

POTTING COMPOSTS

Ready-mixed potting composts, which are well aerated and also water retentive, contain a balanced supply of nutrients and are free of weed seeds as well as soil-borne pests and diseases. Gardeners can prepare their own composts but space is needed to sterilize loam and mix ingredients and savings are made only when the materials are bought in bulk.

There are two main categories of ready-mixed potting compost: soil-based and soil-less. The principal component of soil-based composts is sterilized loam, which is usually mixed with peat and coarse sand, as well as a balanced supply of nutrients. The John Innes formulations, devised by the John Innes Horticultural Institute, cover seed and cutting mixes and three strengths of potting mix: No. 1, for seedlings and cuttings; No. 2, for general purpose; and No. 3, for very vigorous growers. For plants intolerant of lime there is a special ericaceous compost. Rock-garden plants need a lean diet such as one part No. 1 mixed with one to two parts grit.

Until recently, most soil-less potting composts were based on peat, but concern at the environmental impact of large-scale exploitation of peat reserves has led to experimentation with other materials, including bark and coconut fibre. Soil-less composts are available in a range that includes seed, cuttings, standard, all-purpose (sold as suitable for seeds and cuttings as well as for general use) and ericaceous composts. They are light, clean to use, and usually cheaper than soil-based ones. Their nutrient levels fall relatively quickly, however, so that in a normal growing season plants require additional fertilizer (see page 65), and they tend to dry out quickly and are then difficult to re-wet, yet become waterlogged if overwatered.

A trowel is indispensable for the container gardener. A narrow-bladed one is an advantage when working on a small scale but a standard model suits most purposes. A hand fork, secateurs, kitchen scissors and a folding knife are among the tools most useful in the container garden.

ABOVE *Soil-less composts are lightweight, so they are ideal for hanging baskets.*

RIGHT *Plants that are intolerant of lime, including rhododendrons (here* Rhododendron *'Bow Bells'), ling and some heaths, require an ericaceous compost.*

ABOVE *Rock-garden plants need free drainage and they retain their compact growth on a lean diet. Add grit to a soil-based compost low in nutrients.*

LEFT *Soil-based composts maintain their nutrient levels well. Use them for long-term planting and to give stability. This standard* Hydrangea paniculata *needs weight to counterbalance its top growth.*

PLANTING A TREE OR LARGE SHRUB

The enduring beauty of trees and large shrubs gives the container garden an air of maturity. Many of these distinctive plants are easily grown and, once they have been satisfactorily planted, their main requirement is a regular supply of water.

Container-grown specimens can be planted at almost any time of year, although planting in autumn or spring generally gives the best results. The dormant season, however, is best for planting bare-root trees (almost invariably deciduous) and root-balled specimens (often evergreens), which have roots and surrounding soil wrapped in a material such as hessian. Both these types should be planted in the same way as container-grown specimens, except that in the case of root-balled plants the wrapping must be removed from the roots while planting.

For trees and large shrubs, the stability of the planter is important, as is its size. A tub or pot about twice the width and depth of the root ball will allow room for roots to develop and will hold sufficient reserves of nutrients and moisture to sustain healthy growth. Avoid using lightweight containers and those with a narrow base.

Use a soil-based potting compost (lime-free for trees and shrubs that need it), to which a slow-release fertilizer has been added. Standard trees may need staking, in which case insert the stake before planting and secure it to the tree with a buckle-and-spacer tie.

A tall jar, distinguished by its texture and pale green glaze, makes a handsome container for a purple-leaved Japanese maple (Acer palmatum f. atropurpureum). *Since the narrow base of the container is potentially unstable, it must be positioned in a sheltered spot where it is not exposed to strong winds.*

PLANTING A JAPANESE MAPLE

1 *Scrub the terracotta pot, then soak it thoroughly in clean water. If possible, position it in its final site before filling with potting compost, because it will be difficult to move once planted. Put crocks over the drainage holes.*

2 *Fill the pot about one-third full with a soil-based potting compost to which a slow-release fertilizer has been added. Japanese maples thrive in lime-free composts, such as those specially formulated for ericaceous plants.*

3 *Holding the young tree more or less horizontal, ease it out of its original pot, taking care to keep the root ball intact (it is important to check a tree before purchase to see that it is not potbound, for such a specimen will not establish well).*

4 *Set the tree carefully in the new container, gently loosening the root ball. Add potting compost until, when firmed, the tree is at the same depth that it was growing at previously, as indicated by the soil mark on its stem.*

5 *Ensure that the tree remains upright while adding more compost, working it around the roots and firming the tree in. When finished, the level of the potting compost should be 2.5–5cm (1–2in) below the rim of the container.*

6 *Water the planted tree. If it is not already in its final position, do not attempt to move the pot until it has drained fully. Each spring, remove the top 2.5–5cm (1–2in) of potting compost and replace with fresh compost.*

PLANTING BULBS

Bulbs are neatly packaged stores of plant energy that are easy to handle. Whether they are true bulbs (such as daffodils) or plants with corms (crocus) or tubers (cyclamen), most are planted when they are dormant, the main season being autumn. In most cases, they predictably produce a gladdening display several months later without having made any serious demands on the gardener. Snowdrops can also be planted as dry bulbs in autumn, but they are among a small group of bulbs that do better when planted immediately after flowering, while still in leaf.

Since most bulbs require good drainage, the container must have adequate drainage holes. It also needs to be of sufficient depth. Crocuses and other small bulbs should be set 5–8cm (2–3in) deep, while, at the other extreme, stem-rooting lilies, such as *Lilium regale*, require 15–20cm (6–8in) of potting compost above the bulb.

Plant only healthy and undamaged bulbs, preferably in a soil-based potting compost. For bulbs needing particularly sharp drainage, add grit or coarse sand. Provided they are watered regularly, well nourished when in active growth, and allowed to die down naturally, many bulbs will flower satisfactorily in subsequent years. But there is generally a loss of flower quality in daffodils, hyacinths and tulips, making it worth planting fresh bulbs each year.

The sweetly scented, bunch-flowered Tazetta narcissi are much used for forcing, succeeding outdoors only in very mild areas. Some hybrids, including the frilly-centred 'Cragford', are hardier and a dense planting makes a full, wonderfully fragrant display.

PLANTING DAFFODILS IN LAYERS

1 *Plant in early autumn, covering the base of the container with a layer of drainage material 2.5–5cm (1–2in) deep.*

2 *Put in potting compost to a depth of 5–8cm (2–3in) and plant the first layer of bulbs, about 5cm (2in) apart.*

3 *Cover the bulbs with more compost, then plant a second layer above the gaps left between bulbs in the first layer.*

4 *Add more potting compost to a level about 2.5cm (1in) below the container's rim. Gently firm the compost, and water.*

PLANTING TULIPS IN A POT

Plant in late autumn, 2.5–5cm (1–2in) apart, in one or two layers, according to the depth available.

Tulips add a touch of spring glamour to a permanent planting of box in an old copper container (right).

PLANTING LILIES

1 *Place a generous layer of drainage material in the base of the container before planting lilies singly or in small groups.*

2a *Plant stem-rooting lilies about 15–20cm (6–8in) deep to allow for the development of roots above the bulb.*

2b *Plant basal-rooting lilies, which produce no roots above the bulbs, about 10–15cm (4–6in) deep.*

The stem-rooting regal lily (Lilium regale) *is an easy bulb to grow and its magnificent trumpets are richly scented.*

PLANTING A BASKET OF IVY AND CROCUSES

1 *Plant dwarf bulbs in early autumn. Line a wicker basket about 20cm (8in) across with plastic sheeting, slitting the plastic for drainage.*

2 *Half-fill the basket with potting compost, then plant in it three small-leaved ivies. Evenly space them around the perimeter of the basket.*

3 *Insert 10 crocus corms, about 5cm (2in) deep, between the ivy plants. Add potting compost until it reaches a level about 2.5cm (1in) below the rim of the container when gently firmed.*

4 *The ivy foliage is attractive all winter, and in late winter or early spring the crocuses will push through its variegated leaves, opening their goblet-shaped flowers in warm sunlight.*

PLANTING SMALL BULBS

Plant spring-flowering small bulbs such as puschkinias or scillas in early autumn. For a dense display set the bulbs close, but not touching, at a depth of about 5cm (2in).

PLANTING WINDOW BOXES

The classic sequence for window box displays consists of an autumn planting of bulbs for spring and a late spring or early summer planting of long-season summer flowers that will continue blooming until early autumn, or even later. Many variations can be introduced by using, for example, shrubs for a long-term display or making several changes between spring and autumn. If frequent changes are contemplated, it is worth having two rigid liners per window box. While one is used for the current display, the other can be planted in readiness for the changeover.

To plant a window box or rigid liner, follow the method demonstrated on these pages for the small terracotta trough, which is filled with a hart's-tongue fern (*Asplenium scolopendrium*) and New Guinea hybrid impatiens for a shady position. If there are no drainage holes in a window box or they are too small for good drainage, they must be pierced or enlarged (*see page 55*). A plastic sheet liner may be useful for some boxes, because it will slow down water loss in a terracotta window box and extend the life of a wooden one (*see page 54*). It is often easier to plant a window box on a bench or open area in the garden before placing it in position. Heavy window boxes and those that would be awkward to manoeuvre are better positioned before being filled.

PLANTING A SMALL TERRACOTTA WINDOW BOX

1 *After scrubbing the window box and soaking it in clean water, put crocks over the drainage holes to prevent any potting compost being washed out.*

2 *Cover the bottom of the window box with a layer of gravel 2.5–5cm (1–2in) deep to ensure good drainage. A layer of crocks is a suitable alternative.*

3 *Half-fill the window box with a soil-less potting compost. In this case granules of a slow-release fertilizer have already been added to the potting compost.*

4 *Without removing plants from their pots, arrange them in different ways until you find a satisfactory layout. Keep in mind the formal design on the front of the window box.*

5 *Ease the fern out of its pot, gently loosen its roots, and position it in the centre of the window box. Work potting compost around the roots until the fern is planted at its original depth.*

6 *Insert a New Guinea hybrid impatiens on one side of the fern, removing or adding compost until the impatiens is set at its original depth.*

7 *To create the symmetry of this formal arrangement, position a similar hybrid impatiens at the front of the container, to the other side of the fern.*

8 *Continue planting symmetrically, with New Guinea hybrid impatiens at the back of the window box and variegated plectranthus in the front corners.*

9 *Add potting compost so that when it is gently firmed the surface is about 2.5cm (1in) below the box's rim. Water thoroughly, then allow the window box to drain before positioning it.*

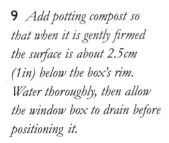

PLANTING A PLASTIC-LINED WOODEN WINDOW BOX

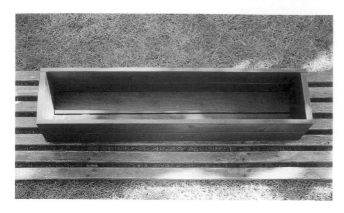

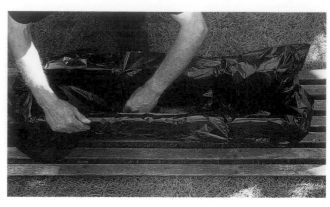

1 *Wooden window boxes are constructed in a variety of ways. The drainage is sometimes provided by a central slit instead of by a series of small holes.*

2 *Lining the box with sheet plastic may prolong the life of a wooden container. Place the plastic in position, allowing a generous overlap, and make slits in its base.*

3 *Cover the bottom of the container with drainage material, such as crocks and a layer of washed gravel about 2.5cm (1in) deep. Half-fill the box with a soil-less potting compost.*

4 *Without removing the plants from their pots, position them so that they are displayed to best effect. Begin planting, starting with the key plant of the arrangement – here, a tellima.*

5 *Position the other plants – pansies, monkey flowers and creeping jenny – around the tellima. Firm gently, adding compost to a level about 2.5cm (1in) below the rim of the window box.*

6 *When the planting has been completed, trim the sheet plastic to just above the rim and neatly tuck in the remainder down the sides of the window box.*

Dark-centred rudbeckias dominate the planting in this simple wooden window box, whose own trailing ivy merges with the ivy that clothes the house front. But it is the contrasts in flower size that give this cheerful, single-colour theme its special charm. The window box itself is supported on brackets below the sill, so that plants do not cut out too much light from the room.

PREPARING A PLASTIC WINDOW BOX FOR PLANTING

Plastic window boxes are often sold with the drainage holes marked but not pierced. Use a sharp implement, such as a screwdriver, to make holes where indicated.

Some plastic window boxes have sides that bow slightly inwards when empty, but these will expand when they are filled with potting compost and plants.

PLANTING HANGING BASKETS

Hanging baskets are generally most effective when planted with bushy and trailing plants that overwhelm and obscure the container. Planting through the sides and top of a hanging basket – easy to do with wire-framed baskets – makes the plant cover even more complete. If you are using the traditional lining material, sphagnum moss (increasingly replaced by substitutes), simply make a hole in it and work young plants through to the potting compost underneath. When using rigid, preformed liners, cut holes for trailers. Most of the other liners, made from materials such as matted fibres, foam plastic and wadding, come in the form of circular sheets cut radially almost to their centre. The segments formed by these cuts overlap when the liner is laid in the basket. Planting through the sides of the hanging basket is best done where sections overlap.

Be practical in choosing a site for your hanging basket. Do not hang it where it will be in the way, and bear in mind how it is to be watered. Avoid exposed positions. There will always be rapid loss of moisture in a breezy location, and high winds could bring a basket down.

The considerable weight of a planted basket makes it essential that it should be securely fixed. While the basket is still empty, try it in the position where it is to hang, make sure that the support is secure, and, if necessary, adjust the lengths of the chains or cords that attach it to its support. Make sure you can reach it for watering.

RIGID LINER

Preformed shapes of various materials come in standard sizes. Positions for holes are usually scored in the sides.

LINER OF MATTED FIBRES

Liners made of matted natural fibres such as coconut are usually cut so that the segments overlap when laid in a basket.

WADDING LINER

Thick liners of natural and synthetic materials are also often cut so that the segments overlap.

LINING A BASKET WITH LOOSE FIBRE

1 *Dyed coconut fibre is a natural lining material with a loose texture similar to that of sphagnum moss, for which it is used as a substitute.*

2 *Tease out the fibre and lay it inside the basket at a uniform thickness. The fibre can be used in conjunction with a plastic sheet pierced for drainage.*

3 *Half-fill the basket with a soil-less potting compost. Push plants through the sides and gently firm them in before adding more compost.*

PLANTING A SHEET-LINED BASKET WITH TRAILING PLANTS

1 *Support the hanging basket during planting by resting it on an empty bucket or an upturned pot. Place a liner (a synthetic capillary matting liner is used here) in the basket and arrange so that the segments overlap.*

2 *Mix granules of slow-release fertilizer with a soil-less potting compost. These are better suited to hanging baskets than composts that are soil-based because they are lighter. Half-fill the basket with compost. Do not compact by pressing.*

3 *To ensure that the frame is covered, plant trailers in the side of the basket where the liner segments overlap. Use a pair of scissors or a sharp knife to make a small lateral cut in the edge of the liner so that plants can be inserted easily.*

4 *Using both hands, work the root system of a trailing plant such as a lobelia through the liner where the cut has been made. Add potting compost around the roots and firm lightly. Repeat this operation at intervals around the basket.*

5 *Add about 5cm (2in) of compost before planting the top of the basket. A large, bushy plant such as impatiens makes a good centrepiece. Begin with this, working compost around its roots and firming gently before putting in other plants.*

6 *Complete planting from the top, making sure that plants are positioned to give a balanced display. Work potting compost around the roots and firm gently. Add compost so that the final level is just below the basket's rim.*

7 *When planting is finished, remove any damaged leaves and stems, and then water the basket thoroughly. Leave standing for about 10 minutes while excess water drains away before moving the basket to the position where it will hang.*

PLANTING ROCK GARDEN PLANTS

Many of the exquisite dwarf plants that thrive in mountainous areas and other rocky places can be cultivated successfully in containers as well as in raised beds and rock gardens. Whether they are grown in stone troughs or sinks, concrete or composition-stone planters, terracotta pots or even window boxes, the conditions most require are full sun and free drainage. The low terracotta planter, 35cm (14in) across and 17cm (7in) deep, shown being filled on the opposite page, is a good size for a small collection of these lovely miniatures.

Autumn and early spring are the best times to plant, spring being preferable in areas that experience cold winters. Heavy containers should always be positioned before planting; they need a spot where they are exposed to maximum sun. To ensure free drainage, put a layer of stone chippings or gravel in the base of the container. Use a soil-based compost and add one-quarter to one-third of its volume in grit or gravel. Cover the surface with a layer of gravel, to keep the necks of plants clear of moist potting compost. Plants will not need additional fertilizing if a little slow-release fertilizer is added to the potting compost. In subsequent years, top-dress the plants in early spring: remove the gravel and set aside, replace the top 2.5cm (1in) of potting compost with fresh compost containing slow-release fertilizer, then cover again with gravel.

Stone is a sympathetic material for a container planted with rock garden plants. This roughly hewn planter, its weathered surface encrusted with lichens, holds a small collection including phlox, sedums and thrift, arranged around a mossy stone.

CREATING A MINIATURE ROCK GARDEN IN A PLANTER

1 *Scrub the planter and soak it in clean water in order to rehydrate it. If possible, position it where it is to be displayed – which should be in a sunny spot – and put crocks over the drainage hole.*

2 *Cover the crocks and the bottom of the planter with a layer of well-washed grit or gravel about 5cm (2in) deep. If the container is very deep, increase the amount of drainage material.*

3 *Half-fill the planter with slightly moist, soil-based potting compost containing a slow-release fertilizer and to which grit or gravel (up to one-third by volume) has been added.*

4 *Without taking them out of their pots, experiment with arrangements for plants, including here dwarf juniper, sisyrinchium, dianthus and sempervivum, and stones, by moving them around the container.*

5 *Embed the large stones in the potting compost, then begin planting, starting with the shrubby plants. Loosen the root ball slightly before inserting into a prepared hole. Add compost, if necessary, and firm.*

6 *Add the remaining plants, working potting compost around them and firming them. When this stage is completed, the surface of the potting compost should be about 5cm (2in) below the planter's rim.*

7 *Top-dress with well-washed grit or gravel to just below the planter's rim, working the chippings around the neck of plants to ensure sharp drainage and so reduce the risk of rot.*

8 *Water the rock garden gently with a hose or watering can until excess water runs out of the drainage hole. If the container is to be repositioned, move it only when it has drained fully.*

9 *Although most rock garden plants need free drainage, they also require plenty of moisture, especially during the growing season, so water regularly. Trim excessive or untidy growth.*

PLANTING HERB AND STRAWBERRY POTS

A traditional planter commonly used for herbs consists of a terracotta pot with planting holes at two or three levels in the sides. A similar container of larger size is used for strawberries. Purpose-made planters that accommodate plants arranged vertically are also available in other materials. Among these are wooden tubs with a series of holes drilled in the sides large enough to take plants, usually strawberries. A gardener with only moderate practical skills can drill the holes to make a strawberry barrel.

The method of planting is essentially the same for all these containers. They require drainage material in the base, over which potting compost is added to just below the lowest holes. From the outside, push the root ball of a plant through each hole and firm it in the compost. When the holes at one level are filled, add potting compost to just below the next level of holes. Follow the same procedure until the holes at every level are planted.

Herbs must have even exposure to light, so rotate the pot regularly; light is not as critical for strawberries. Less conventional plantings can be made of ornamental plants. In a large, heavy pot that is not easily rotated, plant one side with sun-lovers, the other with shade-tolerant plants.

PLANTING A TERRACOTTA HERB POT

1 *Scrub and soak the pot in clean water, then put crocks over the drainage holes and add a layer of drainage material.*

2 *Fill the pot to just below the lower holes with a soil-based potting compost containing added grit to ensure good drainage.*

3 *Push the root balls of plants through the lower holes and firm in. Then add more compost to just below the upper holes.*

4 *Repeat for the upper holes. Small stones packed around plants will prevent compost leaking out. Add 5cm (2in) more compost.*

5 *Add a final plant in the top of the pot. Work compost around it and firm so the final level is 2.5cm (1in) below the pot's rim.*

6 *Place the pot in position and water thoroughly. Rotate every five to seven days to ensure that all plants get plenty of light.*

Alpine strawberries bear small, rather dry fruit of distinctive flavour throughout the summer. The fruit is not readily available in stores so it is well worth growing plants, and in a purpose-made pot pierced with holes you can easily supply the conditions they need. The more familiar large-fruited strawberries, which bear prolific crops in summer, can be grown in the same way.

PLANTING A WATER GARDEN

An attractive miniature water garden can be created in a watertight container no more than 45cm (18in) in height and diameter. Glazed ceramic pots are ideal containers except in frost-prone areas, where they may be shattered by freezing water. Even where the winters are cold they can be used outdoors in summer and moved under cover from autumn to spring, although you may need to empty the container in order to move it.

Metal and wood are the most suitable materials for year-round exposure. Metal is best treated with a rubber-based paint, because if left uncovered it may be harmful to plants and fish. Wooden half-barrels and tubs will usually remain fairly watertight once the wood is thoroughly soaked and has had a chance to swell. Plastic and fibreglass make good watertight containers, but since they are less visually pleasing you may wish to mask them with plants, or disguise them in some other way.

When planting, aim to strike a balance between the different groups of plants. Those that cover the surface, such as water lilies (*Nymphaea*), block out the light that encourages discolouring algae. Several water lilies are happy in as little as 45cm (18in) of water. Waterside plants, such as the dwarf cat-tail (*Typha minima*), with only their feet in water, soften the edge, while submerged plants help to clean and oxygenate the water – especially important if fish are to be introduced.

Even a small water garden can be enlivened by the sound and movement of flowing water. Here an old water pump has been converted into an ornamental feature brightened by a variegated moisture-loving grass. An electric-powered submersible pump is used to circulate the water.

POTTING AQUATICS

1 *Plant aquatics in spring, using open-sided plastic baskets (lined with hessian if the holes are large) and a specially formulated aquatic compost.*

2 *Use a sharp knife to trim the roots if necessary. Insert the plant deep in the container, working the compost around it and firming it in gently.*

3 *Top-dress the compost with a layer of washed gravel about 2.5cm (1in) deep. Water newly planted baskets before introducing them to a pool.*

PLANTING A WATER GARDEN IN A TUB

1 *Position the tub in its final sunny spot, checking that it is level on the ground. Then cover the base of the tub with a 5cm (2in) layer of washed gravel.*

2 *Add the aquatics planted in open-sided baskets, raising the waterside plants on bricks around the edge and resting the water lily on the base of the tub.*

3 *Slowly fill the tub with water, directing the flow from the hose at the wall of the tub. If water is added too quickly, it will disturb the potting compost in the baskets.*

4 *Rapid growth by the water lily and the waterside plants should soon largely mask the pots. Add water from time to time, always doing this slowly and gently.*

WATERING

Plants in containers depend on the gardener for their water supplies. Even in rainy weather watering may be necessary, either because the canopy of foliage sheds rainwater outside the container or because the pot sits in an area of rain shadow. Failing to water can quickly prove fatal to plants but overwatering can also make plants sicken. Drip trays and saucers left unemptied will cause waterlogging.

Check moisture levels frequently by pushing a finger below the surface of the potting compost. Do this at least once a day in summer, when plants are making vigorous growth. Even in cloudy weather, winds speed up water loss. When the compost is nearly dry, water thoroughly until water runs out of the bottom of the container.

In hot, sunny weather avoid splashing water on the leaves, which otherwise may scorch. Tap water is usually satisfactory but, if it is hard, use rainwater or distilled water for rhododendrons, camellias and other lime-haters. For hanging baskets it may be necessary to use alternatives to the standard hose or watering can (*see below*). Automatic drip-feed irrigation systems are a boon when large numbers of containers need watering.

Measures to slow down water loss include lining terracotta pots with sheet plastic, adding water-retaining granules to the compost, covering the surface of the compost with a gravel mulch and spraying plants such as conifers with an anti-desiccant. Self-watering containers are available.

OVERHEAD WATERING

AUTOMATIC IRRIGATION

FAR LEFT *Rigid hose extensions with a curved nozzle simplify the watering of hanging baskets and window boxes (or you can improvise using a bamboo cane tied to the end of a hose). Pump-action compression units are useful if there are only a few pots to water.*

LEFT *Drip-feed, sometimes known as trickle, systems of automatic irrigation incorporate a unit to reduce the pressure. They also include a filter but the tubes feeding water into individual containers still need regular cleaning. For efficient operation use these systems in conjunction with a timer to regulate the water supply.*

REVIVING WILTING PLANTS

LEFT *Act promptly if container-grown plants begin to wilt because watering has been neglected. Stand the container in a vessel of water in a position out of strong sunlight. Leave for about 30 minutes. When the compost is thoroughly wet, take out the pot and stand to drain. Some plants are remarkably resilient and revive quickly but others soon reach the point of no return once the compost is allowed to dry out.*

FEEDING

Standard potting composts contain a balanced supply of nutrients but the reserves in the small amount of compost in a pot or planter can be used up quickly by plants. They are also leached out by watering. The application of fertilizers, simply referred to as feeding, is a way of maintaining the level of nutrients.

The fertilizers used are either organic, that is, derived from plant or animal material, or inorganic, usually man-made from various minerals. Proprietary formulations of inorganic fertilizers are particularly useful in the container garden. They have a balanced supply of the major minerals required for plant growth – nitrogen (N), phosphorus (P) and potassium (K) – together with minute quantities of trace elements. The label should state the constituents and their relative proportions. These fertilizers fall into two main categories. Quick-acting formulations are sold in liquid or soluble powder form and applied at regular intervals throughout the growing season. Slow-release fertilizers, usually in granular form, are incorporated in the potting compost at the beginning of the growing season. Their nutrient value lasts over a long period.

In applying fertilizers, always follow the manufacturer's instructions closely. Do not be misled into thinking that exceeding the recommended rates and frequencies of application will result in bigger and better plants. Over-application may be harmful and is certainly wasteful.

SLOW-RELEASE FERTILIZERS

Slow-release inorganic fertilizers, generally manufactured in granular form, are particularly useful when preparing a topdressing for trees or shrubs.

FOLIAR FEEDING

Plants respond quickly to applications of a liquid foliar feed. Use a pump-action spray gun to apply and avoid spraying in hot, sunny conditions, which might result in leaf scorch.

APPLYING A LIQUID FERTILIZER

Water quick-acting soluble fertilizers into containers at the rate and the frequency recommended by the manufacturer. Avoid wetting the leaves of the plant.

TIDYING AND DEADHEADING

On the intimate scale of container gardening it is easy to keep a close eye on plants and by pleasurable grooming maintain them in prime condition. Occasionally it may be necessary to pinch back straggly stems to encourage more compact growth. Sometimes plants other than climbers need discreet support to keep them from flopping or to ensure a balanced arrangement of stems and foliage. Use carefully placed split canes and tie with soft twine. Remove dead leaves and flowers promptly and you will not only keep the container garden looking attractive but reduce the risk from pests and diseases. Deadheading, the removal of faded blooms, is a particularly important aspect of grooming because so many container plants, popular on account of their long flowering season, start to give up once their energies go into producing seed or fruit. In many cases the spent flowers or flower heads can simply be removed by hand or cut off with scissors. For plants with strong stems, such as roses, use sharp secateurs.

SPRING CLEANING

Many evergreens, including ivies, need to have damaged leaves and shoots removed in spring. Pinching back the stems will encourage dense, leafy growth.

DEADHEADING ROSES

To encourage further blooms on roses, remove whole clusters of faded flowers, cutting back to a bud or shoot.

DEADHEADING VIOLAS

Small-flowered violas and large-flowered pansies bloom over a long season if they are prevented from seeding. Pick off flowers as soon as they fade.

Verbenas and the blue marguerite (Felicia amelloides) are among many invaluable summer-flowering plants that bloom over a long season provided they are regularly deadheaded.

LONG-TERM CARE OF SHRUBS AND TREES

Until it reaches maturity, a container-grown shrub or tree will usually outgrow its pot every one or two years. Move it on to a new container that is about one and a half times the size of the old. Use fresh, soil-based potting compost (ericaceous for those, like rhododendrons, that are intolerant of lime), that incorporates a slow-release fertilizer.

The root system of established shrubs and trees eventually becomes congested in containers, so repotting of mature specimens is advisable every three or four years.

Once their roots have been cut back, the established plants can usually be replanted in the same container. Begin by laying the container on its side to ease out the plant. Discard the surface potting compost and tease out the roots, cutting back those that are non-fibrous by a half to two-thirds. Repot at the original depth, using fresh compost. To replenish nutrients for shrubs and trees that are not repotted, top-dress annually in spring, using fresh compost that incorporates a slow-release fertilizer.

REPOTTING A SHRUB

1 *If a shrub needs to be moved to a larger container, repot in spring. First water it thoroughly, and leave to drain.*

2 *One-third fill a clean container with fresh potting compost before easing the shrub out of its old container.*

3 *Position the shrub in its new container at its original depth, top up with fresh compost, and water well.*

TOP-DRESSING A SHRUB

1 *Top-dress annually in spring if not repotting. First remove the top 5–10cm (2–4in) of compost in the container.*

2 *Add a slow-release fertilizer to a soil-based potting compost, at the rate prescribed by the manufacturer.*

3 *Add sufficient fresh compost to bring the level up to the original height, then water thoroughly.*

PRUNING

Many container-grown shrubs, climbers and trees require little if any pruning. When you do need to prune, use sharp, clean secateurs and, for larger branches, loppers or a pruning saw. Make clean cuts so that pruning wounds heal rapidly. If you are not pruning back to a main stem, make the cut above a vigorous side-shoot or growth bud. If plants have opposite shoots, make a straight cut immediately above a pair of buds or shoots (one bud or shoot can be removed if growth is needed in one direction only). If plants have alternate buds or shoots, make an angled cut just above a selected bud or shoot.

Formative pruning, often already done on nursery-raised stock, may be necessary to shape a young plant. In the dormant season remove weak shoots and badly placed stems, especially if these clutter the centre of a bush, and aim to build up a balanced framework of main branches or shoots. Heavy corrective pruning at a later stage is rarely necessary and should be avoided as it stimulates growth.

To maintain a plant's vigour, remove promptly any dead, diseased or damaged wood. Cutting back to healthy living wood will reduce the risk of diseases gaining entry or of infections spreading. Annual pruning of some popular and mainly deciduous flowering shrubs and climbers im-proves their display. Those that flower in spring or early summer usually do so on wood produced in the previous growing season. Cut out the old wood as soon as the flowers fade to encourage vigorous new growth to flower the following year. If flowers are produced on the current season's growth, prune in winter or early spring. A number of shrubs, including lavender, that become bare at the base if allowed to grow unchecked, can be kept compact and vigorous by annual pruning. Plants that are pruned heavily benefit from feeding in spring.

Most fruit trees and climbers also require annual pruning to encourage the formation of fruit-bearing wood. After the initial training of apples, build up fruiting spurs by shortening the side shoots. In autumn or winter cut these back to two buds. The pruning of grape vines is based on establishing a framework and pruning annually to encourage the production of new wood that will carry fruit the next year. A convenient way of growing a vine in a container is to train a standard and to prune shoots at the head back to one bud during the dormant season.

Variegated shrubs sometimes produce non-variegated shoots. Cut out these reverted shoots as soon as they develop, otherwise they will eventually dominate the plant.

BASIC CUTS

Make angled pruning cuts with sharp, clean secateurs on plants such as roses that have alternate growth buds or leaves. Cut to a bud that will make growth in the desired direction, beginning the cut opposite the base of the bud and sloping it so that it finishes about 5mm (¼in) above the bud.

Use secateurs to make a straight pruning cut on plants that have opposite buds or leaves, such as hydrangeas. Make the cut just above strong buds or shoots, without damaging them. If growth is wanted in one direction only, remove the unwanted bud or shoot after making the cut.

HARD PRUNING TO KEEP PLANTS COMPACT

1 *Several shrubs, including lavender and cotton lavender, become straggly and deteriorate if not cut hard back regularly. Prune lavender in mid-spring, just as new shoots are forming, or, in areas with a mild climate, in autumn.*

2 *Use sharp secateurs or hand shears to cut off flower heads and most of the growth made in the previous season. Spring-pruned plants can have flower heads removed in autumn. Avoid cutting into old wood, as this rarely produces new growth.*

3 *When making cuts, follow the natural domed outline of the plant, to prevent bareness at the base. When pruning is finished, remove all trimmings, brushing over the bush to shake off any loose shoots remaining. Repeat this pruning annually.*

PRUNING TO MAINTAIN VIGOROUS GROWTH

1 *Begin pruning shrubs, for example a mophead hydrangea, by removing all dead, diseased, weak and damaged wood. Take out a stem or stems if branches are crossing, which would otherwise result in congestion and wounds that could be entry points for diseases.*

2 *Many shrubs benefit from additional pruning to encourage new growth. Some shrubs flower on new wood, and the aim of pruning is to take out wood once it has flowered. A number of shrubs, including mophead hydrangeas, flower on old wood, but they still need some pruning to ensure a succession of vigorous growths.*

3 *Cut a proportion of old stems back to base or to strong shoots low down on the bush and lightly trim other stems to healthy buds. Prune more drastically shrubs, including roses, that flower on the current season's growth.*

TOPIARY

In the traditional garden craft of topiary, trees and shrubs are sheared into geometric or representational forms. Container-grown specimens in the shape of pyramids, cones, obelisks and spheres are ideal for defining formal arrangements, while birds, animals and even more fanciful representations will add a whimsically humorous note to the garden.

The most suitable candidates for topiary are small-leaved evergreens that tolerate trimming and hold their shape with one, or at most two, prunings in the growing season. In temperate climates the favourite for small and medium-sized specimens is box (*Buxus sempervirens*) and,

for larger specimens, yew (*Taxus baccata*). Other evergreens with larger leaves that are suitable for simple shapes include many hollies (*Ilex*), sweet bay (*Laurus nobilis*), and Portugal laurel (*Prunus lusitanica*). Oval-leaf privet (*Ligustrum ovalifolium*), although responding to trimming, is too fast growing to hold its shape well.

Plants for topiary need shearing from an early age to encourage dense, even growth from low down. A formal shape can be built up gradually or carved out of a plant that is already loosely shaped. In the initial stages of training representational specimens, tails and other narrow extensions need to be trained to supports.

Specimens of topiary box (Buxus sempervirens), *clipped into standard mopheads and other forms, have a different kind of container allocated for each shape. They are ranged with many-* *sided containers of sedums in formal ranks like chess pieces. The formal effect is further emphasized by the background line of pleached trees and geometric lawn shapes .*

PRUNING A BOXWOOD SPECIMEN INTO A SPIRAL

1 *A dense five-year-old specimen of a variegated box (*Buxus sempervirens *'Elegantissima'), roughly conical in outline, is suitable for shaping into a spiral. Do the initial training in mid- to late summer, with the plant positioned on a stable surface or at ground level.*

2 *Having assessed that there is room for two turns of the spiral and a topknot, trim to shape freehand, using sharp, manually operated hedge shears. Powered tools work so fast that it is easy to make unwanted cuts that cannot be rectified. Start from the base, slowly defining the lower turn.*

3 *Work upwards, initially cutting out the two turns of the spiral roughly and then clipping more closely. Make many small cuts rather than taking fewer but larger bites that might distort the shape. Stand back from time to time to check by eye that the spiral is balanced.*

4 *Complete the shape by finishing with a topknot. Separate the topknot from the spiral by using the hedge shears to cut through to the central stem just above the top turn of the spiral. Trim the topknot to a conical shape, ensuring that it is in proportion to the spiral.*

5 *Shake and ruffle the plant gently to dislodge any cut pieces of stem that have become stuck among the leaves. Check that the cutting is even and make any necessary adjustments. If there are stray ends remaining, trim these off with the hedge shears or secateurs.*

6 *Maintain the specimen at the same height in subsequent years by annual pruning with hedge shears in mid- to late summer. Top-dress annually in spring with fresh potting compost containing a slow-release fertilizer and repot every two or three years.*

FALSE TOPIARY

A simple and relatively quick method of forming both geometric and representational shapes with plants is to train small-leaved climbers over frames. Once the frame is densely covered with leaves, these shapes look very much like traditional topiary, which is why the technique is referred to as false topiary. In a more elaborate form of training, the frame is used not only to define the shape but also to hold a material, such as sphagnum moss, into which small plants are densely planted.

Commercially produced frames that provide a skeleton for climbing plants are usually made of sturdy galvanized or enamelled wire. Bold, stylized shapes are not difficult to fashion out of chicken wire over a simple framework of heavy-gauge galvanized wire. All frames need feet that can be inserted firmly in the container, and a soil-based potting compost is required to provide a solid foundation.

In temperate gardens the most versatile plants to use for training over shapes are the small-leaved common ivies (*Hedera helix*), which have flexible stems and neat foliage, and form dense growth when pinched back. In one growing season, a single plant will usually give good cover to a simple frame 30–45cm (12–18in) high. To achieve even cover on a large frame with a broad base, use two or three plants spaced out around the frame. The climbing fig (*Ficus pumila*) is also a good plant for training, but it needs warmer conditions.

The small-leaved cultivars of the common ivy have flexible stems that are easily trained over frames and make a dense evergreen cover if bare lengths of stem are trimmed back. A bird shape in wire, with a small head, plump body and angled tail, can easily be recognized without the need for fine detail. A single ivy plant will be sufficient to clothe the smaller frame in green, while two or three plants will be required to achieve quick results on each of the larger frames.

TRAINING IVY ON A WIRE FRAME

1 In spring plant a well-branched small-leaved ivy in a pot containing soil-based potting compost. After watering in, allow the pot to drain, then insert the frame over the ivy. Make sure the foot of the frame is firmly embedded in the compost.

2 Gently pull the stems of the ivy through the base of the frame so that they hang outside it. Before training them upwards, tease out the stems, then drape the longest stems over the frame, distributing them evenly over the wires.

3 Twist the ivy stems around the wires of the frame to keep them in position. In the early stages it may be necessary to hold the stems in place with a few inconspicuous ties of plastic-coated wire or tarred twine.

4 Train the shorter stems up the outside of the frame, spacing them evenly and twining them around the wires. Continue to train these stems as they make growth, tucking them into the frame.

5 Water regularly and apply liquid fertilizer every two weeks during the growing season. Tuck in new growth and trim any excess. A small frame such as this will be covered in two or three months.

TRAINING CLIMBERS

Growing climbers in flat-sided containers is a good solution to clothing walls where a paved surface means that there is no bare earth for planting. Container-grown climbers flourish independently of walls, either trailing freely or else trained over a support system fitted into the pot or planter. Climbers grown on integral supports need heavy, deep containers and should be put in a sheltered position. Use a soil-based potting compost for all climbers.

The kind of support a climber needs depends on its manner of growth. Those that cling by means of adhesive pads or aerial roots, ivies among them, do best on a solid surface such as a house or garden wall. Although vigorous and tenacious once established, these self-clingers are often slow to get started. Secure young stems against the surface they are to climb until the aerial roots begin to

grip. Many climbers, like the common jasmine (*Jasminum officinale*) are twiners, while others, such as sweet peas, hold on to supports by tendrils. Both these categories of climbers need supports they can work round, such as wires, netting, trellis or a wigwam of canes. Secure wall supports firmly, allowing a gap of about 5cm (2in) so that air can circulate. Some purpose-made supports are available that can be fitted into planters, and you can make your own with trellis or bamboo canes. Put them in before planting. Twiners and tendril climbers need to be guided and lightly tied in until they start to surge upwards.

Roses need to have their lax stems regularly tied into netting or trellis supports. Train in the main stems as near the horizontal as possible, to encourage free flowering. Check ties often to see that they are secure but not too tight.

MAKING A CLIMBING FRAME FOR SWEET PEAS

1 *A wigwam of bamboo canes inserted in a tub or half-barrel makes an effective support for annual climbers such as sweet peas and beans. In a tub that is 45–60cm (18–24in) across, evenly space six canes 1.8–2.5m (6–8ft) long.*

2 *Between the tall canes, insert other canes that are approximately half their length. Tie the tall canes together at the top and then tie twine around all canes at a height of about 23cm (9in) and 60cm (2ft).*

ABOVE *Sweet peas can easily hoist themselves up a columnar support consisting of bare twiggy branches that are lightly trimmed and tied together. Before planting, insert the support in a heavy container filled with a soil-based potting compost.*

ABOVE *Transplanted sweet peas tend to flop about unless they are tied to a support, and they are easily attached using twist ties. Twiners and tendril climbers benefit from initial training.*

ABOVE *Fix climbing roses to trelliswork, netting or other supports using twine secured in a figure of eight or plastic ties. Check ties often and loosen them before they become too tight.*

BELOW *A golden hop* (Humulus lupulus 'Aureus') *is trained to grow over an attractive homemade wicker frame. This vigorous climber will have completely hidden its support by mid-summer.*

ABOVE *Where paving runs to the walls, containers offer the only way of growing climbers. Large pots planted with jasmines and clematis have softened the architecture of this paved courtyard.*

BELOW *Many moderately vigorous clematis, including the spring flowering* C. macropetala, *are superb grown without supports.*

TRAINING STANDARDS

Standards give height in the container garden, and a well-shaped head on a clear stem makes a pleasing contrast to low-growing, rounded or more spreading shapes. One method of forming standards, used for roses and some other woody plants, is to train vertically a stem of a suitable rootstock and to bud or graft a selected cultivar at the desired height. This specialized technique is usually carried out by the nursery, and the plants you buy have the head partly or fully formed.

The method that is more relevant to the amateur gardener involves training the plant stem vertically, cutting back the tip at a given height, encouraging the development of a bushy head by pruning, and removing shoots and leaves from the stem below the head. This technique can be used on many woody plants and on sub-shrubs such as fuchsias. The soft young growth of sub-shrubs can usually be pinched out between finger and thumb, a method of shortening stems often known as 'pinch pruning'. In frost-prone areas, you must keep standard fuchsias and other plants that are not frost-hardy – including marguerites (*Argyranthemum*), heliotrope (*Heliotropium*), and pelargoniums – under glass through winter.

Fuchsias are among the easiest plants for the amateur gardener to train as standards. The combination of standard and bush fuchsias in the one container is often highly successful, the two kinds providing a display of dangling flowers that continues through much of the summer and well into autumn.

TRAINING A STANDARD FUCHSIA

1 *In autumn, select a healthy rooted cutting taken in late summer to train as a standard and pot it up individually. In winter keep in a well-lit position at a minimum temperature of 10°C (50°F).*

2 *When the young fuchsia reaches a height of 20–25cm (8–10 in), insert a cane in the pot and, using simple twist ties, secure the stem of the plant so that it continues to make strong vertical growth.*

3 *Continue to tie in the stem, using a longer cane if necessary. Begin removing leaves from the lower part of the stem only when the plant has nearly reached the height at which it is to be stopped.*

4 *When the plant has reached the desired height, pinch out the tip of the terminal shoot. This stimulates branching that will form the framework of the head. Once a strong stem has been formed, strip off all leaves below the head.*

5 *To support a well-branched head, standard fuchsias need to be tied to a permanent stake. Build up the head by pinching out the growing tips of stems three or four times, removing completely any stems that are weak or badly placed.*

PESTS AND DISEASES

There is no need to wage a constant battle to control pests and diseases in the container garden. In dealing with them, strike a balance between tolerating minor imperfections and checking problems by using chemical and other controls. It often pays to be ruthless and discard plants that are sickly. Chemical controls must be used responsibly to avoid harming people, animals and the environment. Always follow the manufacturer's instructions strictly, and keep to the following guidelines:

• Mix chemicals in the open or a well-ventilated place.
• Avoid contact with skin and eyes; do not inhale sprays.
• Apply chemicals in calm, dry weather and do not spray in hot, sunny conditions, which may cause scorching.
• Dispose of surplus mixed chemicals carefully and wash equipment thoroughly after use.
• Store chemicals in their original containers, out of the reach of children and animals, and always retain instructions on their use and disposal.
• Any pesticides used should comply with the latest edition of the *UK Pesticide Guide*.

SAP-SUCKING PESTS

These often cause stunted growth and will transmit virus diseases from infected to healthy plants. Sooty moulds grow on the sticky honeydew which some excrete. They often prove difficult to control except by chemical means. Some insecticides, such as the organic derris and pyrethrum, kill pests that come into direct contact with a spray or dust. Systemic insecticides are absorbed and carried through the whole plant by the sap.

Aphids (blackfly and greenfly) Winged or wingless insects, about 5mm (¼in) long, that form fast-growing colonies on young shoots, buds and undersides of leaves.
Leafhoppers Insects up to 2.5mm (⅛in) long that cause spotting to the upper surfaces of leaves. Spray undersides of leaves.
Mealy bugs Aphid-like pests, covered by waxy white filaments, found on many plants in greenhouses and outdoors in warm climates.
Scale insects Insects covered by blister-like scales up to 5mm (¼in) long found on the undersides of leaves or the stems of shrubs and trees.
Thrips (thunderflies) Small dark insects and their yellow-orange nymphs, both less than 2.5mm (⅛in) in size, that fill the air in hot, dry conditions, and cause a silvery discoloration on leaves and white flecking on flowers.
Whitefly Tiny white-winged insects found under leaves of plants. Biological control is only practicable under glass.

PESTS THAT EAT LEAVES, FLOWERS AND STEMS

Although they cause conspicuous damage, these pests are often the most easily controlled by nonchemical means.
Caterpillars The immature stage of various butterflies and moths that feed on the foliage of a wide range of plants. Remove by hand.
Earwigs Yellowish-brown, pincer-tailed insects up to 2cm (¾in) long that eat leaves and flowers. Trap in pots stuffed with straw, then destroy.
Snails and slugs Slimy-bodied molluscs that feed voraciously on leaves and flowers, mainly at night or in rainy weather. Remove by hand, or lay slug pellets containing, for example, metaldehyde.
Vine weevils Dark-coloured beetles about 1cm (½in) long that leave jagged holes in the margins of leaves; the white grubs feed on roots. Remove adults by hand. A biological control is available to destroy grubs.

DISEASES

A large number of fungal and viral diseases affect plants, of which the following are the most common.
Black spot A common fungal disease of roses. Small black spots develop into larger patches before the leaves drop off. Remove infected leaves and dead foliage in autumn. Spray infected plants promptly with a fungicide.
Botrytis (grey mould) A fungal disease that attacks leaves, stems, flowers and fruit, often showing as a furry mould. Prevent by clearing away dead plant material and making clean pruning cuts. Burn affected parts, or whole plants such as bulbs, and spray with a fungicide.
Damping off A fungal disease that in close conditions causes seedlings to collapse. Prevent by maintaining strict hygiene, ensuring good ventilation and watering seedlings occasionally with a copper-based fungicide.
Powdery mildew Fungal diseases that affect a wide range of plants, a white powdery growth showing on the leaves. Prevent by keeping susceptible plants well watered. Remove and burn parts that are affected and spray with a fungicide.
Rust Fungal diseases that attack a wide range of plants, red-brown pustules developing on the undersides of leaves. Prevent by growing rust-resistant strains of plants if available. Remove and burn parts that are affected and spray with a fungicide.
Viruses Numerous diseases causing distorted, stunted growth and often discoloration and marking of flowers and leaves. Prevent by using virus-free stock and controlling sap-sucking pests. Remove and burn infected plants.

SAP-SUCKING PESTS

Aphids (blackfly)

Aphids (greenfly)

Leafhopper

Leafhopper damage

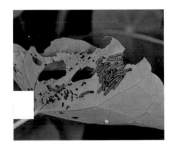

Mealy bugs

Scale insects

Thrips

Whiteflies

PESTS THAT EAT LEAVES, FLOWERS, AND STEMS

Caterpillars

Earwig

Slug

Vine weevil

DISEASES

Black spot

Botrytis damage

Damping off

Powdery mildew

Rust on pelargonium leaf

Rust on rose leaf

Virus damage to foliage

Virus damage to flower

PROPAGATING FROM SEED

It is not difficult for amateur gardeners to raise many of their own plants. Propagating from seed is a simple and cheap way of raising large numbers of hardy and half-hardy annuals, mainstays of the summer garden. Except in areas with very mild winters that are not affected by frosts, the normal pattern is to start seeds of annuals in warmth during late winter or early spring for planting outdoors in late spring or early summer. Good germination results can be achieved on a window sill using plastic flower pots filled with seed compost. Cover the pot with a clear polythene bag until seed has germinated. A more sophisticated version of this is the unheated propagator.

To give plants the best chance in life sow thinly, scattering very fine seed on the surface and just covering larger seeds with a layer of seed compost. Germination of most annuals takes two to three weeks. Move seedlings on as soon as they are large enough to handle.

The process of lifting and replanting seedlings is known as pricking out or pricking off. Once the pricked-off seedlings are making good growth, harden them off by gradually exposing them to conditions outdoors over a period of two or three weeks in readiness for planting them out. A cold frame makes an ideal halfway house in which the increase in ventilation can be controlled.

SOWING SEED IN A PROPAGATOR

1 *Fill the seed tray of a propagator with a layer of seed compost. Level the surface of the compost and lightly firm it with the hand or with a piece of wood.*

2 *Sow all seed thinly. To ensure an even distribution, use a finger of one hand to tap the seed out of the other, or sprinkle seed carefully from a folded piece of paper.*

3 *Cover seeds with a layer of fine compost equal in depth to the size of the seed. Place the tray gently in a pail or sink filled with shallow water until the compost is thoroughly moistened.*

4 *Allow the tray to drain, then cover it with the propagator lid. Keep in a position that is warm but not exposed to direct sunlight until the seeds germinate.*

PRICKING OUT

1 *To grow seedlings on, prick them out when they are large enough to handle. Use a label or a knife blade to ease them out of the tray, holding them by the leaves.*

2 *Plant the seedlings individually in compartmented packs or evenly spaced about 4cm (1½in) apart in larger pots filled with gently firmed potting compost.*

PLANTING LARGE SEEDS

1 *Sow large seeds such as nasturtiums two to a small pot filled with seed compost. Water gently from above or below.*

2 *Nasturtiums can be moved into their final container once they are large enough to handle. Harden them off before they go outdoors.*

The scarlet nasturtium 'Empress of India' has a purplish-blue tinge to the foliage that is brought out by the unusual colour of this pot. Nasturtiums can be sown directly outdoors in mid- to late spring, two seeds per station. Thin out seedlings, removing the weakest.

RAISING PLANTS FROM CUTTINGS

Stem cuttings provide material for propagating a wide range of shrubs and sub-shrubs commonly grown in the container garden. This method of propagation is particularly useful to gardeners who want to overwinter stocks of fast-growing plants such as fuchsias and pelargoniums that will not endure frost. Cuttings are usually classified according to the maturity of the wood: softwood, semi-ripe, and hardwood cuttings.

Hormone-rooting powders or solutions, which often contain a fungicide that checks rotting, usefully speed up the rooting of all but the easiest plants to grow from cuttings. Use sparingly, according to the instructions given.

Good garden hygiene is essential to minimize the risk of fungal and viral diseases. Always prepare cuttings on a clean surface. A razor blade is ideal for trimming them to size. It is worth buying a ready-made cuttings compost which is reasonably moisture-retentive but of open texture and free-draining. Keep cuttings in a warm, moist atmosphere, preferably with bottom heat, to encourage quick root formation. Good results can be achieved even without a heated propagator. A simple way of creating a humid atmosphere is to secure a clear plastic bag over a pot, using short canes to keep the plastic away from the leaves. Lift the covers every seven to ten days to water the cuttings and allow air to circulate. Once the cuttings have rooted, pot them up individually.

TAKING SEMI-RIPE CUTTINGS OF AN EVERGREEN

1 *Take semi-ripe cuttings of evergreen shrubs, such as the box shown here, in late summer or early fall, selecting shoots made in the current season.*

2 *Using a sharp blade, trim just below a joint so that cuttings are 10–15cm (4–6in) long. Take off the tip if it is still soft and remove the lower leaves.*

3 *Dip the base of the cutting in hormone-rooting powder, shaking off the surplus. Insert with other cuttings in a pot filled with moist cuttings compost.*

4 *Place the container in a propagator or cold frame and leave. Lift the cuttings to pot them up individually once they are showing signs of growth and are well rooted.*

TAKING SEMI-RIPE CUTTINGS OF PELARGONIUMS

1 *Take softwood cuttings in spring from overwintered plants or semi-ripe cuttings in late summer. Select healthy, non-flowering shoots.*

2 *Place the cutting on a clean surface and, using a razor blade or sharp knife, trim with a straight cut just below a leaf joint to leave a cutting 10–15cm (4–6in) long.*

3 *Remove lower leaves before inserting the cutting in the compost. The top leaves are needed to produce food for the cutting.*

4 *Make holes 2.5–5cm (1–2in) deep in a pot of moist cuttings compost, insert and firm in the cuttings. Place in a warm position.*

TAKING SOFTWOOD CUTTINGS OF FUCHSIAS

1 *Take fuchsia cuttings for overwintering at any time between spring and late summer, selecting non-flowering shoots from a healthy plant.*

2 *Trim the stem below a leaf joint and remove the lower leaves before inserting in a pot of cuttings compost. Keep in a warm, moist atmosphere until the cuttings are rooted.*

PROPAGATING BY DIVISION

The easiest way to increase stocks of many herbaceous perennials is by division. This method of vegetative propagation can also be applied to shrubs that produce suckers on their own roots and to bulbs and corms, most of which naturally produce offsets. When bulbous plants are lifted, the offsets can be detached and grown on until they reach flowering size. This may take several years, so for the container garden, where space is usually at a premium, it is only worth growing on offsets of bulbous plants that are unusual and difficult to obtain.

Over several years perennials tend to become either woody, and then they produce little growth at the centre, or else congested, with the result that they make poor growth and produce fewer flowers. Division is an important way of rejuvenating plants as well as of propagating them. Because they are growing in cramped conditions, perennials in containers should be lifted and divided every one or two years. Fibrous-rooted perennials such as heucheras are the easiest to deal with. To divide large crowns of hostas and other perennials with tough rootstocks, it is generally best to lift or tip the plant out of its container and divide by cutting with a spade.

DIVIDING FIBROUS-ROOTED PERENNIALS

1 *Lift the perennials to be divided in autumn or in early spring. Discard the old, unproductive centre but retain growth from the outer part of the plant.*

2 *Divide by hand into as many viable sections as you need, if necessary cutting thick roots with a sharp knife. Make sure that each piece has vigorous shoots as well as healthy roots.*

3 *Remove any damaged leaves or stems and either pot up individually to grow on or replant directly with other ornamentals, using fresh soil-based potting compost.*

4 *Water thoroughly. If the plant was large enough to break up into several portions, repeat the process of division followed by that of replanting.*

WINTER PROTECTION

In frost-prone areas many plants in containers need protection in winter. One solution is to move container-grown tender plants under glass in the autumn. Even unheated greenhouses, conservatories and glassed-in porches will give some protection but with heating a wider range of plants can be overwintered successfully.

The most convenient way of overwintering many tender perennials and shrubs is in the form of rooted cuttings. If plants of marginal hardiness are being left outdoors, it is always worth overwintering a few cuttings under glass in case the parent plant is lost. Pelargoniums can be lifted and stored through the winter (*see below*) and planted up the following spring or used to provide material for cuttings. Keep all plants overwintered under glass nearly dry and at the minimum temperature they will tolerate, since moisture and warmth stimulate premature growth.

Even reasonably hardy plants may need protection when left outdoors, since container-grown specimens are more vulnerable to frost than those in the open ground. Wrap a shrub and its container in some form of insulation, such as straw inside a hessian cover, to minimize the risk of damage caused by alternating freeze and thaw.

OVERWINTERING PELARGONIUMS

1 *Lift pelargoniums before there is a risk of frost, shaking potting compost off the roots. Cut back the stems just above a joint about 8–15cm (3–6in) from the base.*

2 *Trim the roots back so that they are not more than 5–8cm (2–3in) long. Check that all the remaining growth is healthy and free of pests.*

3 *Prepare a container such as a wooden box with drainage holes, line it with polythene (slit at the base) and half-fill with a soil-less potting compost.*

4 *Put in the plants, close but not touching, and top up with more compost. Water the compost and let it drain thoroughly before storing the box in a frost-free but light position.*

MODEL
PLANTINGS

Beautiful and interesting container plantings are achieved by a combination of
sound garden practice and a feel for putting plants together creatively. The
practical skills are easily acquired, and a flair for planting comes from
experience and by taking inspiration from successful models.

The following section provides instructions for thirty-five different
container plantings. Each double page begins with an introduction
describing the theme of the planting or plantings. This is followed by
advice on when best to plant and how to maintain each scheme. There is a
list of the ingredients used, and a step-by-step guide clearly shows how
each one is put together.

Some gardeners may want to reproduce the plantings more or less exactly
as they are illustrated. Others may wish to use the ideas and information as
the inspiration for planting plans of their own creation. Using a container
of a different material or colouring, or even a slightly different size or shape,
changes the character of a planting. Daffodils, fuchsias, petunias and tulips
are among the many plants with numerous cultivars that can be chosen
according to taste and availability. Substituting plants with characteristics
similar to those illustrated is another interesting way to give your container
garden a personal stamp. A selection of plants listed by characteristics is
given on pages 204–5.

Fuchsias produce masses of flowers over a long season from mid-summer into autumn.
Here, the bushy fuchsia 'Tom Woods' and the trailing cultivar 'Jack Shahan' complement
one another perfectly in a traditional terracotta pot decorated with a basketwork pattern.
The trailing foliage of Salvia discolor, *which thrives in hot conditions, adds a silvery*
note in the foreground. Details of this planting are given on page 114.

DEEP PINKS FOR SPRING

For colourful variety and reliability in spring, bulbs are unbeatable. After planting in autumn, they require little attention until their brilliant explosions transform the container garden. They can, of course, be planted alone, but for extra interest try combining them with other spring-flowering plants. Plants that go well with bulbs include some long-lived herbaceous perennials, among them Lenten roses. Those that are hardy can be planted at the same time as the bulbs. Others can be added in early spring, but mark the position of the bulbs planted in autumn.

A POT WITH LENTEN ROSES

Plant in early to mid-autumn, in sun or shade, leaving space for the dwarf primulas. Apply liquid fertilizer when the hyacinths and primulas come into flower, and again two weeks later. It is possible to maintain Lenten roses and ivy permanently in pots, but the hyacinth bulbs and the primulas should be replanted in the open garden after flowering.

Terracotta pot, diameter 20cm (8in), depth 13cm (5in)

Crocks

Soil-based potting compost incorporating a slow-release fertilizer

3 pink hyacinths (*Hyacinthus orientalis* 'Pink Pearl'), page 156, **A**

2 Lenten roses (*Helleborus orientalis*), page 156, **B**

3 pink dwarf primulas (*Primula*), page 139, **C**

1 small-leaved ivy (*Hedera helix* 'Donerailensis'), page 181, **D**

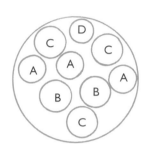

1 Scrub the pot and soak it in clean water.
2 Put crocks over the drainage hole and fill with potting compost to a depth of 5cm (2in).
3 Plant the hyacinth bulbs (**A**), then add more compost so that the bulbs are nearly covered.
4 Position a Lenten rose (**B**) on either side of the central hyacinth, and insert them at their previous growing depth.
5 Plant the primulas (**C**) and the ivy (**D**), then add potting compost to a level about 2.5cm (1in) below the pot's rim. Firm in the plants.
6 Water well.

TULIPS IN A MIXED PLANTING

Plant the bulbs in late autumn. Place in full sun, and add the other plants in spring. Apply liquid fertilizer when the tulip leaves emerge and again as the buds open. Replant in the open garden after flowering.

Terracotta pot, diameter 45cm (18in), depth 35cm (14in)

Crocks

Soil-based potting compost incorporating a slow-release fertilizer

12 pink tulips (*Tulipa* 'Garden Party'), page 157, **A**

2 variegated daylilies (*Hemerocallis fulva* 'Kwanzo Variegata'), page 141, **B**

2 pink double ranunculus (*R. asiaticus*), pages 163–4, **C**

1 white double ranunculus (*R. asiaticus*), pages 163–4, **D**

2 large-flowered, deep pink, double daisies (*Bellis perennis*), page 156, **E**

2 small-flowered, deep pink, double daisies (*Bellis perennis* 'Pomponette'), page 156, **F**

3 deep pink, double primroses (*P. vulgaris*), page 139, **G**

1 pink dicentra (*D.* 'Stuart Boothman'), page 160, **H**

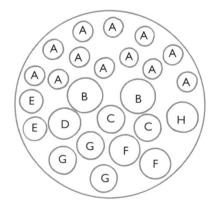

1 Scrub the pot and soak it in clean water.

2 Put crocks over the drainage holes, and fill the pot with potting compost to a depth of 5–8cm (2–3in).

3 Plant the tulip bulbs (A) in a dense group at two depths at the back of the pot. Add the daylilies (B) in the centre.

4 Completely fill the back half of the pot with potting compost, marking the position of the tulips. Fill the front half two-thirds full with compost.

5 When the tulips begin to appear the following spring, remove 8–10cm (3–4in) of the potting compost in the front of the pot. Plant the ranunculus (C, D), then the daisies (E, F), primroses (G) and dicentra (H). Work potting compost around the roots and add more compost to a level about 1in (2.5cm) below the pot's rim. Firm in all the plants.

6 Water well.

SPRING FRESHNESS

There is a refreshing charm about plants which retain the simplicity of their wild ancestors. One of the most beautiful recent introductions from China falls in this category. *Corydalis flexuosa* (*below*) has fern-like foliage, sometimes grey-green or purple-green with red markings, and showers of curiously tilted blue flowers that succeed one another throughout most of the spring. The cowslip (*opposite*) is more familiar, and is one of the classic wild flowers of spring. Small-flowered violas have an unaffected beauty that makes them perfect companions for both cowslips and corydalis. All these plants thrive in partial shade.

Elaborate containers can overwhelm simple plants. Here, the corydalis and violas are planted in a plain terracotta pot. In the case of the terracotta trough, a pale blue wash tones down the relief decoration and makes it part of the overall colour scheme.

CORYDALIS AND VIOLAS

Plant in late winter or early spring, positioning in partial shade. Apply liquid fertilizer three weeks after planting and again two weeks later. Deadhead the violas to keep them flowering.

When the corydalis has stopped flowering, move it to the open garden. If the violas are still in flower, leave them in the pot as an addition to a summer planting; otherwise discard them.

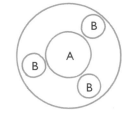

Terracotta pot, diameter
   25cm (10in), depth 17cm
   (7in)
Crocks
Soil-based potting compost
1 corydalis (*C. flexuosa*),
   page 172, **A**
3 violas (*V.* 'Johnny Jump Up')
   page 143, **B**

1 Scrub the pot and soak it in clean water.
2 Put crocks over the drainage holes, and fill the container with potting compost to a depth of 8–10cm (3–4in).
3 Plant the corydalis (**A**) in the centre of the pot, ensuring that it is at its previous planting depth.
4 Space the violas (**B**) evenly around the edge of the pot, then add compost to a level 2.5–5cm (1–2in) below the pot's rim. Firm in the plants.
5 Water well.

COWSLIPS AND VIOLAS

Plant in late winter or early spring and position in partial shade. The cowslips flower for weeks in mid-spring; the violas, provided they are deadheaded, have a longer season. Apply liquid fertilizer three weeks after planting and every two weeks throughout the violas' flowering season. When the cowslips have finished flowering, plant them in the open garden. The violas can be retained as an edging for a replacement planting.

Terracotta trough, length 45cm (18in), depth and width 15cm (6in)

Crocks

Soil-based potting compost

3 cowslips (*Primula veris*), page 139, **A**

6 violas (*Viola* hybrids), page 143, **B**

1 Scrub the trough and soak it thoroughly in clean water.
2 Put crocks over the drainage holes, and fill the trough with potting compost to a depth of 8–10cm (3–4in).
3 Plant the three cowslips (**A**), evenly spaced, along the length of the trough.
4 Plant a viola (**B**) at each front corner and on the same front line plant two more between the cowslips. Plant the last two violas in the back on either side of the centre cowslip.
5 Add potting compost to a level 2.5–5cm (1–2in) below the rim of the trough. Firm in the plants.
6 Water well.

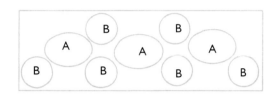

TULIP TIME

Tulips are among the most versatile of spring bulbs and invaluable in the container garden. The numerous hybrids offer a colour range that is matched by few flowers of any description. Their season extends for about three months, reaching its peak in mid- to late spring. Tulips are also easy to grow, requiring little attention between planting in late autumn and flowering in spring. Choosing among them according to when they bloom, flower colour and shape, even foliage markings, is a matter of personal taste, although for window boxes and other containers in exposed positions it is best to use the shorter-growing kinds.

Provided the container is deep enough, it is worth planting the bulbs at two levels, to make a dense display. The effect of the tulips can also be enhanced by a skirt of companion plants. In the plantings here, dwarf yellow flowers and yellow and purple violas are combined with scarlet single tulips to make a bold arrangement (*below*), while the centres of double white daisies echo the rich colour of double yellow tulips (*opposite*). Tulips tend to deteriorate in flower size and quality after their first season. Use fresh bulbs in containers and, once they have flowered, move them to the open garden.

TULIPS AND DWARF WALLFLOWERS

Plant tulip bulbs and wallflowers in late autumn for this mid-spring display, which needs a sunny spot. Violas can be tucked in when available in early spring. Apply liquid fertilizer as the tulip leaves emerge and again as the buds open. Discard the wallflowers and violas after flowering. Save the tulips for planting in the open garden.

Terracotta pot, diameter 25cm (10in),
    depth 17cm (7in)
Crocks
Soil-based or soil-less potting compost
6 red single tulips (*Tulipa* 'Red Riding
    Hood'), page 151, **A**
6 dwarf yellow wallflowers, page 138, **B**
2 violas (*V.* 'Johnny Jump Up'),
    page 143, **C**

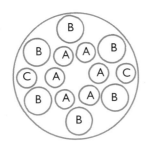

1 Scrub the pot and, to rehydrate it, soak it thoroughly in clean water.
2 Put crocks over the drainage holes, and add potting compost to a depth of 8–10cm (3–4in).
3 Arrange the tulip bulbs (**A**) so that they are evenly spaced and separate, and cover with potting compost.

4 Plant the wallflowers (**B**) and violas (**C**) around the edge. Add potting compost to 2.5–5cm (1–2in) below the rim. Firm in the plants.
5 Water well.

DOUBLE TULIPS AND DAISIES

*For this mid- to late spring
display, which requires a sunny
spot, plant the tulip bulbs in
mid-autumn. In mild climates,
the daisies can be planted at
the same time. Where winters
are more severe, add the daisies
in early spring: remove 5cm
(2in) of the potting compost,
insert the plants and replace
the compost, working it
around the roots. Apply liquid
fertilizer as the tulip leaves
emerge and again as the buds
open. Discard the daisies after
flowering, but replant the tulip
bulbs in the open garden.*

Terracotta pot, diameter and
    depth 30cm (12in)
Crocks
Soil-based or soil-less
    potting compost
15 double yellow tulips (*Tulipa*
    'Gold Medal'), page 140, **A**
4 white double daisies (*Bellis
    perennis*), page 156, **B**

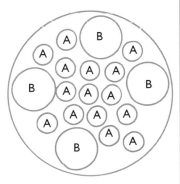

1 Scrub the pot and soak it in clean water.
2 Place a layer of crocks in the base of the pot,
covering the drainage holes, and add potting compost to
a depth of 10cm (4in).
3 Evenly space eight tulip bulbs (**A**) to form the first
layer, and cover with potting compost so that the tips
are just showing.

4 Arrange the remaining seven bulbs between the tips
of those already planted. Add potting compost until it is
8–10cm (3–4in) below the planter's rim.
5 Evenly space the four daisies (**B**) around the edge of
the pot, adding potting compost until it is 2.5–5cm
(1–2in) below the rim. Firm in the plants.
6 Water well.

ORNAMENTAL VEGETABLES

Among the many plants with decorative foliage are several ornamental vegetables. These can be used imaginatively with flowers or other foliage plants to create unusual designs. Red-leaved Swiss chard, often listed as ruby chard or rhubarb chard, has crimson stems and dark foliage which make a good match for red and purple flowers, such as many of the petunias (*below*). The flower-like rosettes of ornamental cabbages will remain attractive for weeks and are especially useful in autumn or winter as a replacement for summer ornamentals. Here, they have been used as underplanting for a mopheaded standard box (*opposite*). Chard is edible, but ornamental brassicas (cabbages and kale) are not good to eat. They are raised for the decorative appeal of their variegated leaves, in various combinations of green, red, pink, white and cream, and often beautifully cut, crinkled and waved.

RUBY CHARD WITH PETUNIAS

Ruby chard makes an ideal centrepiece for a late spring planting of purple petunias, which will bloom all through the summer until autumn. Position in full sun. Water regularly and apply a liquid fertilizer every two weeks, starting two to three weeks after planting. Discard after flowering.

Glazed terracotta pot, diameter 30cm (12in), height 30cm (12in)
Crocks
Soil-based or soil-less potting compost
1 ruby chard (*Beta vulgaris* Cicla Group), page 200, **A**
5 purplish-red petunias, page 170, **B**

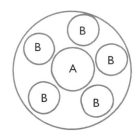

1 Scrub the pot and soak thoroughly in clean water.
2 Put crocks over the drainage holes, and fill the container with potting compost to a level 8cm (3in) below the rim.
3 Plant the ruby chard (**A**) in the middle, and work compost around the roots. Space five petunias (**B**) evenly around it.
4 Add potting compost until it is about 2.5cm (1in) below the planter's rim. Firm in the plants.
5 Water well.

BOX MOPHEAD WITH CABBAGES

In this scheme, box balls are planted in smaller pots to repeat the rounded shape of the mopheaded standard. Lifting the head of a topiary specimen, by growing it on a short stem, leaves room for generous underplanting. Discard the cabbages once they are past their prime.

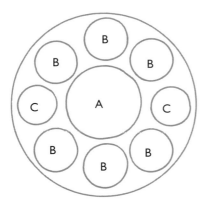

Terracotta pot, diameter 50cm (20in), height 50cm (20in)

Crocks

Soil-based potting compost incorporating slow-release fertilizer

1 standard box (*Buxus sempervirens*), page 179, **A**

6 red and 2 white ornamental cabbages (*Brassica oleracea* Capitata Group), pages 186 and 189, **B** and **C**

1 Scrub the pot and soak it thoroughly in clean water.
2 Put crocks over the drainage holes, and fill the container with potting compost to a depth of about 35cm (14in).
3 Plant the box (**A**) in the middle, at its previous planting depth.
4 Add potting compost to 8cm (3in) below the pot's rim. Plant the red and white cabbages (**B, C**) around the edge.
5 Work more compost around the cabbages until it is 2.5–5cm (1–2in) below the pot's rim. Firm in the plants.
6 Water well.

YELLOW FOR SUN AND SHADE

Trailing plants that flower well are invaluable in containers. Some, such as nasturtiums and creeping jenny, spill decorously over the pot's sides, their foliage and flowers masking the hard edge of the pot. Others, including bidens, are free-branching and create a swirl of colour that floats around a container without appearing to be confined by it.

In a partially shaded trough (*below*) the golden-leaved creeping jenny works harmoniously with an attractive range of bedding plants and herbacous perennials that all prefer moist conditions. A vivid scarlet double nasturtium and airy sprays of yellow *Bidens ferulifolia* (*opposite*) escape the confines of a narrow container in a sunny wall niche.

A WOODEN TROUGH FOR PARTIAL SHADE

Plant this moisture-loving mixture in late spring or early summer. Regular deadheading of the pansies and monkey flowers will help to sustain the display well into summer. Water regularly and apply a liquid fertilizer every two weeks, starting three weeks after planting. At the end of the season, save the tellima and the creeping jenny by replanting in another pot or in the open garden.

Wooden trough, length 90cm (3ft), width and depth 20cm (8in)

Black plastic sheet for liner

Soil-based potting compost

1 tellima (*T. grandiflora*), page 182, **A**

6 red-faced yellow pansies, page 143, **B**

12 monkey flowers (*Mimulus* Malibu Mixed), page 147, **C**

6 golden creeping jenny (*Lysimachia nummularia* 'Aurea'),
    page 185, **D**

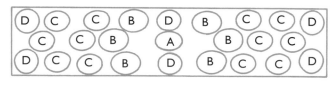

1 Insert the plastic sheet to line the trough completely. Cut drainage holes in the base. Fill the container with potting compost until it is 10cm (4in) below the rim.
2 Plant the tellima (**A**) in the centre, and place three pansies (**B**) in an arc on each side of it. Plant a group of six monkey flowers (**C**) towards each end of the trough.
3 Tuck in the creeping jenny (**D**), one at each corner and the remaining two on either side of the tellima.
4 Add potting compost to 2.5cm (1in) below the trough's rim. Firm in the plants.
5 Water well.

A POT OF SUN-LOVING TRAILERS

If planted in late spring or early summer, this bright mixture will flower freely until autumn. Water regularly through the summer and apply a liquid fertilizer every two weeks, starting three weeks after planting. Tie in the fuchsia stems as necessary. Discard plants after flowering, but overwinter cuttings of the fuchsia (see pages 82–3, 85).

Terracotta pot diameter 30cm
    (12in), height 40cm (16in)
Crocks
Soil-based potting compost
    with slow-release fertilizer
1 red fuchsia (*F.* 'Thalia'),
    page 153, **A**
1 double scarlet nasturtium
    (*Tropaeolum majus* 'Hermine
    Grashoff'), page 149, **B**
1 bidens (*B. ferulifolia*), page
    140, **C**
1 *Lotus berthelotti* x *maculatus*,
    page 147, **D**
2 dark blue salvias
    (*S. discolor*), page 176, **E**
2 grey-leaved helichrysums
    (*H. petiolare*), page 193, **F**
4 75cm (30in) bamboo canes

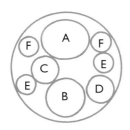

1 Scrub the pot and soak it thoroughly in clean water.
2 Put crocks over the drainage hole, and add potting compost to within 10cm (4in) of the pot's rim.
3 Plant the fuchsia (**A**) at the back of the pot, at its previous planting depth. Centre a well-grown nasturtium (**B**) in the front of the pot, with the bidens (**C**) to its left and the lotus (**D**) to its right. Tuck in the salvias and helichrysums (**E, F**) at the sides.

4 Add potting compost to a level 2.5–5cm (1–2in) below the rim of the pot.
5 Firm in the plants. Water well, then allow to drain.
6 Before placing the pot in a sunny place, insert canes around the fuchsia to serve as supports for the plant as it develops.
Note: such a tall pot may need to be wedged in position to prevent it from being blown over.

A WHITE-BASED PLANTING

Of all the single-colour planting themes, white is the most consistently successful, making flowery containers dazzling in full sun, and giving them a light freshness that stands out in gloomy shade, and retains a ghostly beauty as darkness falls. Skilfully applied touches of colour make a planting distinctive, without detracting from the overall impression of whiteness. Here, single and double white marguerites establish the white theme but shades of pink – soft in another double daisy and deeper in the trailing plants that form the skirt – give the planting an individual character.

WHITE WITH SHADES OF PINK

Plant this scheme during late spring. Place the pot in full sun and it will flower all through the summer and autumn, until stopped by frost. Deadhead the plants regularly, and cut back marguerite stems with yellowing foliage to vigorous new shoots. Apply weak liquid fertilizer every two weeks, starting three to four weeks after planting. It is worth overwintering rooted cuttings of all these plants (see pages 82–3, 85).

Terracotta pot, diameter 50cm (20in),
    depth 60cm (2ft)
Crocks
Soil-based potting compost
1 white single marguerite (*Argyranthemum foeniculaceum* of gardens), page 131, **A**
1 pink double marguerite (*Argyranthemum* 'Mary Wootton'), page 158, **B**
1 white double marguerite (*Argyranthemum* 'Mrs F. Sander'), page 131, **C**
1 reddish-pink verbena (*V.* 'Sissinghurst'), page 165, **D**
1 malvastrum (*M. lateritium*), page 148, **E**

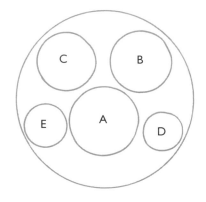

1 Scrub the pot and soak it thoroughly in clean water.
2 Put crocks over the drainage holes, and fill the container with potting compost to a level 13cm (5in) below the rim.
3 Plant the white single marguerite (**A**) slightly forward of the centre, working potting compost around the roots. Behind it, plant the pink double marguerite (**B**) to its left and the white double (**C**) to its right, adding sufficient compost to hold these in place.
4 At the front edge, plant the verbena (**D**) left of the centre and the malvastrum (**E**) right of the centre.
5 Add potting compost until it is about 2.5–5cm (1–2in) below the pot's rim, working it around the plants. Firm in the plants.
6 Water well.

SUBTLE GREYS

Grey foliage, despite its apparent reticence, is often the making of successful container plantings. It is particularly useful as a moderator, calming mixtures of vibrant and even clashing colours and showing off to advantage more subdued plantings, especially in shades of pink, mauve, purple and blue. When intensified to silver, as it is in some of the most finely cut grey foliage plants, it makes a lovely eye-catching accent among flowers.

The richly felted and splendidly hoary senecio *S. cineraria* is a popular grey-leaved plant for summer schemes. The bleached filigree beauty of the cultivar 'Silver Dust' shows up well in a densely planted pot that also contains a curry plant, which has fine pewter-grey leaves (*below*). One of the most widely used plants with grey foliage is *Helichrysum petiolare*, which is a major component in a delightfully interwoven mixture featuring shades of pink (*opposite*). It sometimes produces cream flowers, which tone in well with this planting.

1 Scrub the pot and soak it thoroughly in clean water.
2 Put crocks over the drainage holes and fill with compost to within 10cm (4in) of the rim.
3 Position the two salvias (**A**). Draw potting compost around them to keep them in place.
4 Place the flossflower (**B**) at the front with the curry plant (**C**) and senecio (**D**) on either side.
5 Add the two verbenas (**E**), one beside each of the salvias.
6 Add compost until it is about 2.5cm (1in) below the rim of the pot. Firm in the plants.
7 Water well.

SHADES OF GREY

Plant in late spring or early summer for a display that will last through to the autumn. Keep the pot in an open, sunny position. The dense planting of annuals and perennials will make frequent watering necessary. Apply a liquid fertilizer every two weeks, starting two to three weeks after planting. Deadhead regularly. After flowering, remove the curry plant to the open garden and discard the rest.

Terracotta pot, diameter 25cm (10in), depth 17cm (7in)
Crocks
Soil-based potting compost
2 dark blue salvias (*S. farinacea* 'Victoria'), page 176, **A**
1 compact flossflower (*Ageratum houstonianum*), page 173, **B**
1 curry plant (*Helichrysum italicum*), page 193, **C**
1 silver senecio (*S. cineraria* 'Silver Dust'), page 195, **D**
2 purple verbenas (*V. tenuisecta*) , page 171, **E**

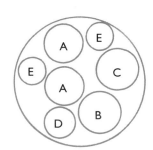

PINK WITH GREY

Plant in early summer. Place in a sunny position, water well and apply a liquid fertilizer every two weeks, starting two to three weeks after planting. After flowering, discard the petunias and verbenas and move the diascias to the open garden. Overwinter the plectranthus and nemesias and take cuttings of the marguerite and divisions of the helichrysum (see pages 82–5).

Wooden planter, 50cm (20in) long and wide, 45cm (18in) deep
Rigid, fitted plastic liner
Crocks
Soil-based potting compost
3 white osteospermums (*O.* 'Blue Streak' and 'Silver Sparkler'), page 135, **A**
1 white double marguerite (*Argyranthemum* 'Qinta White'), page 130, **B**
1 white petunia, page 136, **C**
1 pink osteospermum (*O.* 'Pink Whirls'), page 135, **D**
2 pink verbenas (*V.* 'Silver Anne'), page 165, **E**
2 pink diascias (*D. vigilis*), page 160, **F**
1 grey-leaved helichrysum (*H. petiolare*), page 193, **G**
3 nemesias, 2 mauve and 1 purple (*N. caerulea*), page 169, **H**
2 plectranthus (*P. madagascariensis* 'Variegated Mintleaf'), page 187, **I**

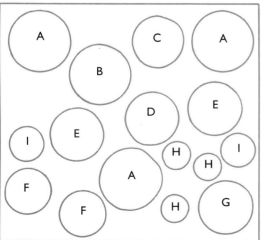

1 Scrub out the plastic liner and position it inside the planter.
2 Place crocks over the drainage holes. Fill the liner with potting compost to within 13cm (5in) of the rim.
3 Plant the white osteospermums (A), one in each back corner and one in the centre near the front. Add compost around them.
4 Place the marguerite (B) and the petunia (C) between the two osteospermums in the back. In front of this row plant the pink osteospermum (D) with a verbena (E) on either side of it.
5 Put the two diascias (F) in the front left corner and the helichrysum (G) with nemesias (H) in an arc around it on the right.
6 Add the two plectranthus (I), one on either side of the planter.
7 Add potting compost to 5cm (2in) below the rim. Firm in plants.
8 Water well.

PURPLE FOLIAGE

Deep purple foliage is uncommon among the plants most often used in container mixtures, but it is well worth including, because it seems to intensify the colour of flowers that are placed close to it. Here, in a simple terracotta pot, a magnificently rich magenta petunia meets its match in a purple-leaved sweet basil (*below*). A wooden trough planted with a conventional mixture of scarlet nasturtiums and dwarf French marigolds is transformed by the addition of sultry purple-leaved cabbages (*opposite*). The daring mix of scarlet and orange flowers with the large, plum-purple leaves of the interlopers from the vegetable garden creates a stunning effect.

A POT OF BASIL AND PETUNIAS

Plant in late spring and place in a sunny, sheltered spot. Water regularly, but allow the potting compost to become almost dry between waterings. Apply a liquid fertilizer every two weeks, starting three to four weeks after planting. Pinch back the basil flowers as they develop, and deadhead the petunias regularly. Discard all the plants in the autumn.

Terracotta pot, diameter 20cm (8in), height 17cm (7in)
Crocks
Soil-based potting compost
1 purple-leaved sweet basil (*Ocimum basilicum* 'Purple
  Ruffles'), page 196–7, **A**
2 magenta petunias, page 170, **B**

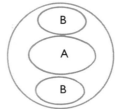

1 Scrub the pot and soak it thoroughly in clean water.
2 Put crocks over the drainage holes.
3 Half-fill the container with potting compost. Position the basil (**A**) in the centre of the pot with a petunia (**B**) on either side of it.
4 Add compost to 2.5–5cm (1–2in) below the rim. Firm in the plants.
5 Water well.

A TROUGH OF ANNUALS WITH CABBAGES

Put the trough in position, in full sun, before filling it. Planted in late spring, this combination will be attractive through most of the summer and into the autumn. Water regularly and apply a weak liquid fertilizer every two weeks, starting two to three weeks after planting. Deadhead the marigolds and nasturtiums and tidy the leaves of both these plants and the cabbages frequently. Discard all the plants in the autumn.

Wooden trough, length 1.35m (54in),
  width 30cm (12in), depth 25cm
  (10in)
Crocks
Soil-based or soil-less potting compost
9 purple-leaved cabbages (*Brassica
  oleracea* Capitata Group),
  page 189, **A**
18 dwarf French marigolds (*Tagetes*
  'Paprika'), page 148, **B**
5 scarlet-flowered nasturtiums
  (*Tropaeolum majus* 'Empress of
  India'), page 155, **C**

1 Scrub the trough thoroughly.
2 Place a layer of crocks over the bottom of the trough, making sure that the drainage holes are covered.
3 Fill with potting compost to within 10cm (4in) of the rim.
4 Plant the cabbages (**A**), placing one at each corner and one in the centre at the back; distribute the other four in the remaining space.
5 Add a group of five French marigolds (**B**) in the front left of

the trough and another group of five at the back, to the right of the centre cabbage. Then add two groups of three marigolds, one in front of the centre cabbage and one in the front right. Finally, position another two marigolds at the back left.

6 Plant the nasturtiums (C), two at the back beside the

corner cabbages and one in the middle of each end between the cabbages. Add another one off-centre, to the front and left of the centre cabbage.

7 Add potting compost to about 2.5–5cm (1–2in) below the rim of the trough. Firm in the plants.

8 Water well.

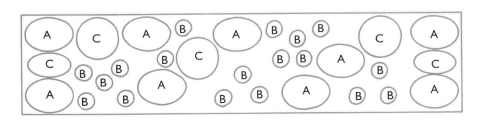

FOCUS ON AROMATIC FOLIAGE

When planting a window box, which needs to make an impression from both inside and out, it is especially important to pay attention to texture and scent as well as to flower and foliage colour. The aromatic cream-variegated foliage of *Pelargonium* 'Lady Plymouth' forms the core of this window box planting (*below*), while the small purple flowers of *Heliotropium* 'Chatsworth' provide delicious fragrance that will waft into the room over a long season.

The unusual copper urn (*opposite*) merited a highly original planting. The key plant in the scheme is a scented-leaved pelargonium (*Pelargonium* 'Atomic Snowflake'), whose large leaves have a creamy margin. An interesting contrast is provided by another scented-leaved pelargonium (*P. crispum* 'Variegatum'), with variegated foliage that is tightly crinkled. These pelargoniums have pink flowers, in keeping with the colour theme of the whole planting.

A FRAGRANT WINDOW BOX

This window box for full sun could be filled in its final position or, since it is made of light plastic, moved after planting, which should be done in late spring or early summer. Water regularly and apply a liquid fertilizer every two weeks, starting two to three weeks after planting. Dig up the plants in the autumn and move the diascias to the open garden. Overwinter cuttings of the pelargoniums and heliotropes in a frost-free place (see pages 82–3, 85).

Plastic window box, length 1m (40in), width and depth
   20cm (8in)

Crocks

Soil-based or soil-less potting compost

2 cream-variegated pelargoniums (*P.* 'Lady Plymouth'), page 187, **A**

2 grey-leaved helichrysums (*H. petiolare*), page 193, **B**

3 pale mauve pelargoniums (*P.* 'L'Elégante'), page 170, **C**

2 heliotropes (*Heliotropium* 'Chatsworth'), page 169, **D**

2 salmon-pink diascias (*D. rigescens*), page 160, **E**

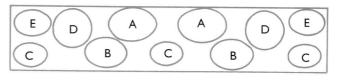

1 Cover the drainage holes with crocks and half-fill the box with potting compost.

2 Plant the cream-variegated pelargoniums (**A**) at the back, one on either side of the centre. In front of these, add the two helichrysums (**B**) with one mauve pelargonium (**C**) between them.

3 Plant a heliotrope (**D**) on either side of this group, and add a diascia (**E**) at each end in the back. Insert a mauve pelargonium at each of the two front corners.

4 Add potting compost to a level about 2.5cm (1in) below the rim of the box. Firm in the plants.

5 Water well and allow the container to drain before moving into position.

VARIEGATED LEAVES WITH PINK FLOWERS

Plant in late spring or early summer and place in full sun. Water regularly and apply a liquid fertilizer every two weeks, starting three to four weeks after planting. Overwinter the anisodontea, and also cuttings of the pelargoniums and the verbenas, under glass. Plant the diascias in the open garden, and keep the ground ivy in pots for next spring.

Copper urn, diameter of bowl at opening 50cm (20in), depth 45cm (18in)

Crocks

Gravel

Soil-based potting compost

1 anisodontea (*A. capensis*), page 158, **A**

2 pink verbenas (*V.* 'Silver Anne'), page 165, **B**

1 variegated small-leaved pelargonium (*P. crispum* 'Variegatum'), page 187, **C**

3 bright pink diascias (*D. cordata*), page 160, **D**

3 variegated scented-leaved pelargoniums (*P.* 'Atomic Snowflake'), page 187, **E**

2 variegated ground ivy (*Glechoma hederacea* 'Variegata'), page 186, **F**

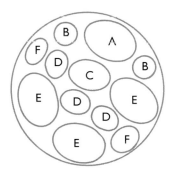

1 Clean the urn thoroughly. Put crocks over the drainage holes, and cover the base with an 8cm (3in) layer of gravel.

2 Add potting compost to a level 10–15cm (4–6in) below the container's rim.

3 Plant the anisodontea (**A**) towards the back of the urn, the verbenas (**B**) on either side of it and the small-leaved pelargonium (**C**) in front of it.

4 Set the diascias (**D**) in a curving line in the centre of the container. Plant one scented-leaved pelargonium (**E**) at the edge of the urn behind this line and two in front. Then add the two ground ivy (**F**), one near the front, the other further back.

5 Add potting compost to within 5cm (2in) of the urn's rim. Firm in the plants.

6 Water well.

FOLIAGE CONTRASTS

Though flowers usually steal the limelight, it is often the skilful use of foliage that ensures the success of a container planting. The warm shades of the verbena 'Peaches and Cream' add their chameleon charm to this hanging basket. But the underlying strength of the planting is based on contrasts of foliage texture, leaf shape and colour, summed up in the rich mixture of the coleus.

BASKET OF BRIGHT FOLIAGE

Plant this hanging basket in late spring for a display that will last throughout the summer. Hang in a sunny, sheltered position. Water the plants regularly and apply a liquid fertilizer every two weeks, starting two to three weeks after planting. Pinch out the coleus flowers as soon as they start to form, and deadhead the verbenas. Dismantle the planting in the autumn, saving the heuchera for planting out in the open. Rooted cuttings of the helichrysum can be overwintered under glass.

Wire-framed hanging basket,
    diameter 45cm (18in)
Coir fibre (or other) liner, page 56
Soil-based or soil-less potting
    compost
1 clump of purple-leaved heuchera
    (*H. micrantha* var. *diversifolia*
    'Palace Purple', page 189, **A**
3 dark-leaved coleus
    (*Solenostemon*), page 191, **B**
3 warm-coloured verbenas (*V.* 'Peaches
    and Cream'), page 149, **C**
3 helichrysums with yellow-green
    leaves (*H. petiolare* 'Limelight'),
    page 184, **D**

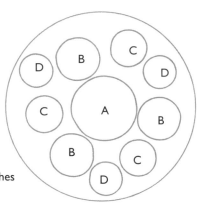

1 Position the hanging basket on an empty pail or large pot to give a stable base. Detach one chain. Place the liner in the hanging basket.

2 Fill the lined basket three-quarters full with potting compost.

3 Place the heuchera (**A**) in the centre and and space the coleus (**B**) evenly around it. Add the verbenas (**C**) between the coleus and tuck the helichrysums (**D**) between the coleus and the verbenas.

4 Add more potting compost, to about 2.5cm (1in) below the rim of the basket. Firm in the plants.

5 Water well. Allow to drain before arranging the chains and hanging the basket in a sheltered but open and sunny position.

PLANTINGS IN IMPROVISED CONTAINERS

The blemishes of recycled containers sometimes need to be masked by planting, but when improvised pieces are of the quality of this oval terracotta vessel (*below*), originally intended for salting pork, or the fine old copper (*opposite*), used for washing clothes, the planting should complement and not obscure the container. Both of these containers have drainage holes drilled in their bases.

A limited palette of pinks and purples has been used in the oval container. The copper is outstanding for its simple full shape, the regular pattern of its riveting and above all for its magnificent patina. Trailing magenta petunias and deep purple heliotropes seem to intensify its blue-green hue, making a richly coloured base to which marguerites in white and pink provide a light topping.

AN OVAL CONTAINER

Planted up in late spring for an open, sunny position, this scheme will continue through summer into autumn. Water well and feed with a liquid fertilizer every two weeks, starting three weeks after planting. Deadhead regularly. Overwinter cuttings of the pelargoniums, helichrysum and verbenas (see pages 82–3, 85).

Terracotta container, length 50cm (20in), maximum width and depth 25cm (10in)
Crocks
Soil-based potting compost
1 white marguerite (*Argyranthemum*), page 130, **A**
2 white pelargoniums, page 135, **B**
2 trailing convolvulus (*C. sabatius*), page 174, **C**
1 grey-leaved helichrysum (*H. petiolare*), page 193, **D**
4 white verbenas (*V. tenuisecta f. alba*), page 136, **E**

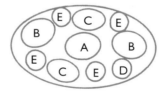

1 Scrub the container thoroughly and soak it in clean water.
2 Place crocks over the drainage holes, and fill with compost to within 10cm (4in) of the rim.
3 Position the marguerite (A) in the centre and two pelargoniums (B) at either end. Draw potting compost around them.
4 Put in the convolvulus (C), one on either side of the marguerite. Place the helichrysum (D) at one end of the trough. Add the verbenas (E).
5 Add compost to 2.5–5cm (1–2in) below the rim. Firm in all plants.
6 Water well.

A BLUE-GREEN COPPER

Set the copper in a sunny position before planting in late spring to provide a display that will continue through summer and into autumn. Water regularly but allow the compost to become nearly dry between waterings. Feed with liquid fertilizer every two weeks, starting two to three weeks after planting. Deadhead regularly. Overwinter cuttings of the hibiscus, marguerites and heliotropes (see pages 82–3, 85).

Copper, diameter 55cm (22in), depth 45cm (18in)
Crocks
Soil-based potting compost
3 white marguerites (*Argyranthemum foeniculaceum* of gardens), page 131, **A**
1 lilac hibiscus (*Alyogyne huegelii*), page 158, **B**
2 pink double marguerites (*Argyranthemum* 'Vancouver'), page 158, **C**
2 dark purple heliotropes (*Heliotropium* 'Princess Marina'), page 169, **D**
2 magenta-flowered trailing petunias, page 170, **E**

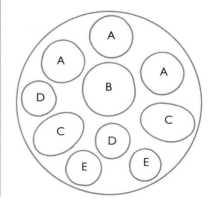

1 Scrub the copper and wash it thoroughly in clean water.

2 Place a layer of crocks in the base, covering the drainage holes, and fill to within 13cm (5in) of the rim with potting compost.

3 Set one white-flowered marguerite (A) at the back of the copper and the other two on either side and in front of it, adding potting compost around them to keep them firmly in position.

4 Plant the lilac hibiscus (B) in the centre and the two pink marguerites (C) on either side and in front of it.

5 Add potting compost to about 5cm (2in) below the rim and firm in the plants.

6 Plant one heliotrope (D) in front of the lilac hibiscus and the other at one edge behind a pink-flowered marguerite. Add the two petunias (E) to trail over the front of the copper. Firm in the plants.

7 Water well.

EYE-CATCHING REDS

These two plantings, very different in scale, both have prominent foliage centrepieces with brightly coloured flowers assembled around them. In the window box planting (*below*) a hart's-tongue fern is surrounded by bright red New Guinea hybrid impatiens, extremely useful plants that provide bright colours over a long season and do best in partial shade. Their foliage is also an attractive feature: sometimes it is variegated and sometimes a dark purplish red. The imposing scheme in the large pot (*opposite*) features red pelargoniums and a spiky cordyline, in a spectacular display suitable for a sunny patio or terrace. Pelargoniums come in a good range of vibrant reds and also flower prolifically over a long season, but they need a position in full sun.

A WINDOW BOX FOR PARTIAL SHADE

Because the window box is light, it can be filled before being positioned. Place in partial shade in early summer. Water well and apply liquid fertilizer every two weeks, starting three to four weeks after planting. Deadhead the impatiens and pinch back plectranthus shoots (cuttings can be overwintered, see pages 82–3, 85). Discard the impatiens at the end of the season. The fern can be used in another planting.

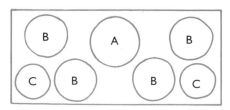

Terracotta window box, length 60cm (2ft), width and depth 25cm (10in)
Crocks
Soil-based potting compost
1 hart's-tongue fern (*Asplenium scolopendrium*), page 179, **A**
4 red impatiens (*I.* New Guinea Hybrids), pages 161–2, **B**
2 variegated plectranthus (*P. madagascariensis* 'Variegated Mintleaf'), page 187, **C**

1 Scrub the window box and soak it thoroughly in clean water. Put crocks over the drainage holes, and fill the container three-quarters full with potting compost.
2 Plant the fern (**A**) as a centrepiece, slightly to the back, then surround it with the impatiens (**B**), two in the front and one on either side. Position the plectranthus (**C**) at the front corners of the window box.
3 Add potting compost to about 2.5cm (1in) below the rim of the window box. Firm in the plants.
4 Water well.

110

A SPECTACULAR POT OF VIBRANT COLOUR

Plant in late spring or early summer with the pot in its final position in full sun. Water regularly. If a slow-release fertilizer is incorporated into the potting compost, further applications of fertilizer should be unnecessary. The pelargoniums and the canna rhizomes can be overwintered (see page 85) and the cordyline reused in a subsequent planting.

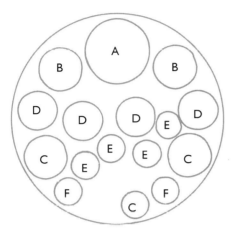

Terracotta pot, diameter 60cm (2ft), height 65cm (26in)

Crocks

Soil-based potting compost with slow-release fertilizer

1 mature purple-leaved cordyline (*C. australis* Purpurea Group), page 189, **A**

2 red cannas (*C.* 'Roi Humbert'), page 109, **B**

3 red Ivy-leaved pelargoniums (*P.* 'Yale'), page 154, **C**

4 red Zonal pelargoniums (*P.* 'Paul Crampel'), page 154, **D**

4 lime-green flowering tobacco plants (*Nicotiana* 'Lime Green'), page 142, **E**

2 red salvias (*S. fulgens*), page 155, **F**

1 Scrub the pot and soak it thoroughly in clean water. Place crocks over the drainage holes, and half-fill the pot with potting compost.

2 Arrange the plants so they get maximum light on the side that provides the main view. Plant the cordyline (**A**) in the centre but towards the back of the container. Position the cannas (**B**) on either side of it. Draw potting mix around them to hold them in place.

3 Position the Ivy-leaved pelargoniums (**C**), evenly spaced and tilted outwards, around the edge of the pot. Plant the Zonal pelargoniums (**D**) along the centre line. Position the flowering tobacco plants (**E**) and the salvias (**F**) in front of the Zonal pelargoniums.

4 Add potting compost to about 5cm (2in) below the pot's rim. Firm in the plants.

5 Water well.

PLANTING FOR THE SETTING

These two plantings are appropriate for their setting, yet could be adapted to fit happily into other contexts. Both benefit from being raised on tree-stump pedestals. The plain terracotta pot (*below*) is planted with grey foliage, a magenta petunia and sprawling fan flowers. It is mounted at the boundary between the ordered garden and a wilder area. The colour harmony extends the theme of the garden but the asymmetry of the plants is in keeping with the gentle wildness beyond. Helichrysum and an upright grass add height to a container planting in a yellow, cream and mauve colour theme that is radiant against a blue and yellow backdrop (*right*).

GREY FOLIAGE WITH FAN FLOWERS AND PETUNIAS

Plant in late spring for an open sunny position. Water regularly and feed with a weak liquid fertilizer every two weeks, starting three to four weeks after planting. Deadhead frequently. It is worth over-wintering cuttings of the plecostachys and the fan flower (see pages 82–3, 85).

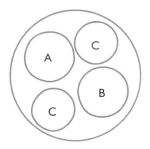

Terracotta pot, diameter 35cm (14in), height 30cm (12in)
Crocks
Soil-based potting compost
1 magenta petunia, page 170, **A**
1 plecostachys (*P. serpyllifolia*), pages 194–5, **B**
2 fan flowers (*Scaevola aemula* 'Blue Fan'), page 176, **C**

1 Scrub the pot and soak it thoroughly in clean water.
2 Cover the drainage holes with crocks. Fill with potting compost to within 10cm (4in) of the rim.
3 Set the petunia (**A**) and the plecostachys (**B**) on either side of the centre of the pot. Place the two fan flowers (**C**) nearer to the edges.
4 Add potting compost to 5cm (2in) below the rim. Firm in the plants.
5 Water well.

A YELLOW, CREAM, AND MAUVE PLANTING

Plant in late spring for a summer-long display suitable for an open, sunny position. This dense planting will need frequent watering and should be fed with a liquid fertilizer every two weeks, starting two to three weeks after planting. Mix water-retaining granules with the potting compost to even out fluctuations in moisture content. Deadhead petunias and trim back untidy or excessive growth. When the planting is dismantled, discard the petunias and tobacco plants. It is worth overwintering the gardener's garters and cuttings of the other plants (see pages 82–3, 85).

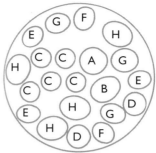

Ceramic container, diameter 50cm (20in), depth 40cm (16in)

Crocks

Soil-less or soil-based potting compost, with water-retaining granules incorporated

1 yellow petunia, page 142, **A**

1 white petunia, page 136, **B**

5 dwarf white tobacco plants (*Nicotiana* 'White Bedder'), page 135, **C**

2 thymophyllas (*T. tenuiloba*), page 143, **D**

3 grey-leaved helichrysums (*H. petiolare*), page 193, **E**

2 variegated helichrysums (*H. petiolare* 'Variegata'), page 193, **F**

3 gardener's garters (*Phalaris arundinacea* var. *picta*) page 187, **G**

4 brachyscomes (*B. multifida*), page 173, **H**

1 Scrub the container and wash it thoroughly.

2 Cover the drainage holes with crocks and fill to within 10cm (4in) of the rim with potting compost.

3 Position the petunias (A and B) and the tobacco plants (C) in slightly off-centre groups.

4 Space the thymophyllas (D) and both the grey-leaved (E) and the variegated (F) helichrysums around the rim.

5 Add the gardener's garters (G), two towards the back of the container and one at the front right. Tuck in the brachyscomes (H), two at the back and two towards the front.

6 Add potting compost to 5cm (2in) below the rim. Firm in the plants.

7 Water well.

CASCADING FUCHSIAS

With elegant, pendulous flowers carried over a lengthy season, the hybrid fuchsias make an invaluable group of shrubs for containers. Fuchsias with lax stems are particularly good as trailers for pots and hanging baskets, but even on more upright fuchsias the prettily shaped flowers dangle gracefully. Upright and trailing fuchsias can be combined together successfully, as they have been in the handsome lattice-pattern terracotta pot (*see page 87*),

with a trailing fuchsia forming a broad skirt. Bushy fuchsias help to complete the crown of a hanging basket (*right*) which includes several trailing plants, other fuchsias among them. Some especially beautiful fuchsias bear long tubular flowers with small, pointed petals. In another lattice-pattern pot (*pages 116–17*), *Fuchsia* 'Gartenmeister Bonstedt' glows among cool swirls of grey helichrysums and blue lobelias.

A POT OF FUCHSIAS

See illustration page 87.

Plant in late spring in full sun. Insert bamboo canes around the bush fuchsia at planting time and as the fuchsia stems develop tie them to the canes. Water regularly and apply a liquid fertilizer every two weeks, starting two to three weeks after planting. Overwinter cuttings of the fuchsias and the salvia (see pages 82–3, 85).

Terracotta pot, diameter 43cm (17in),
    height 50cm (20in)
Crocks
Soil-based potting compost
1 bush fuchsia (*F.* 'Tom Woods'),
    page 168, **A**
1 trailing fuchsia (*F.* 'Jack Shahan'),
    page 161, **B**
1 dark-flowered salvia (*S. discolor*),
    page 176, **C**
2–3 bamboo canes

1 Scrub and soak the pot.
2 Cover the drainage holes with crocks. Fill with potting compost to 13cm (5in) below the rim.
3 Plant the bush fuchsia (**A**) at the back, the trailing fuchsia (**B**) in the centre, and the salvia (**C**) in front.
4 Add potting compost to 5cm (2in) below the container's rim. Firm in the plants.
5 Insert the canes around the bush fuchsia.
6 Water well.

FUCHSIAS IN A HANGING BASKET

Plant in mid-spring. Fix a strong support in a sunny, sheltered spot (see page 43). Add water-retentive granules to the potting compost and water frequently, applying a liquid fertilizer every two weeks. Deadhead and trim regularly. Cuttings of the fuchsias, marguerites and pelargoniums can be overwintered (see pages 82–3, 85).

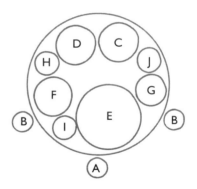

Wire-framed hanging basket, diameter 45cm (18in)
Synthetic liner
Soil-less potting compost with water-retentive
    granules
1 variegated ground ivy (*Glechoma hederacea*
    'Variegata'), page 186, **A**
2 mauve-pink variegated Ivy-leaved
    pelargoniums, page 170, **B**
1 white bush fuchsia, page 132, **C**
1 pink marguerite (*Argyranthemum* 'Pink
    Australian'), page 158, **D**
1 red trailing fuchsia (*F.* 'Marinka'), page 153, **E**
1 white-and-pink trailing fuchsia, page 133, **F**
1 red Ivy-leaved pelargonium (*P.* 'Rote Mini-
    Cascade'), page 154, **G**
1 pink Ivy-leaved pelargonium (*P.* 'Madame Crousse'),
    page 163, **H**
1 grey-leaved helichrysum (*H. petiolare*), page 163, **I**
1 lime-green-leaved helichrysum (*H. petiolare*
    'Limelight'), page 184, **J**

1 Detach one of the chains from the basket.

2 Place the basket on an upturned pot. Put a liner inside the basket and half-fill it with potting compost.

3 Just above the compost level, cut the liner horizontally for 5cm (2in) at the centre front of the basket. Make similar cuts on either side.

4 From outside the basket, push the root ball of the ground ivy (A) through the centre slit. Push the two variegated pelargoniums (B) through the side slits. Add potting compost to 10cm (4in) below the basket's rim.

5 Plant the bush fuchsia (C) against the back of the basket and the marguerite (D) to its left. Place the red trailing fuchsia (E) in the centre towards the front, the white-and-pink trailing fuchsia (F) to its left and the red pelargonium (G) to its right.

6 Tuck in the pink pelargonium (H) and the helichrysums (I, J). Firm in the plants and add potting compost to 2.5cm (1in) below the rim of the basket.

7 Water well and allow to drain.

8 Attach the chain and hang the basket.

A RED FUCHSIA WITH GREYS AND BLUES

This planting is well suited to a prominent position. Symmetrical planting ensures that, through the free-flowing lines of the helichrysum veiling the other plants, the pot will look balanced from any angle. If planted in late spring, this scheme will provide an attractive display through summer into autumn. All the plants need full sun. Water regularly and apply a liquid fertilizer every two weeks, starting three weeks after planting. Rooted cuttings of the helichrysums and the fuchsia can be overwintered (see pages 82–3, 85). Discard the lobelias after flowering.

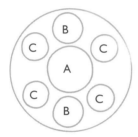

Terracotta pot, diameter 43cm (17in), height 50cm (20in)

Crocks

Soil-based potting compost

1 red bush fuchsia (*F.* 'Gartenmeister Bonstedt'), page 153, **A**

2 grey-leaved helichrysums (*H. petiolare*), page 193, **B**

4 blue-flowered lobelias, pages 175–6, **C**

1 Scrub the pot and soak it thoroughly in clean water.

2 Cover the drainage holes with crocks and fill the container with potting compost to 13cm (5in) below the rim.

3 Plant the fuchsia in the centre of the pot. Set the two helichrysums on either side and space the four lobelias evenly around it.

4 Add compost to 2.5–5cm (1–2in) below the pot's rim. Firm in the plants.

5 Water well.

SOFT ORANGES AND YELLOWS

Intense orange can be magnificent when seen in brilliant sunlight but where the sun shines less fiercely, paler shades of peach and apricot are easier to manage. These colours, which are well represented in a large number of summer-flowering tender perennials and shrubby plants that enjoy sunny positions, combine well with many other colours, including soft shades of yellow or cream, as shown here in a subtly restrained planting (*below*).

The appeal of the grand planting in the large container (*opposite*) lies partly in its fullness and in the wide range of plants included, but it could easily be simplified to take account of available plants and to suit a smaller pot.

A POT OF PEACHES AND CREAM

In this planting the verbena is placed against a background of the taller Sphaeralcea ambigua. *Plant in late spring, in a sunny position, for a display that will last through summer and into autumn. Water regularly and feed with a liquid fertilizer every two weeks, starting three weeks after planting. Deadhead the verbena throughout the summer. It is worth overwintering cuttings of the sphaeralcea (see pages 82–3, 85).*

Terracotta pot, diameter
    23cm (9in), depth
    17cm (7in)
Crocks
Soil-based potting compost
1 sphaeralcea (*S. ambigua*),
    page 148, **A**
2 warm-coloured verbenas
    (V. 'Peaches and Cream'),
    page 149, **B**

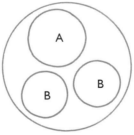

1 Scrub the pot and soak it thoroughly in clean water.
2 Put crocks over the drainage holes and half-fill with potting compost.
3 Set the sphaeralcea (**A**) to form the background to the planting, drawing compost around it. Place the verbenas (**B**) in front.
4 Add compost to come 5cm (2in) below the pot's rim. Firm in the plants.
5 Water well.

A LARGE POT OF TENDER PERENNIALS

Plant this mixture when there is no longer a risk of frost and it will give a display that lasts through summer and into autumn. Place this heavy pot in its final position, which should be open and sunny, before planting. Most of the plants are reasonably drought-tolerant, but the planting is dense and frequent watering is essential. Feed with a liquid fertilizer every two to three weeks, starting two weeks after planting. Deadhead the flowers regularly through summer and autumn. When dismantling the planting, keep the artemisia to plant in the open garden, or for use in a subsequent container planting. Cuttings of the marguerites, osteospermum and pelargoniums can be overwintered (see pages 82–3, 85).

Terracotta pot, diameter 55cm (22in),
    depth 60cm (24in)
Crocks
Soil-based potting compost
1 creamy-yellow osteospermum
    (*O.* 'Buttermilk'), page 135, **A**
1 white marguerite (*Argyranthemum
    gracile* 'Chelsea Girl'), page 131, **B**
2 yellow marguerites (*Argyranthemum
    callichrysum* 'Prado'), page 140, **C**
3 peach-pink pelargoniums, page 147, **D**
1 cigar plant (*C. ignea*) page 146, **E**
3 African daisies (*Arctotis* x *hybrida*
    'Apricot'), page 145, **F**
2 bidens (*B. ferulifolia*), page 140, **G**
1 grey-leaved artemisia
    (*A. stelleriana*), page 192, **H**
1 Swan River daisy (*Brachysome
    iberidifolia*), pages 173–4, **I**

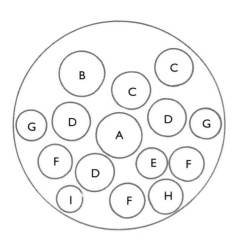

1 Scrub the pot and soak it thoroughly in clean water.

2 Put crocks over the drainage holes, and add potting compost to within 13cm (5in) of the rim.

3 Position the osteospermum (A) in the centre of the pot, adding compost around it to hold it in position. Place the white and yellow marguerites (B and C) behind the osteospermum.

4 Position the pelargoniums (D) and the cigar plant (E) to the front and sides of the osteospermum, forming two-thirds of a circle. Set the three African daisies (F) to make an arc in the foreground.

5 Position the bidens (G) on the centre line at the rim and tuck in the artemisia (H) and Swan River daisy (I) at the edge in the foreground.

6 Add more compost, working it around the plants, to about 5cm (2in) below the rim of the pot. Firm in the plants.

7 Water well.

VIBRANT COLOURS

Flamboyant reds and yellows tend to dominate the garden during the second half of summer. A few annuals or perennials gathered together, as in these terracotta pots, can create an incandescent display.

Sunflowers tower over a red and yellow mixture, the fiery tone set by one of the most strongly coloured of the strawflowers combined with dwarf rudbeckias and coreopsis (*below*). All the components of this planting could be raised from seed sown in warmth in mid-spring.

A more subdued planting of perennials skilfully links foliage colour with plants in the open garden (*right*). Bronze-purples in the garden are picked up in the arching leaves of the phormium and in the heuchera with its irregularly cut, heart-shaped leaves, which have a metallic sheen. A dwarf form of the short-lived blanket flower provides a radiant mix of red and yellow.

A FIERY MIXTURE

Whether you raise these bright annuals from seed or buy them as young stock, you should plant the pot in late spring. This planted container is positioned to show it off from one angle and to expose all the plants to maximum sunlight. Water regularly and apply liquid fertilizer every two weeks, starting two to three weeks after planting. Discard plants at the end of their flowering season.

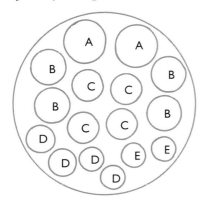

Terracotta pot, diameter 45cm
   (18in), height 50cm (20in)

Crocks

Soil-based potting compost

2 medium sunflowers (*Helianthus annuus* 'Valentine'), page 141, **A**

4 dwarf coreopsis (*C. tinctoria*), page 141, **B**

4 dwarf rudbeckias (*R. hirta* Rustic Dwarfs), page 148, **C**

4 strawflowers (*Helichrysum bracteatum* 'Hot Bikini'), page 146, **D**

2 oncosiphons (*O. grandiflorum*), page 142, **E**

1 Scrub the pot and soak it in clean water. Put crocks over the drainage holes and fill with potting compost to within 10cm (4in) of the rim.
2 Plant the sunflowers (**A**) at the back of the pot with the coreopsis (**B**) on either side. Add rudbeckias (**C**) in the centre, strawflowers (**D**) in front of them, and the oncosiphons (**E**) to the right.
3 Add compost to within 5cm (2in) of the pot's rim. Firm in the plants.
4 Water well.

A POT OF PURPLE, YELLOW AND RED

Plant in mid-spring for a summer display in full sun. Water regularly and apply a liquid fertilizer every two weeks, starting two to three weeks after planting. At the end of their flowering season, dig the plants up and move them to the open garden.

Terracotta pot, diameter 50cm (20in),
   height 40cm (16in)

Crocks

Soil-based potting compost

1 bronze-leaved phormium (*P.* 'Bronze Baby'), page 190, **A**

1 purple-leaved heuchera (*H. micrantha* var. *diversifolia* 'Palace Purple'), page 189, **B**

3 dwarf blanket flowers (*Gaillardia* 'Kobold'), page 146, **C**

1 variegated aquilegia, page 167, **D**

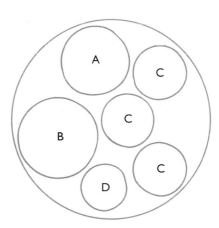

1 Scrub the pot and soak it in clean water. Put crocks over the drainage holes and fill with potting compost to 10cm (4in) below the rim.
2 Plant the phormium (**A**) off-centre, at the back, and the heuchera (**B**) in front of it, at their previous planting depths. Space the blanket flowers (**C**) evenly, and place the aquilegia (**D**) at the front.
3 Add compost to 2.5–5cm (1–2in) below the rim. Firm in the plants.
4 Water well.

A PLANTING FOR WINTER AND SPRING

Where the climate is sufficiently mild, dwarf evergreen shrubs, especially those that carry berries or flower in the coldest part of the year, make outstanding container plants for winter displays. Skimmias are compact, slow-growing, shade-tolerant evergreens that bear male and female flowers on different plants. With oval, leathery, pale or darker green leaves, they are good foliage plants throughout the year, but their glory lies in the brilliant globular red berries, borne in tight clusters, that make the female plants so ornamental from winter through to spring.

To produce good crops of berries the female skimmias need a male plant close by. The ideal arrangement is to use two or three female plants, spangled with polished red berries set among glossy foliage, as a skirt to a taller male skimmia. In the planting here the low-growing *Skimmia japonica* subsp. *reevesiana* is matched with the more vigorous male plant *S. j.* 'Rubella'. The latter has sweetly scented white flowers that open from pink buds in spring, and is also eye-catching from early to mid-winter, when the beautiful buds, reddish-brown in the early stages, are clustered on red stalks (*below*). The addition of a spring-flowering bulb, such as a white hyacinth, gives the planting a boost in spring (*opposite*). Skimmias need repotting only when their roots become congested.

EVERGREEN FOLIAGE WITH FLOWERS
AND BERRIES

Plant this arrangement in early to mid-autumn. In winter and spring it can be in a sunny site, but in summer it must have shade. Move the hyacinths to the open garden when they fade.

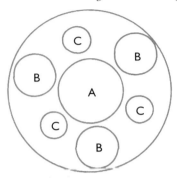

Terracotta pot, diameter 30cm (12in), depth 25cm (10in)
Crocks
Ericaceous compost incorporating slow-release fertilizer
1 male skimmia (*S. japonica* 'Rubella'), page 203, **A**
3 female skimmias (*S. j.* subsp. *reevesiana*), page 203, **B**
3 white hyacinths (*H. orientalis* 'Carnegie'), page 129, **C**

1 Scrub the pot and soak it thoroughly in clean water.
2 Put crocks over the drainage holes. Half-fill the container with compost.
3 Position the male skimmia (**A**) in the centre with the female plants (**B**) around it. Insert the hyacinths (**C**) between the female skimmias at a depth of 10cm (4in).
4 Add compost until it is 2.5–5cm (1–2in) below the pot's rim. Firm in the plants.
5 Water well.

COLOUR FOR LATE WINTER

Numerous dwarf bulbs shorten the long winter months by flowering well before the main flush of spring daffodils and tulips. Their effect is sometimes lost in the open garden but in containers they create a concentrated, vivid display. The flowers of irises, crocuses and dwarf daffodils, star performers in late winter, appear fragile but stand up surprisingly well to cold, rough weather. Evergreen foliage with yellow or cream variegation makes a sunny addition to winter containers, and relieves the starkness of bulbs.

Place containers planted with these delightful fore-runners of spring in prominent positions where they can be seen in comfort from indoors, or beside paths and doors that are used regularly. The displays put on by the late-winter bulbs may not be long-lived, but they are very heartening while they last. Where there is room, a succession of plantings can be held in reserve. Bring containers out as plants begin to bloom and replace them when the flowering is over.

DECORATED POT WITH DWARF DAFFODILS AND IRIS

The yellow variegation of the osmanthus and ivy is seen at its best in an open, sunny position. Plant these perennial foliage plants in autumn, at the same time as the bulbs. Where winters are severe, plant them in spring, adding the bulbs in early autumn. Replace the bulbs annually. Repot the foliage plants every two years, top-dressing with fresh compost in the year between.

Glazed and decorated pot, diameter 20cm (8in),
    depth 15cm (6in)

Crocks

Soil-based potting compost

1 yellow-variegated osmanthus (*O. heterophyllus* 'Goshiki'), page 185, **A**

2 green ivies, pages 180–81, **B**

1 yellow-variegated ivy (*Hedera helix* 'Golden Ingot'), page 184, **C**

2 dwarf daffodils (*Narcissus* 'Tête-à-Tête'), pages 138–39, **D**

4 yellow dwarf iris (*I. danfordiae)*, page 144, **E**

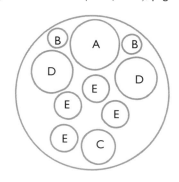

1 Scrub the pot and soak it thoroughly in clean water.
2 Put crocks over the drainage holes, and fill to within 5cm (2in) of the rim with potting compost.
3 Position the osmanthus (**A**) and the plain green ivy (**B**) at the back of the pot and the variegated ivy (**C**) in front.
4 Add potting compost to about 2.5cm (1in) below the rim of the pot, firming in the plants.
5 Plant the daffodil bulbs (**D**) on either side of the osmanthus and place the dwarf irises (**E**) in front of them. Use a sharp stick or a pencil to make holes so that they are set 5–8cm (2–3in) deep. Firm the surface.
6 Water well.

124

IRIS AND CROCUS WITH THYME

The thyme and bulbs in this planting do best in an open, sunny position, and need a free-draining potting compost. Where the climate allows, plant the thyme in autumn, at the same time as the bulbs. Trim the thyme after flowering to keep it neat, but discard when plants become straggly, after three or four years. Use new bulbs each year. Top-dress with fresh compost in spring.

Black plastic pot, diameter
   20cm (8in), depth 15cm
   (6in)
Crocks
Soil-based potting compost
   with added grit
1 yellow-variegated thyme
   (*Thymus serpyllum*
   'Goldstream'), page 185, **A**
15 blue Reticulata iris
   (*I.* 'Harmony'), page 177, **B**
10 deep yellow crocus
   (*C. chrysanthus* 'Gipsy
   Girl'), page 144, **C**

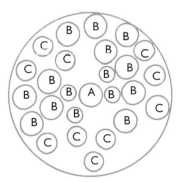

1 Scrub the pot and soak it thoroughly in clean water.
2 Place crocks in the base of the pot, covering the drainage holes, and fill to within 5cm (2in) of the rim with potting compost.
3 Plant the thyme (**A**) in the centre of the pot, adding potting compost so that when firmed the surface is about 2.5cm (1in) below the rim of the container.
4 Plant the iris (**B**) and crocus bulbs (**C**) all around the thyme. Lift the foliage of the thyme and use a sharp stick or a pencil to make holes so that the bulbs are set 5–8cm (2–3in) deep.
5 Water well.

PLANTS FOR CONTAINERS

This directory to more than a thousand plants, all of which can be grown by the amateur gardener with no specialist skills, groups entries in various categories. The first and largest section covers the many plants, ranging from low-growing trailers to large shrubs, that are grown principally, although usually not exclusively, for their flowers.

To help you design attractive schemes, the plants are grouped according to flower colour. Ornamental plants with attractive foliage are covered in the second section and grouped according to the colour of their leaves. The third section describes useful plants that can be grown successfully in containers, with sub-sections for herbs, vegetables and fruit. Finally, there is a small section on berrying plants and grasses. Within each sub-section of the directory, plants are listed alphabetically according to botanical (Latin) name but the common name is given at the head of each entry. Where there is more than one entry for plants (tulips, for example, have several entries because of their wide colour range) a cross-reference in bold type indicates the entry containing advice on cultivation.

Plants marked poisonous contain certain compounds that may prove toxic to people or pets. There is still much work to be done in this field, so it should not be assumed that plants not described in this way are non-poisonous.

Many of the simplest but most effective planting schemes in containers rely on a happy combination of flowers and foliage. The sprightliness of these starry pelargoniums, their flowers elegantly poised above beautifully cut and marked foliage, makes them a valuable addition to one of the most useful groups of summer flowers for containers. A coral and salmon fuchsia emerges here from a subtly textured and coloured base formed from its own foliage, the scented-leaved pelargonium 'Lady Plymouth' and the grey-leaved, trailing Helichrysum petiolare.

Whether you are looking for individual specimens of refined beauty, dazzling additions to give a lift to mixtures or collections for all-white schemes, you will find a wide range of plants among the whites. Extending this range are the many near-whites in which tints or stains provide links with stronger colours. The creams are particularly beautiful, almost as luminous as white in the evening light, but softer and warmer in full sun.

SPRING

ARABIS

Arabis alpina subsp. *caucasica* 'Flore Pleno'

EVERGREEN PERENNIAL   ZONE 5

This spreading evergreen, often listed as *A. caucasica* 'Flore Pleno', makes a mat of grey-green leaves about 50cm (20in) wide (*below*). The double white flowers, clustered on stems 23cm (9in) high in late spring and early summer, look somewhat like miniature stocks.

Plant arabis so that it trails over the edge of a trough filled with other sun-loving rock-garden plants, using a gritty, free-draining, soil-based compost. Deadhead and trim back straggling stems after flowering.

Arabis *Arabis alpina* subsp. *caucasica* 'Flore Pleno'

Camellia *Camellia japonica* 'Alba Plena'

CAMELLIA

Camellia japonica

EVERGREEN SHRUB   ZONE 8

Camellias are outstanding shrubs for containers, treasured for their polished dark green leaves as well as for their elegant flowers. Flower colour is predominantly pink or red, but there are several white forms, with flowers ranging from single through semi-double to fully double.

The single 'Alba Simplex' has conspicuous stamens, while the petals of the fully double 'Shiragiku' (syn. *C. j.* 'Purity') are arranged with formal precision. An impressive formal double with overlapping petals is the bushy 'Alba Plena' (*above*). 'Lady Vansittart' is a semi-double, with white petals streaked pink.
*See also pages 150, **156**.*

CLEMATIS

Clematis

CLIMBER   ZONE 3   POISONOUS

Many of the spring-flowering clematis are too vigorous to do well in containers, but those that are less rampant add an appealing dimension to the garden when they are trained up supports, or look very attractive when allowed to trail.

C. alpina var. *sibirica* has a green-tinged selection, 'White Moth', which produces masses of nodding double flowers in late spring. It rarely exceeds 1.8m (6ft) in height. *C. florida* 'Sieboldii' (Zone 6) has double

flowers, white with a hint of green surrounding a purple boss. Cut both back lightly when the flowers fade. *See also pages **131–2**, 156, 159, 167, 174.*

CROCUS

Crocus vernus 'Jeanne d'Arc'

CORM   ZONE 4

This large Dutch crocus blooms in early spring, producing sturdy flowers up to 13cm (5in) high. The tongues of orange styles are eye-catching in the white bowls formed by rounded petals.

Plant in autumn, using a free-draining soil-based or soil-less compost (add coarse sand). Set corms just over 5cm (2in) deep and close to one another but not touching. Use alone or plant with other spring flowers in pots or a sunny window box. *See also pages 137, **138**, 144, 149, 166, 171, 177.*

SNAKE'S-HEAD FRITILLARY

Fritillaria meleagris var. *alba*

BULB   ZONE 4   POISONOUS

The netting and veining on the drooping bells of the snake's-head fritillary give this white variety a lovely, green-tinged pallor (*below*). It is as beautiful in containers as when naturalized in grass. Plant in autumn among mixed spring flowers.
*See also page **166**.*

Snake's-head fritillary *Fritillaria meleagris* var. *alba*

HYACINTH

Hyacinthus orientalis

BULB ZONE 5

The densely packed, waxy flower heads of all hyacinths are intensely fragrant. Two popular whites, 'Carnegie' and 'L'Innocence', both have spikes about 20cm (8in) high. 'Carnegie' produces tightly packed spikes of pure white in mid-spring. 'L'Innocence', less congested, has ivory-white flowers.
*See also pages 138, 150, 156, **172**; illustrations pages 41, 123.*

DAFFODIL, NARCISSUS, JONQUIL

Narcissus

BULB ZONE 4

The bewitchingly fragrant *N. papyraceus* (*N.* 'Paper White', Zones 9–10), with bunches of white, starry flowers, though deservedly popular as an indoor pot plant for winter, is too tender to be grown outdoors except in very mild areas. However, there are many white daffodils that are more robust.

Early spring brings 'February Silver', a Cyclamineus daffodil that is usually less than 35cm (14in) tall. The trumpet, surrounded by milky petals, fades from lemon-yellow to cream. 'Ice Follies', only 40cm (16in) in height, is more heavily built and useful for exposed gardens. Creamy petals surround a frilled cup, which fades from primrose to near-white as it ages.

In mid-spring, 'Dove Wings' produces flowers with milky white, swept-back petals and a pale yellow trumpet on a stem rarely more than 30cm (12in) high. 'Petrel', only 25cm (10in) high and ideal for a window box, produces two or three stems per bulb, each carrying as many as five small-cupped flowers of pure white.

'Actaea', a hybrid of the poet's narcissus (*N. poeticus*), blooms in late spring and is sweetly scented (*right*). Growing to a height of 50cm (20in), it has glistening white petals surrounding a small yellow cup with an orange rim. 'Cheerfulness', also late flowering and sometimes more than 50cm (20in) tall, bears one to three double flowers per stem. They are cream with a yellow centre and have a delicious scent. 'Silver Chimes' (Zone 5) is slightly more tender. Stems 35cm (14in) high carry about six flowers each; the small cup is pale yellow and the petals are pure white.
*See also pages **138–9**, 144, 145.*

MOSS PHLOX

Phlox subulata 'White Delight'

EVERGREEN PERENNIAL ZONE 3

In mid- to late spring, the moss phlox is a mound of flat, starry flowers, mainly in pinks, mauves and reds. The mat of small linear leaves obscured at this season is not more than 10cm (4in) high, but can have a spread of over twice this. The vigorous 'White Delight' is a dazzling selection.

Grow in a gritty, soil-based compost with the container positioned in full sun. Trim plants after flowering to keep them compact.
See also page 163.

PIERIS

Pieris

EVERGREEN SHRUB ZONE 5

The medium-sized and occasionally large shrubs that make up this evergreen genus are often remarkable for the brilliant colouring of their young foliage in spring as well as for their sprays of waxy flowers, which are usually attractive in bud throughout the winter months. As container-grown plants they are reasonably compact but spreading at the base and therefore best planted alone. None tolerates alkaline soil, so grow in a pot or tub filled with an ericaceous compost.

P. formosa var. *forrestii*, of which there are several named forms, is relatively

Daffodil *Narcissus* 'Actaea'

tender (Zone 8) and needs a sheltered position. When container grown, it is unlikely to exceed a height and spread of 1.8m (6ft). In spring, it produces brilliant scarlet young leaves, which then pass through pink and pale yellow before turning dark green. The sprays of white lily-of-the-valley flowers often coincide with the most vivid phase of the foliage.

Of similar size are several selections of the hardier *P. japonica*. Their young foliage is generally either bronze tinted or reddish, and lax sprays of fragrant white flowers, attractive in bud, open to white or pink flowers. A good example is 'Scarlett O'Hara', with reddish young foliage and pure white flowers.

Plant alone in a large pot, using a lime-free compost. Place in a lightly shaded, sheltered position. Pruning is rarely needed, but remove the seed pods as soon as they start to develop.

RHODODENDRON, AZALEA

Rhododendron

SHRUB ZONE 5

'Palestrina', an evergreen or semi-evergreen azalea (Zone 7), makes a bush about 1.2m (4ft) in height and spread, which in late spring carries masses of funnel-shaped flowers. Faint green stripes give their whiteness a cool distinction.

'Silver Sixpence' is one of the *R. yakushimanum* hybrids (Zone 4). Although it can have a spread of 1.5m (5ft), it is rarely more than 90cm (3ft) high. In late spring and early summer, trusses of creamy flowers prettily marked with lemon spots stud the evergreen foliage.
*See also pages 139, 142, 145, 148, 150, **156–7**, 167, 173.*

TULIP

Tulipa

BULB ZONE 3

White and cream tulips strike a distinctive note in the container garden. Shapely singles in unadulterated white and cream create a formal effect. Much less restrained are the doubles and also the many forms, both doubles and singles, that are streaked and feathered with other colours.

T. turkestanica is a starry-flowered species that mixes well with rock-garden plants. Blooming in early spring, its slender stems up to 30cm (12in) high, carry six or seven white

Tulip *Tulipa* 'White Triumphator'

flowers, marked cream and green on the outside and with a yellow centre.

Flowering in early to mid-spring is 'Diana', a single with pure white, egg-shaped blooms on sturdy stems 35cm (14in) high. 'Purissima', also known as 'White Emperor', flowers at the same time. Strong stems, 45cm (18in) high, carry beautifully shaped, milky, single flowers with yellow centres. In the same period comes 'Carnaval de Nice', a double with a densely packed bowl of white petals streaked with red. The stems, 40cm (16in) high, carry the flowers over variegated leaves.

In mid-spring, 'Schoonoord', a stocky double 30cm (12in) high, has peony-like flowers of milky whiteness; it is suitable for a window box. 'Mount Tacoma' is a long-lasting double for mid- to late spring with pure white flowers on stems 45cm (18in) high.

White tulips for late spring include 'Maureen', a milky white, tall single up to 60cm (2ft) high, and, at the same height, 'Estella Rijnveld', also a single, but such a confection of twisted and fringed petals streaked red and white that the shape appears to dissolve.

'Shirley' flowers in late spring, its stems 50cm (20in) or more high carrying single ivory-white blooms with delicate purple feathering. 'White Triumphator' (*above*) is one of the elegant Lily-flowered tulips, with gracefully curving, pointed petals. The single flowers are carried on stems 65cm (26in) high in late spring.
*See also pages 140, 145, **150–1**, 157, 167; illustration page 8.*

SUMMER

AFRICAN LILY

Agapanthus
PERENNIAL   ZONE 8
A. campanulatus var. *albidus* is a white variety of the more familiar blue African lily. Strap-shaped leaves and heads of numerous attractive white funnels are held on erect sturdy stems that are 60cm (2ft) high.
*See also page **173**.*

MOUNT ATLAS DAISY

Anacyclus pyrethrum subsp. *depressus*
PERENNIAL   ZONE 6
Low shrubs and prostrate perennials with a long flowering season are especially useful in troughs and other containers featuring rock-garden plants. The Mount Atlas daisy, a native of Morocco, may prove short-lived, but makes up for this shortcoming by flowering profusely throughout summer. Ground-hugging stems about 30cm (12in) long, which provide the framework for mats of finely cut leaves, radiate from a central rootstock. The up-turned stem tips carry white daisy flowers, which are rusty red in bud.

Plant in a sunny position in early autumn or mid-spring, using gritty, free-draining, soil-based compost.

ANTHEMIS

Anthemis punctata subsp. *cupaniana*
EVERGREEN PERENNIAL   ZONE 5
This relative of the common chamomile makes aromatic silvery cushions up to 30cm (12in) wide and high, composed of finely dissected leaves. Single daisies 5cm (2in) wide, or more, are borne profusely in late spring and summer.

Plant in gritty, soil-based potting compost and position in sun, among other rock-garden plants. Deadhead the blooms regularly to ensure a long flowering season.

SNAPDRAGON

Antirrhinum majus 'White Wonder'
HALF-HARDY ANNUAL
A. majus 'White Wonder' has flower spikes 45cm (18in) high (*right*). The flowers, white with a yellow throat, are of classic snapdragon form, tubular with five flared petal lobes about the closed mouth.
*See also pages 140, **151**, 158, 167.*

AFRICAN DAISY

Arctotis
HALF-HARDY ANNUAL
The sprawling *A. fastuosa* 'Zulu Prince' (*Venidium fastuosum* 'Zulu Prince'), with a height and spread of 60cm (2ft), has grey woolly leaves and large cream daisies, up to 10cm (4in) wide, with a black ring and centre. *A. venusta* (syn. *A. stoechadifolia*) has grey-green leaves and flowers that are blue in bud, opening white to show a blue centre surrounded by a yellow ring.
*See also page **145**.*

MARGUERITE, PARIS DAISY

Argyranthemum
EVERGREEN PERENNIAL   ZONE 9
The marguerite (sometimes listed under its former name of *Chrysanthemum frutescens*) is one of the most useful standbys of the container garden, with a non-stop display of white daisy flowers through summer and into autumn. In its native Canary Islands and in similarly mild areas, it will flower outdoors throughout most of the year. Elsewhere, it can be overwintered under glass, but is commonly treated as an annual, young plants being bought in late spring or early summer and discarded in autumn.

This sub-shrubby perennial grows 45–90cm (18–36in) high, with a spread of up to 75cm (30in). Specimens can be trained as standards to a height of about 1.5m (5ft). The feathery foliage,

Snapdragon *Antirrhinum majus* 'White Wonder'

either grey-green or dark green, is often nearly hidden by the daisies, which are 5cm (2in) across.

A similar and equally free-flowering marguerite is *A. foeniculaceum* of gardens, which is distinguished by its finely dissected, blue-green leaves. *A. gracile* 'Chelsea Girl' is another pretty white single and 'Blizzard', 'Mrs F. Sander' and 'Qinta White' (also listed as *A.* 'Sark') are all good doubles, with a height of 60cm (2ft) and a spread of 45cm (18in).

Plant singly in containers (this is the best way to grow standards) or combine them with other sun-loving plants, using soil-based compost. Deadhead regularly throughout the flowering season to keep plants blooming. If over-wintering large specimens under glass, cut back hard in autumn and trim in spring. *See also pages 140, 158; illustrations pages 10, 20, 98, 101, 108, 109, 119.*

BROWALLIA

Browallia

HALF-HARDY ANNUAL/PERENNIAL ZONE 9
The blue forms of browallia are the best known, but 'White Troll' makes a useful variation for mixed plantings in hanging baskets, window boxes and other containers in sunny, sheltered positions. These compact plants, with a height and spread of 25cm (10in), flower through summer and into autumn. *See also page 174.*

HEATHER, LING

Calluna vulgaris

EVERGREEN SHRUB ZONE 4
There are many forms of this dwarf shrub, with a wide range of flower and foliage colour. Those with white flowers provide an attractive variation on the more familiar purples and mauves.

'White Lawn', only 5cm (2in) high but often with a spread of more than 30cm (12in), is ideal for softening the hard edge of a container. An upright alternative with grey foliage is 'Anthony Davis', 45cm (18in) high. Both flower in late summer and autumn. *See also pages 159, 183.*

BELLFLOWER

Campanula

PERENNIAL ZONE 3
The lovely bellflower *C. carpatica* subsp. *turbinata* f. *alba* makes a clump of toothed leaves, rarely more than 15cm (6in) high but 25cm (10in) or so wide,

covered in mid- to late summer with exquisite, saucer-shaped flowers, their whiteness tinged by the merest suspicion of blue. Its exquisite pallor is a match for stronger blues.

For the second half of summer, another pretty rock-garden plant is *C. cochleariifolia* subsp. *alba*, which is usually less than 15cm (6in) in height. However, it spreads so vigorously that it is not a suitable companion for really choice miniatures. Little bells of dazzling white hang down from wiry stems. *See also page 174.*

Madagascar periwinkle *Catharanthus roseus* 'Pretty-in-White'

VINCA, MADAGASCAR PERIWINKLE

Catharanthus roseus

HALF-HARDY ANNUAL POISONOUS
With their phlox-like flowers, the Madagascar periwinkles make a delightful contribution to mixed plantings in window boxes, hanging baskets and pots. In 'Pretty-in-White' (*above*) a yellow eye relieves the purity of the petals. Another cultivar, 'Parasol', has a red eye.

MEXICAN ORANGE BLOSSOM

Choisya ternata

EVERGREEN SHRUB ZONE 7
Glossy aromatic leaves, boldly divided into three, make *C. ternata* an impressive shrub year round. The leaves are at their best when showing off the large clusters of pure white, fragrant

Mexican orange blossom *Choisya ternata*

flowers in spring (*above*) and often again at the end of summer, or even in late autumn or a mild winter. The main display is particularly prolific, flowers studding plants that in pots are usually less than 1.5m (5ft) high and 1.8m (6ft) across at the base.

Plant singly, using soil-based compost, in full sun or light shade, sheltered from cold winds. Cut out frost-damaged shoots in early spring, and trim any straggling stems in late spring or early summer, when the flowers have faded.

CLEMATIS

Clematis

CLIMBER ZONE 3 POISONOUS
Clematis are among the most versatile of climbers, and there are single and double varieties in a wide colour range for most seasons. In the container garden, those of moderate vigour are more useful than their rampant cousins. Those to be trained upwards need supports on which leaf tendrils can grip. They can also be grown trailing from tall containers.

The following white-flowered clematis are fairly restrained in their growth and in containers are unlikely to exceed 3.7m (12ft).

'Marie Boisselot', sometimes listed as 'Madame Le Coultre', is a large-flowered hybrid of beautiful form; its flowers are pure white, although pink

131

tinged when opening, and appear in early summer and sometimes again later. 'Henryi', another large-flowered hybrid, may produce its pure white single flowers in late as well as early summer. In late summer and early autumn, 'Alba Luxurians' (*below*), a lovely *C. viticella* hybrid, produces its nodding flowers, green at the tips.

Plant in autumn or spring, using a soil-based compost. Provide supports for training. Prune early-flowering clematis lightly in early summer, after flowering. In early spring prune late-flowering clematis hard. In mid-spring prune lightly large-flowered hybrids that repeat. Top-dress with fresh compost in spring.
See also pages 128, 156, 159, 167, 174.

Clematis *Clematis* 'Alba Luxurians'

CUP-AND-SAUCER VINE, MONASTERY BELLS
Cobaea scandens 'Alba'
ANNUAL/PERENNIAL CLIMBER   ZONE 9
This vigorous but tender climber attaches itself with tendrils to a support and can reach great heights – up to 5m (15ft) in a single growing season. Specimens grown as perennials in frost-free areas flower from spring through to early winter, while those

Cup-and-saucer vine *Cobaea scandens* 'Alba'

grown as annuals in temperate climates flower from late summer to autumn, when started in early spring under glass. The bell-shaped, nodding flowers bloom one to a stem; 'Alba' (*above*) has greenish-white bells with a green calyx.
See also pages 167–8.

COSMOS
Cosmos
HALF-HARDY ANNUAL
Cosmos are easy and rewarding annuals, providing an airy display of single, dahlia-like flowers over finely cut leaves in summer and autumn. They are most commonly grown as mixtures, with pinks and reds predominating. 'Sonata', with gold-centred white flowers, is a good choice for containers, since it has sturdy stems and grows to 60cm (2ft).

Raise from seed, sowing in warmth in early spring. Plant in groups, using soil-based or soil-less compost. Remove faded blooms to keep plants flowering. Do not feed generously as this will encourage foliage at the expense of flowers.
See also pages 152, 159–60; illustration page 23.

PINK
Dianthus
PERENNIAL   ZONE 4
Despite their common name, there are several enchanting white forms of these drought-tolerant, sun-loving perennials with their distinctive grey-green foliage. Many of the old-fashioned pinks that have been in cultivation for many years have a ravishing scent. Among them is 'Musgrave's Pink' (also known as 'Charles Musgrave'), a green-eyed, single white with prettily fringed petals. 'Mrs Sinkins', a rather loose double white, is said to have the most powerful scent of all. In some pinks, the form of the flower is emphasized by dark markings: 'Dad's Favourite', for example, has a white ground with purple lacing.

The faster-growing modern pinks flower mainly in early to mid-summer, but often flower again in autumn. A splendid example is the fully double white 'Haytor'.
*See also pages 152–3, **160**.*

AFRICAN DAISY, STAR OF THE VELDT
Dimorphotheca sinuata
HALF-HARDY ANNUAL
Sometimes listed as *Osteospermum aurantiacum*, this sun-loving daisy is normally grown as a summer-flowering annual. 'Glistening White' is compact, usually less than 25cm (10in) high, with silky petals that contrast with the slate-blue centre. The flowers do not open in shade or when the weather is dull. For a bold effect, use on its own in a low container.

To raise from seed, sow under glass in early spring in Zone 8 and colder areas, in either soil-based or a soil-less compost. Position in full sun and deadhead regularly.

FUCHSIA
Fuchsia
SHRUB   ZONE 10
The dangling flowers of many fuchsia hybrids are bicoloured, the tube and four waxy sepals being of one colour and the skirt of petals another. All those selected here have white petals.

The following three cultivars usually produce plants with a height and spread of no more than 60–90cm (2–3ft) in a season. 'Annabel' is a double in which all the parts of the flower are white. 'Hawkshead' (Zone 8), a single, has white petals and the rest of the flower is also white but with a green tinge. 'Madame Cornelissen' (Zone 8), is a semi-double with cerise-veined white petals; the rest of the flower is pale pink. These last two are often listed as hardy fuchsias.

Among the trailing hybrids, ideal for hanging baskets and window boxes, is 'Sophisticated Lady'(Zone 9), a double in white and pale pink. 'Swingtime' (Zone 9), another double, has creamy white petals; the rest of the flower is red.
*See also pages 153, 160–61, **168**; illustration page 115.*

SUN ROSE
Helianthemum 'Wisley White'
EVERGREEN SHRUB ZONES 6–9
A pretty sun rose that has grey-green leaves and grows 25cm (10in) high with a spread of 30cm (12in); this cultivar has white flowers with yellow centres, giving an overall effect of cream.
*See also pages **141**, **146**, 161.*

HYDRANGEA
Hydrangea
SHRUB ZONE 6
H. macrophylla 'Madame Emile Mouillère' is a fine white mophead hydrangea with a long flowering season, and is ideal for planting in a formal situation, such as in matched containers.

H.m. 'Lanarth White', a compact lacecap hydrangea, has flower heads with small fertile florets in the centre, surrounded by large sterile florets.

Other deciduous hydrangeas suitable for containers include *H. quercifolia* (Zone 5) and *H. paniculata* (Zone 4). *H. quercifolia* has handsome lobed leaves, which colour well in autumn, and in mid-summer produces pyramid-shaped, milky white flower heads, which take on a purplish tint as they age. In containers it has a height and spread of about 1.2m (4ft). The most widely grown selection of *H. paniculata* is 'Grandiflora', which can reach 2.5m (8ft) or more in a container. Sterile cream flowers in dense pyramids are often 38cm (15in) or more long, and take on a pink tinge as they age.

Plant in spring, using a soil-based potting compost. Repot every two or three years, top-dressing with fresh compost in other years. Prune in spring.
See also pages 161, 175; illustrations pages 37, 45.

CANDYTUFT
Iberis
HARDY ANNUAL
Few plants add such startling whiteness to summer containers as candytuft. *I. amara* 'Giant Hyacinth Flowered White' has stems up to 38cm (15in) high, crowded with fragrant, long-lasting flowers. The globe candytuft (*I. umbellata*) is difficult to obtain in single colours, but it is often available in mixtures that include white. The Fairy Series, a colour selection that includes pinks, reds and lavenders as well as white, provides bushy plants 23cm (9in) high.

Raise from seed sown in autumn or spring, or buy plants in spring. Use either soil-based or a soil-less compost. Deadhead regularly in order to prolong the flowering season.

JASMINE
Jasminum
CLIMBER ZONE 8
The summer-flowering common white jasmine (*J. officinale*) is a favourite deciduous or semi-evergreen climber, capable of twining up supports to a height of 9m (30ft) or more. Individual flowers, pink in bud but opening white, are small, but they bloom in pretty clusters over a long period and are deliciously scented. Although vigorous, and so not totally suitable as a container plant, it can be grown successfully in a big tub.

A more manageable climber in containers is the tender *J. polyanthum* (Zones 9–10), which reaches a height of about 3m (10ft). Where the climate is too harsh for it to be grown outdoors, it makes a superb greenhouse plant, with clusters of sweetly fragrant, white or pale pink flowers. It can start flowering in late winter, continuing into early summer, but in cooler conditions flowering does not usually begin before the spring.

Plant in soil-based compost and ensure that there are adequate supports for the jasmine to climb up. Reduce congested growth after flowering, but avoid heavy pruning.

SWEET PEA
Lathyrus odoratus
HARDY ANNUAL/BIENNIAL CLIMBER
POISONOUS
Sweet peas are most often sold in mixed pastel colours, but some named

forms are available in single colours. Good whites include the fragrant 'White Supreme'.

Among the creams are 'Hunter's Moon', with sweetly scented and frilly flowers, and 'Lillie Langtry', lightly scented with prettily waved blooms.
*See also pages **162**, **169**, **175**.*

COMMON WHITE LAVENDER
Lavandula angustifolia 'Alba'
EVERGREEN SHRUB ZONE 6
The lavenders, easy sun-loving shrubs with aromatic foliage and flowers, are best known in their grey-blue or purple-blue forms, but *L. angustifolia* 'Alba' makes an attractive white variation. The eye-catching flower spikes produced in late summer cover a grey-green bush about 45cm (18in) high.
*See also page **169**.*

MALLOW
Lavatera trimestris 'Mont Blanc'
HARDY ANNUAL
One of the most brilliant whites in late summer to autumn is the annual mallow 'Mont Blanc' (*below*), which is best appreciated when grown in groups in large troughs or tubs in full sun.

Sow seed *in situ* in spring. Thin to 15cm (6in) apart by early summer.
*See also page **162**.*

Mallow *Lavatera trimestris* 'Mont Blanc'

LILY

Lilium

BULB ZONE 3 POISONOUS

Lilies are the most important group of summer-flowering bulbs, and the majority are suitable for growing in containers. Ideally, lilies should be moved into an eye-catching position when they are coming into flower and withdrawn once their season is over. Place in sun or in partial shade.

In the following selection lilies are described as basal rooting or stem rooting. Basal-rooting lilies produce roots from only the bulb, while stem-rooting kinds also produce roots above the bulb and require deeper planting.

L. candidum (Zone 4), the Madonna lily, has been cultivated for centuries and still holds its own as a supremely beautiful ornamental. In early to mid-summer, stems up to 1.5m (5ft) tall bear numerous fragrant trumpets with golden anthers. It is basal rooting.

'Casa Blanca' (Zone 4) is a stem-rooting lily that flowers in mid- to late summer. Stems up to 1.2m (4ft) high carry several large fragrant flowers. Orange-brown anthers stand out against the white petals, which have wart-like bumps and a yellowish midrib.

'Mont Blanc', only 60cm (2ft) high, is a useful short-growing lily with creamy white flowers that are slightly spotted in the centre. It is basal rooting.

L. regale (Zone 3), the regal lily (*below left*), is one of the easiest lilies to grow and one of the most splendid, fully living up to its name. Stems 1.2–1.8m (4–6ft) high carry clusters of fragrant trumpets in mid-summer. The glistening white flowers have a yellow centre, and the backs of the petals are stained purple and deep pink. Purer whites can be found in the Album Group. All of these are stem rooting.

L. speciosum is another richly fragrant, stem-rooting species. Between 5 and 10 bowl-shaped flowers with turned-back, wavy petals are carried on stems 1.2–1.8m (4–6ft) high. In *L. s.* var. *album* (Zone 4) the flowers are clear white.

'Sterling Star' (Zone 3), a basal-rooting lily, has starry flowers in mid-summer on stems 90cm (3ft) high. Orange-brown anthers and dark speckling stand out against the white petals.

Buy undamaged, plump bulbs in autumn and plant promptly, either singly or in groups of three or more. Consider stability as well as depth when choosing containers. The depth of compost needed above basal-rooting lilies is 13–15cm (5–6in) and above stem-rooting kinds is about 20cm (8in). Lilies planted in groups should be about 8cm (3in) apart. Use soil-based compost and ensure drainage is free. *L. candidum* is an exception: plant in late summer, just covering the bulbs with compost.

Repot lilies in small or medium-sized containers annually in late winter or spring. Repot those in tubs and other large containers every other year, and add more compost and give a slow-release fertilizer in alternate years. Do not water lilies when dormant, and avoid overwatering during the growing season.

Viral diseases, transmitted by sucking insects such as aphids, can be a serious problem with lilies, so regular spraying against these pests is advisable. The most troublesome disease of lilies, especially of *L. candidum*, is botrytis, but fungicides can provide an effective control.

See also pages 142, 147, 153, 162; illustrations pages 7, 14, 18, 24, 50.

Regal lily *Lilium regale*

LOBELIA

Lobelia erinus 'Snowball'

HALF-HARDY ANNUAL POISONOUS

Lobelias are highly valued as trailing plants, especially in hanging baskets, and as edging. 'Snowball' is a compact selection with large clear white flowers. An occasional pale blue plant makes a pretty rogue.

See also pages 153, 169, 175–6; illustration page 25.

SWEET ALYSSUM

Lobularia maritima

HARDY ANNUAL

The honey-scented sweet alyssum is a long-standing favourite and a useful filler for the edges of containers planted to last through summer and into autumn. 'Carpet of Snow' makes a low mound up to 10cm (4in) high, with a spread of 38cm (15in). The flowers are small, giving an attractive white-and-green effect. 'Snow Crystal' is more spreading with larger flowers. Sweet alyssum is often also sold in mixtures. Mixed Wonderland includes pinkish-red and purple as well as white.

Raise from seed or buy plants in spring. Use either soil-based or soil-less compost. To extend the season, trim off flowers as they fade.

See also page 162.

COMMON MYRTLE

Myrtus communis

EVERGREEN SHRUB ZONE 9

Glossy aromatic foliage is a year-round attraction of common myrtle

Common myrtle *Myrtus communis*

(*below*), which, in containers, rarely grows to more than 1.2m (4ft) high and 60cm (2ft) across. In late summer, it carries fragrant white flowers with a brush of thin stamens; these are followed by purplish-black berries. *M. c.* subsp. *tarentina* is more compact than the species, and has small, narrow leaves.

Plant in late spring, using soil-based compost. Choose a warm sheltered position, ideally with the backing of a sunny wall.

Flowering tobacco *Nicotiana* hybrid

TOBACCO PLANT

Nicotiana

HALF-HARDY ANNUAL POISONOUS

One of the most bewitching evening scents of the summer garden is that provided by tobacco plants, *N. ×* *sanderae* and *N. alata* (syn. *N. affinis*). This sticky perennial (*above*), usually treated as an annual, carries long-tubed flowers with starry mouths and grows to 75cm (30in). A well-positioned, large container that is thickly planted will make a major contribution to an intimate small garden.

There is now a versatile range of tobacco plants. In 'Fragrant Cloud', the flowers are large and the evening scent powerful, but the height of plants – at 90cm (3ft) – limits their usefulness in the container garden. 'White Bedder', well scented and pure white, makes bushy plants only 40cm (16in) high, which can be used in window boxes and other small containers. Other compact tobacco plants are available in

colour mixtures that include white. Domino Mixed are hybrids 30cm (12in) high with fragrant, upward-facing flowers in a range of colours. Even shorter growing are the Merlin hybrids, 25cm (10in) high, but branching freely and providing bright colours.

Raise from seed (sow in warmth in early spring, or buy plants in late spring). Use soil-based or soil-less compost.

See also pages 142, 163; illustration page 113.

OSTEOSPERMUM

Osteospermum

PERENNIAL ZONE 9

These sprawling evergreen daisies from South Africa flower freely throughout the summer. They are often grown as annuals or overwintered as cuttings on account of their tenderness.

O. ecklonis, up to 60cm (2ft) high and across, has white flowers, tinged blue on the reverse, and the disc itself is dark blue. 'Blue Streak', its petals washed with blue, and the variegated 'Silver Sparkler' are popular hybrids. 'Whirligig' is an arresting curiosity, with pinched spoon-like petals. Osteo-spermums are also available in a wider colour range, including pink ('Pink Whirls') and pale yellow ('Buttermilk'). All these daisies combine well with a wide range of sun-loving plants and are useful to lighten dark blues and purples.

If you raise from seed, sow in warmth in early spring and plant out in late spring; this is also the time to plant out overwintered cuttings or newly bought stock. Use soil-based or soil-less compost over a layer of drainage material.

See illustrations pages 101, 119.

PELARGONIUM, GERANIUM

Pelargonium

EVERGREEN PERENNIAL ZONE 9

Although most familiar in bright red and many shades of pink, there are several white forms of these classic container plants. The wide colour range among Zonal pelargoniums includes good whites such as 'Arctic Star' and 'Hermione', and there are some other whites available in the single colours of newly introduced seed strains.

Among the trailing, Ivy-leaved pelargoniums, few seed strains are available, but the many cultivars include the pure white 'Snowdrift'.

See also pages 147, 153–4, 163, 170, 181–82, 187, 190, 194; illustration page 108.

PETUNIA
Petunia
HALF-HARDY ANNUAL

Although there are brilliant whites among the petunias – the fringed double 'White Swan' is a dazzling example – the availability of separate colours is restricted and varies from year to year, many strains being sold only as mixtures. Buying plants just coming into flower may offer the surest way of obtaining whites to suit your requirements.

White features prominently in a number of the bicoloured petunias, which can be used in extrovert and hectic displays. In the huge flowers of the Razzle Dazzle mixture, stars in strong colours overlay a white ground, while the Picotee Series has deep colours edged white.
*See also pages 142, 154, 163, 170, **176**; illustrations pages 19, 101, 113.*

ANNUAL PHLOX
Phlox drummondii
HALF-HARDY ANNUAL

A striking example of the taller varieties of annual phlox is the cultivar 'Brilliant', which grows to a height of 50cm (20in). Its petals are white, but the variable centre is a deep rose.

MIGNONETTE
Reseda odorata
HARDY ANNUAL

Although in no way showy, mignonette (*below*) is much loved for the sweet scent of its flowers. Place pot-grown plants in sun among other containers,

Mignonette *Reseda odorata*

in a position where the fragrance can readily be appreciated.

The plants are about 40cm (16in) tall with a spread of 25cm (10in), and they flower between summer and autumn, depending on sowing time. Each loose spire contains a rich profusion of blooms with tiny creamy petals and conspicuous orange-brown stamens.

For flowers in early to mid-summer, sow in containers during early spring. Use any soil-based or soil-less compost (mignonette does well in alkaline soils). Thin seedlings so that those retained are about 15cm (6in) apart. Pinch back the growing tips of young plants to encourage them to branch.

ROSE
Rosa
SHRUB   ZONE 4

The modern ground-cover roses – in effect low mound-forming or prostrate shrub roses – include a number that do well in tubs or other large containers. 'Avon' is one example, with clusters of small, semi-double flowers that are pearly white, sometimes tinged pink. The shrub is only about 30cm (12in) high, but its trailing stems can have a spread of 90cm (3ft). The flowers produce little fragrance, but the season lasts throughout the summer and continues into autumn.

'White Pet' is quite different in character, a light-scented, 19th-century Polyantha rose with neat pompon flowers of pure white in summer. About 60cm (2ft) high and wide, it can also be grown as a short standard.
*See also pages 142, **154**, 164, 170, 203; illustration page 24.*

VERBENA
Verbena
HALF-HARDY ANNUAL

The hybrid verbenas flower over a long season in summer. They make useful container plants, and the mixtures usually include whites.

The purple-flowered trailing species *V. tenuisecta*, with stems about 45cm (18in) long, insinuates itself among other plants. The white form, *V. tenuisecta* f. *alba* has the same beguiling habit; it makes a lovely light touch at the edge of containers or trailing gracefully from a hanging basket.
*See also pages 149, 155, 165, **171**, 176–7; illustration page 108.*

VIOLET
Viola cornuta Alba Group
PERENNIAL   ZONE 5

This white-flowered violet is a jaunty version of the blue-flowered species, and is pretty as an underplanting to shrubs or mixed with other perennials in large containers. It does well in sun or light shade, producing masses of spurred flowers in early summer and if cut back will flower again later.

Plant in autumn or spring in soil-based compost.
*See also pages **143**, 149, 155, 167, 171, 177.*

YUCCA, SPANISH DAGGER
Yucca gloriosa
EVERGREEN SHRUB   ZONE 5

Pointed leaves making a conspicuously jagged clump have given this evergreen (*below*) its picturesque common name. The first flower spike, up to 1.8m (6ft) tall, may not emerge until the plant is five years old. The buds open in autumn to pendulous, creamy white, fragrant flowers that are tinged red on the outside. This arresting plant is seen at its best growing on its own in a large pot placed in a sunny, sheltered position.

Plant in autumn or spring, using soil-based compost.

Spanish dagger *Yucca gloriosa*

Crocus *Crocus chrysanthus* 'Cream Beauty'

AUTUMN AND WINTER

CROCUS
Crocus
CORM ZONE 5
The winter-flowering crocuses are among the loveliest of all the bulbs that give a hint of spring. The white and cream crocuses recommended here all grow to a height of about 8cm (3in).

The many cultivars of *C. chrysanthus* are among the most reliable of the early crocuses. The buttermilk tone of 'Cream Beauty' (*above*) is softly appealing, while 'Snow Bunting' is a stronger white, although its outer petals are creamy with purplish feathering. Both these crocuses have yellow throats and vivid orange stigmas, as has *C. sieberi* 'Albus', whose petals are pure white and pointed.
See also pages 128, 138, 144, 149, 166, 171, 177.

CYCLAMEN
Cyclamen hederifolium f. *album*
TUBER ZONE 6 POISONOUS
In autumn the white flowers of this cyclamen have a freshness that matches the marbled beauty of the silvered leaves. Despite its small size – about 13cm (5in) high, with a foliage spread of 25cm (10in) – it is very effective in lightening shady corners.

Plant cyclamen on their own in a shallow pot, or include them as an underplanting to a shrub in a large container.
See also page 165.

WINTER HEATH
Erica carnea 'Springwood White'
EVERGREEN SHRUB ZONE 6
'Springwood White' is a vigorous example of the many cultivars of this evergreen shrub. Not only is it a useful companion for other acid-loving plants but, unlike most heaths, it tolerates alkaline soil. It will also accept light shade, and so can be used to underplant taller shrubs. Plants are about 15cm (6in) tall, often with a spread exceeding 45cm (18in). The brown stamens are conspicuous within the white flowers, which are produced in late winter and early spring.

Plant in autumn, using soil-based compost. Clip after flowering.
See also pages 155, 165, 171, 183.

HEATH
Erica × darleyensis 'Silberschmelze'
EVERGREEN SHRUB ZONE 7
The named variants of this hybrid, like those of *E. carnea*, tolerate alkaline soil. 'Silberschmelze' ('Molten Silver') grows to about 60cm (2ft), but usually has a wider spread. It flowers throughout winter and into spring, when the pink tips of the young shoots are an added feature.

Plant in autumn, in soil-based compost. Clip over after flowering.
See also page 165.

SNOWDROP
Galanthus
BULB ZONE 3
Classic winter flowers that herald spring, snowdrops all share a strong family likeness, although subtle differences distinguish the species and the many hybrids and cultivars. The white flowers dangle lightly, their three large outer petals enclosing three shorter inner ones, which are usually marked green. Snowdrops do well in shade and are suitable as an underplanting to shrubs in large containers, but growing clumps of plants separately allows their individual characteristics to be appreciated.

One of the largest snowdrops, up to 25cm (10in) high, is 'Atkinsii', which may be in flower by mid-winter. The outer petals are slender and pointed, the inner ones green tipped.

Another large snowdrop is *G. elwesii*, sometimes 30cm (12in) tall, which has broad grey-green leaves. The inner petals of the substantial flowers are green at the tip and also at the base. 'S. Arnott' also has blooms of good substance but is even more valued for its strong and pervasive scent.

The common snowdrop, *G. nivalis* (*below*), has much narrower, strap-shaped leaves and rarely exceeds a height of 15cm (6in). The inner petals are tipped green. In the double cultivar *G. n.* 'Flore Pleno', the numerous inner petals form a green-tipped rosette.

For best results, plant snowdrops 'in the green', just after flowering but while still in leaf, during spring. Alternatively, plant dry bulbs in early autumn. Use soil-based compost with added leaf mould and keep it moist during the growing season. Divide congested clumps after flowering.
See illustration page 20.

Snowdrop *Galanthus nivalis*

Clear yellow flowers introduce sunny splashes that brighten the container garden in all seasons. Combined with orange blooms, yellow creates warm harmonies. For cooler schemes, hints of green are needed. Use yellow with violet for more dramatic effects.

SPRING

BASKET-OF-GOLD

Aurinia saxatilis

EVERGREEN PERENNIAL   ZONE 6

Basket-of-gold (sometimes known as *Alyssum saxatile*) produces a mass of flowers in the second half of spring and early summer. An attractive addition to a tub of sun-loving rock-garden plants, this evergreen is about 30cm (12in) high with a spread of 45cm (18in).

The species is bright gold, as is the dwarf cultivar, 'Compacta', which is rarely more than 15cm (6in) in height. The lemon-yellow of *A.s.* var. *citrina* gives a lighter, cooler effect.

Plant in autumn or early spring in gritty, soil-based compost. Clip plants after flowering.

CROCUS

Crocus × luteus 'Golden Yellow'

CORM   ZONE 4

The vigorous *C. × luteus* 'Golden Yellow' (*below*) comes into flower in early spring, when many crocus species and their hybrids have already finished.

Its rich gold flowers, 10–13cm (4–5in) high, look effective with other strong colours in sunny window boxes and other containers. This crocus is as its best, though, in a pot on its own, making dense clusters of golden cups.

Plant in autumn, using a gritty, soil-based potting compost. Set corms close to one another but not touching, just over 5cm (2in) deep. Position in sun. *See also pages 128, 137, 144, 149, 166, 171, 177.*

WALLFLOWER

Erisymum

BIENNIAL

The wallflowers, sometimes listed as *Cheiranthus*, are short-lived evergreen perennials usually grown as biennials. Bushy plants carry loose clusters of velvety flowers, which are deliciously fragrant, from late spring to early summer. Wallflowers are often mixed with other spring flowers, especially tulips, but they also look good on their own, especially when densely planted in a large container.

Both dwarf and taller wallflowers are often sold as mixtures that include yellow, but some good separate colours are also available. 'Cloth of Gold' is about 40cm (16in) tall and has rich yellow flowers. The more compact 'Primrose Bedder' is about 30cm (12in) high, its flowers a clear yellow.

To raise from seed, sow in a seed bed in late spring or early summer. When the plants are 15cm (6in) tall, pinch back the shoot tips in order to encourage bushy growth. Plant in containers in early to mid-autumn, using a soil-based or soil-less compost. *See also pages 145, 150; illustration page 92.*

SPURGE, EUPHORBIA

Euphorbia myrsinites

EVERGREEN PERENNIAL ZONE 5

The woody but flopping stems of this member of the spurge family (*right*) are about 30cm (12in) long and clothed in fleshy grey-green leaves. They bloom in spring with a head of greenish-yellow flowers held in little saucers of the same colour.

This unusual euphorbia, which needs sun and gritty, soil-based compost, looks best sharing a large container with rock-garden plants.

HYACINTH

Hyacinthus orientalis 'City of Haarlem'

BULB   ZONE 5

This pale yellow hyacinth makes a useful variation on the pinks, blues and white of the large-flowered hyacinths. The dense spikes of fragrant flowers seem tailor-made for sunny window boxes, but the bulbs also look attractive planted alone or mixed with other spring flowers in large containers. *See also pages 129, 150, 156, **172**.*

DAFFODIL, NARCISSUS, JONQUIL

Narcissus

BULB   ZONE 3

Daffodils are among the mainstays of the spring garden, the yellow-flowered species and cultivars introducing a sunny note that triumphs over uncertain weather. The daffodils best suited to containers are those of short or medium height with refined flowers. They include examples with a central cup as well as those with trumpets, some with several flowers to a stem, a few that are double, and many that are scented – some having an exceptionally sweet fragrance. All are easy to grow and do well in sun or partial shade.

Among the Cyclamineus daffodils of early spring, few last longer in flower than 'February Gold'. The blooms, with swept-back petals and elegant poise, stand about 30cm (12in) high. 'Tête-à-Tête', rarely more than 15cm

Crocus *Crocus × luteus* 'Golden Yellow'

Spurge *Euphorbia myrsinites*

Daffodil *Narcissus* 'Rip van Winkle'

(6in) high, is one of the earliest and often has two or three golden flowers with reflexed lemon-yellow petals. A curiosity of similar height is 'Rip van Winkle', with double flowers consisting of lemon-yellow shreds (*above*).

'Jack Snipe', which flowers a few weeks later than those already listed and is 25cm (10in) high, has a long cup rather than a trumpet. Its is pale yellow, with swept-back petals of creamy white.

All the following have several flowers per stem and bloom in mid-spring. 'Hawera', 20cm (8in) tall, has nodding lemon-yellow flowers; the petals ringing the small cups create a starry effect. Although fragrant, it does not have the delicious sweetness of 'Minnow', 20cm (8in) high, also with lemon-yellow cups but creamier petals. Also beautifully scented is 'Yellow Cheerfulness', which blooms from mid- to late spring; the double creamy yellow flowers are carried on stems about 50cm (20in) tall.

Plant all daffodils in late summer or early autumn, the sooner the better, because their roots develop long before there is any sign of growth above ground. Use any kind of potting compost, either soil-based or soil-less, and plant so that bulbs are covered by mix to at least twice their own depth. Deeper planting is advisable for containers in exposed positions. Bulbs can be planted close together and in two layers if a really dense effect is required, but they should not be planted so close that they touch.

Deadhead but allow foliage to die down naturally. To avoid an untidy effect in containers and to allow for replacement planting, bulbs can be lifted as soon as flowering is over and replanted in the garden while their foliage dies down.
See also pages 129, 144, 145; illustration page 124.

POLYANTHUS, PRIMROSE
Primula
BIENNIAL/PERENNIAL   ZONE 5
The perennial English primrose (*P. vulgaris*), itself a plant of unaffected beauty and lovely in a pot, is the parent of a number of cluster-flowered hybrids that are grouped under the name polyanthus. These come in a colour range that includes yellows as well as pinks, reds, blues and white – most having a conspicuous eye. They are usually grown as biennials and discarded after flowering. Crescendo Mixed, with stems up to 30cm (12in) high, is a hybrid available as seed. For specific colours, it is better to buy young plants in autumn or even early spring.

More refined plants in a wonderful range of colours, including dark spice shades, are available in Barnhaven strains, developed in Oregon in the 1930s. There is also a Barnhaven strain of gold-laced kinds, similar to those widely grown in the 19th century, which usually have dark red petals edged with yellow, matching the basal blotch. The perennial cowslip (*P. veris*) appears in early summer.

To raise from seed, sow in late spring or early summer. Pot young plants in autumn, using any soil-based or soil-less potting compost. Grow in an open or lightly shaded position.
See also page 166; illustrations pages 88, 89, 91.

AURICULA
Primula auricula
PERENNIAL   ZONE 3
In the past, auriculas have enjoyed periods of great popularity: in the 18th and 19th centuries, they were raised for showing competitively. There is now renewed interest in this fascinating group of plants, which, as old lists show, covered a wide colour range.

'Old Yellow Dusty Miller' is a border auricula but can be grown in a pot. The grey leaves, which appear to be dusted with white powder (farina),

Auricula *Primula auricula*

form a cluster through which the flower stem grows to a height of about 15cm (6in) in mid- to late spring. The fragrant, clustered flowers are primrose-like but more rounded (*above*).

Plant singly in gritty, alkaline, soil-based compost, and place in a cool, shady position.
See illustration page 14.

RHODODENDRON, AZALEA
Rhododendron
SHRUB   ZONE 5
There are several fine yellow hybrids among the compact spring-flowering rhododendrons and azaleas.

'Bo-peep' (Zone 7) is an evergreen rhododendron flowering in early spring that grows 90–150cm (3–5ft) high and has a spread of about 90cm (3ft). The primrose-yellow, funnel-shaped flowers, tinged green, bloom in small clusters.

The hybrids of the evergreen *R. yakushimanum* (Zone 5) provide some of the best compact spring-flowering shrubs suitable for containers. 'Grumpy' (Zone 4), under 90cm (3ft) but with spreading growth, blooms in mid- to late spring, bearing clustered heads of yellow flowers, tinged pink.

One of the loveliest deciduous azaleas is 'Narcissiflorum' (Zone 6). This makes a bush up to 1.5m (5ft) high, which in spring bears clusters of pale yellow, sweetly scented, double trumpets. The foliage has bronze tints in autumn.
See also pages 129, 142, 145, 148, 150, 156–7, 167, 173.

SAXIFRAGE

Saxifraga
EVERGREEN PERENNIAL ZONE 6
Among the saxifrages are many that are easy and suitable for growing in containers mixed with other rock-garden plants.

The following all make tight rosettes of grey-green foliage that are hoary with an encrustation of lime. The cushions formed by *S. × apiculata* 'Gregor Mendel' (Zone 6) can be more than 30cm (12in) across, and its primrose-yellow flowers, blooming profusely in early to mid-spring, stand 10cm (4in) high. Even earlier flowering is *S. burseriana* 'Brookside' (Zone 4). Its cushion has a spread of about 15cm (6in), and the cup-shaped yellow flowers stand only 5cm (2in) high.

Plant between autumn and early spring, using gritty, preferably slightly alkaline, soil-based compost.
See also page 157.

TULIP

Tulipa
BULB ZONE 4
Although some tulips flower earlier, the climax of the tulip season is in mid- to late spring. Within their colour range are many strong yellows. Others offer attractive combinations and more subtle colours, including the Viridiflora group, with green markings.

Short-growing tulips under 25cm (10in) in height are especially suitable for window boxes. One of the earliest is *T. tarda* (*below*), with up to five flowers per stem, the yellow forming a broad band that leaves the points white.

It is slightly more tender than most tulips (Zone 5). A little later comes 'Stresa', one of the water-lily tulips, whose flowers open out to a star-shape that is yellow inside but with a red base, and flushed red on the outside. A refined species, *T. clusiana* var. *chrysantha*, flowers in mid-spring, the yellow interior contrasting prettily with red on the outside.

Taller-growing yellows include several sturdy singles and doubles. 'Yellow Purissima', 50cm (20in) high, flowers slightly before mid-spring, a satin sheen enhancing its golden single blooms. Mid-spring yellows include the fragrant single 'Bellona', 40cm (16in) high, the double 'Monte Carlo', 40cm (16in) high, with flowers that have deep yellow centres, and another double, 'Gold Medal', up to 50cm (20in) high. 'West Point' is a late-spring Lily-flowered tulip, 50cm (20in) high, with pointed petals that curve sharply outwards at their tip.

All the following tulips, in which yellow is combined with another colour, flower in late spring and are 50–60cm (20–24in) high. The elegant *T. marjoletii* (Zone 6) has pale yellow petals bruised red at their edge, while 'Sweet Harmony' bears lemon-yellow petals with ivory margins.

The Viridiflora tulips flower in late spring. 'Groenland' ('Greenland') grows to 60cm (2ft) and has pink blooms with a green edge. 'Spring Green', 45cm (18in) high, has creamy flowers with green feathering.
See also pages 129–30, 145, 150–51, 157, 167; illustration page 93.

Tulip *Tulipa tarda*

SUMMER

OX-EYE CHAMOMILE

Anthemis tinctoria
PERENNIAL ZONES 4–8
Above a clump of fernlike leaves, the ox-eye chamomile produces a long succession of daisy flowers in summer. 'E.C.Buxton' is a cool, creamy yellow.
See also page 130; illustration page 11.

SNAPDRAGON

Antirrhinum majus 'Yellow Monarch'
HALF-HARDY ANNUAL
The Monarch snapdragons, often sold as mixtures in a wide range of colours, are rust-resistant and are of medium height, growing to about 45cm (18in). 'Yellow Monarch', one of the best single colours, is a good, clear yellow with upright sturdy spikes.
See also pages 130, 151, 158, 167.

MARGUERITE, PARIS DAISY

Argyranthemum
EVERGREEN PERENNIAL ZONE 9
Increasing numbers of marguerites in soft shades of creamy yellow and pink are steadily being added to the familiar white. 'Jamaica Primrose' makes a bush with fern-like leaves and a height and spread of 90cm (3ft), spangled with yellow daisies in summer and into autumn. *A. callichrysum* 'Prado' is shorter growing, with flowers of rich yellow.
See also pages 130, 158; illustration page 119.

BIDENS

Bidens ferulifolia
ANNUAL/PERENNIAL ZONE 9
Although a perennial and grown as such in frost-free areas, *B. ferulifolia* is most frequently treated as an annual. It throws out numerous lax stems up to 75cm (30in) long, which work their way through other plants. They carry light foliage of finely dissected leaves. In full sun its airy display of small bright golden flowers, looking like miniature single dahlias, are carried through summer and into autumn. In full sun the astonishing succession of blooms hardly falters.

Raise from seed (sow in warmth in spring) or buy plants in late spring. Grow in either soil-based or soil-less compost. During the growing season, trim back unruly stems and any excessive growth.
See illustrations pages 9, 97, 119.

SLIPPER FLOWER

Calceolaria integrifolia

ANNUAL/PERENNIAL   ZONE 9

The perennial slipper flower is often grown as an annual bedding or pot plant for its long summer display of pouched yellow flowers in crowded clusters at the end of stems. It displays bushy growth to a height of 60cm (2ft).

Plant in late spring, using either soil-based or soil-less compost.

POT MARIGOLD

Calendula officinalis

HARDY ANNUAL

Orange and yellow continue to be the dominant colours in the cultivars of this old-fashioned plant. All flower throughout summer and into autumn, making bushy aromatic plants. Varieties range in height from 30–60cm (1–2ft).

'Kablouna Gold' is a tall cultivar in the yellow range, with double flowers that have brown tips to the inner petals. 'Sunglow', a dwarf yellow, has masses of bright golden daisies.

See also page 146.

TICKSEED

Coreopsis tinctoria

HARDY ANNUAL

Red centres give a special vividness to the tickseed's yellow daisies. An easy annual for full sun, it grows to 75cm (30in), flowering in summer and early autumn. Sow in warmth in early spring. Harden off and plant out in late spring, using a soil-based potting compost.

See illustration page 120.

SUN ROSE

Helianthemum

EVERGREEN SHRUB   ZONE 6

Among these low-growing rock-garden shrubs there are several with yellow flowers. 'Amy Baring' is a compact variety, usually less than 25cm (10in) high, with buttercup-yellow flowers covering the green foliage. 'Jubilee', slightly more spreading, has drooping double flowers of soft yellow. Plant in gritty soil-based compost and position in sun. Clip after flowering.

See also pages 133, 146, 161.

SUNFLOWER

Helianthus annuus

HARDY ANNUAL

Although the annual sunflower is best known as a giant of the flower garden, short-growing cultivars are better

Sunflower *Helianthus annuus* 'Teddy Bear'

suited to containers. All need sun. Music Box is a mixture in a range from pale yellow to red-brown. Bushy plants no more than 75cm (30in) high produce medium-sized flowers about 13cm (5in) across. 'Teddy Bear' (*above*) is even shorter-growing, no more than 60cm (2ft) high, but the fully double, rich yellow flowers are 15cm (6in) across. 'Valentine', up to 1.5m (5ft) high, has lemon-yellow flowers with black discs.

Raise from seed, sown in early to mid-spring, in their containers, one plant per medium-sized pot. Use either soil-based or soil-less compost, but include a generous layer of drainage material. Set two seeds where one plant is required, removing the weaker plant if both germinate.

See illustration page 120.

DAYLILY

Hemerocallis

PERENNIAL   ZONE 4

The individual flowers of the daylilies, as their common name suggests, are short-lived, but many of the summer-flowering hybrids produce blooms over a long period. The strap-shaped leaves form clumps 45–60cm (18–24in) wide, and they are best planted singly or in small groups in large tubs.

The flowers come in a colour range from yellow to orange-red. In the first half of summer 'Golden Chimes' produces branching sprays of elegant

yellow trumpets with a mahogany exterior. Stems are about 60cm (2ft) high. 'Stella de Oro', only 40cm (16in) high, is exceptional for its long flowering season, from mid-summer until well into autumn. The taller *H. fulva* 'Kwanzo Variegata', 90cm (3ft) high, has white-variegated, light green leaves and produces its tawny-orange flowers from mid- to late summer.

Plant daylilies during spring in soil-based compost and position in sun or partial shade.

See illustration page 89.

LANTANA

Lantana camara

EVERGREEN SHRUB   ZONE 9

POISONOUS

In tropical and subtropical regions, this plant is often considered a noxious weed. But it can be an attractive ornamental, the crowded heads of tubular flowers blooming profusely. Yellow is the most common flower colour, but this ages to brick-red so that flower heads are bicoloured. In the variegated 'Samantha' (*below*) the flower colour is a more consistent yellow. Lantanas can grow to 1.2m (4ft) with a spread of 90cm (3ft), and plants can be trained to make standards.

Lantana is often grown as a pot plant and set out in late spring then discarded at the end of summer. Plant singly in soil-based compost.

Lantana *Lantana camara* 'Samantha'

Lily *Lilium monadelphum*

LILY
Lilium
BULB ZONE 3 POISONOUS
Many fine lilies flowering in early to mid-summer do well in containers. The following are about 90cm (3ft) in height.

A vigorous lily with upward-facing flowers is the basal-rooting 'Connecticut King': a greenish tinge at the centre shows off the clear yellow of the petals. One of the most splendid species in any colour is the fragrant, stem-rooting *L. monadelphum* (*above*). The sturdy stem carries pendent pale yellow flowers, sometimes spotted deep purple or red inside, with purple at their bases and the tips of the petals.
See also pages 134, 147, 153, 162.

FLOWERING TOBACCO
Nicotiana 'Lime Green'
HALF-HARDY ANNUAL POISONOUS
The flowering tobaccos are 75cm (30in) high and flower through summer into autumn. 'Lime Green' remains popular with flower arrangers and container gardeners. Its unusual pale yellowish-green works well with a surprising number of other colours, and alone, it gives a cool, restrained effect.
See also pages 135, 163; illustrations pages 21, 111.

WATER LILY
Nymphaea
PERENNIAL
There are several diminutive water lilies ideal for tubs and similar containers

with a depth of 30–45cm (12–18in). All need still, not flowing, water and an open, sunny position. Air temperatures are not relevant to plants such as water lilies, which have their roots some way beneath the water surface, but the water in which they are growing must not be allowed to freeze.

One of the best dwarf varieties is 'Aurora', which has purple mottling on olive-green leaves. The flowers have a curious colour sequence, each colour lasting a day. They open yellow from creamy buds and turn orange, then red. The truly pygmy *N. × helvola* will grow in less than 30cm (12in) of water.

The best time to plant water lilies is mid-spring. Grow them in open-sided baskets or, if the pool is very small, directly in soil on the bottom. The surface spread of the plants is usually slightly more than the growing depth. Divide the plants in mid- to late spring.
See also page 153; illustrations page 63.

ONCOSIPHON
Oncosiphon grandiflorum
ANNUAL
This sun-loving annual (syn. *Matricaria grandiflorum*), grows to a height of 45cm (18in) and produces button-like bright yellow flower heads in summer. Sow seed outdoors in mid- to late spring, or start earlier under glass and transplant. Use gritty soil-based compost.
See illustration page 120.

PETUNIA
Petunia
HALF-HARDY ANNUAL
The few yellow petunias available as single colours are valuable for creating sunny colour schemes. 'Brass Band' is a Multiflora that produces numerous small single flowers; 'Californian Girl', a Grandiflora with large flowers, is deep yellow with wavy petals; 'Summer Sun' is a strong yellow with large flowers. All three are 30cm (12in) or less in height.
See also pages 136, 154, 163, 170, 176; illustration page 113.

PHLOMIS
Phlomis chrysophylla
EVERGREEN SHRUB ZONE 9
This stiff-branched shrub, with a height and spread of 90cm (3ft), has oval leaves that turn from grey-green to green-gold in summer, when it has two-lipped golden-yellow flowers. Plant in spring in soil-based compost.

RHODODENDRON, AZALEA
Rhododendron 'Summer Fragrance'
SHRUB ZONE 5
The deciduous azalea 'Summer Fragrance' comes into its own in late spring or early summer. This beautifully scented shrub, usually less than 1.8m (6ft) in a container, bears clusters of white flowers that look yellow on account of their blotching.
See also pages 129, 139, 145, 148, 150, 156–7, 167, 173.

ROSE
Rosa
SHRUB ZONE 4
Several yellow roses make fine additions to the container garden, and a valuable repeat-flowering characteristic is shared by the three roses described here.

Most suitable for window boxes and containers of similar size are Miniatures such as the unusual 'Baby Masquerade' with clusters of little flowers in a shifting combination of yellow, pink and red. Bushes grow to a height of 38cm (15in), but this rose may also be grown as a short standard, of about 75cm (30in) high. Slightly larger as a bush is 'Perestroika', a Patio rose that grows to about 45cm (18in) in height and spread. Small yellow double flowers bloom prolifically over dark foliage.

Much more substantial is the Shrub rose 'Graham Thomas', from the 'English roses' group. These show good disease-resistance and flower repeatedly throughout summer and into autumn, carrying blooms in the style of the old-fashioned roses. 'Graham Thomas' can grow to a height of 2.5m (8ft), usually less in a container, and its double flowers are fragrant and rich yellow. It requires a large container, not less than 40cm (16in) deep.
See also pages 136, 154, 164, 170, 203.

MARIGOLD
Tagetes
HALF-HARDY ANNUAL
Marigolds provide an unflagging display of flowers over several months. The colour range includes rust-red, mahogany and orange-brown, often with yellow mixed in. There are also plain yellows. A long-standing favourite among the African marigolds is 'First Lady', a compact plant up to 38cm (15in) high with clear yellow double flowers that are often more than 8cm

Marigold *Tagetes* hybrid

Nasturtium *Tropaeolum majus* 'Whirlybird Gold'

with flowers of a paler yellow.

The showy massed blobs of colour produced by these and other large-flowered marigolds are suitable for bold effects (*above*). More subtle are the small single flowers of 'Lemon Gem', a selection of *T. tenuifolia* var. *pumila* (*T. signata* var. *pumila*). This makes a feathery green mound 23cm (9in) high, almost covered by lemon-yellow stars. The small-flowered French marigold 'Naughty Marietta' is more assertive. Little bushes 30cm (12in) high carry a profusion of deep yellow flowers with a maroon blotch.
See also page **148**; *illustration page 33.*

GOLDEN FLEECE
Thymophylla tenuiloba
ANNUAL/BIENNIAL
This strongly scented, long-blooming plant with small yellow-orange flowers, a native of Texas and Mexico, may be perennial in frost-free areas, but is usually grown as an annual or biennial. Grown in full sun in soil-based compost with added sand, it will reach a height of 50cm (20in). Raise from seed sown *in situ* in spring.
See illustration page 113.

NASTURTIUM
Tropaeolum majus
HALF-HARDY ANNUAL
The nasturtiums are easy and rewarding summer-flowering annuals. All the compact and climbing mixtures include

yellows. The semi-double Whirlybird Mixed, for example, has the vibrant 'Whirlybird Gold' (*above*). Another eye-catching semi-double readily obtainable as seed is 'Peaches and Cream'. This dwarf bushy cultivar bears numerous light yellow flowers with conspicuous scarlet blotches. It flowers most freely in a low-nutrient compost, in full sun.
See also pages **149**, **155**; *illustration page 97.*

CANARY CREEPER
Tropaeolum peregrinum
HARDY ANNUAL CLIMBER
This short-lived perennial, usually grown as an annual, is a native of Peru. It makes rapid growth, racing away to 3.7m (12ft) in a season. Prettily lobed blue-green leaves and curious yellow flowers with wing-like fringed petals make this an attractive plant. It climbs by twisting leafstalks around supports.

Raise from seed, sowing in warmth in early spring or outdoors in mid- to late spring. Sow two seeds where one plant is needed, subsequently removing the weaker seedling. Plants branch naturally, without pinching back.

VIOLA, PANSY
Viola
ANNUAL/BIENNIAL/PERENNIAL   ZONE 5
The summer-flowering garden pansies and violas are among the loveliest and most rewarding low-growing plants for containers. They are easy to please and produce blooms in astonishing quantity

over a long season. The classic pansy has a large rounded flower in a wide range of velvety colours, sometimes richly shaded and often with a conspicuous eye at the centre of a bold mask. The Clear Crystal Series, with a height and spread of 20cm (8in), are strains with a wide range of clean colours, usually sold as a mixture but also by separate colours. There is a good bright yellow, with only fine dark rays marking the centre of the flower.

The violas have smaller, less rounded flowers closer in character to the species from which they are derived. They are rarely more than 15cm (6in) high, although they spread to 20cm (8in). Their neat charm shows well in window boxes and as an underplanting to shrubs. 'Johnny Jump Up' is a good small-flowered yellow and purple bicoloured viola that is cheerfully prolific.

These pansies and violas are readily raised from seed, but others have to be propagated from cuttings, because they do not come true from seed. Among these is the unusually coloured 'Irish Molly', with bronze-yellow flowers tinged green. 'Jackanapes' (*below*) is bicoloured, the lower petals yellow, the upper petals rusty red. Both these pansies grow to 13cm (5in).

Pansy *Viola* 'Jackanapes'

143

Pansies and violas are short-lived perennials. Those raised from seed are normally treated as biennials and sown outdoors in summer for flowering the following year. They can also be grown as annuals, sown under glass between mid-winter and early spring and planted out, after being hardened off, in late spring or early summer. Propagate plants that do not come true from seed by taking basal cuttings in mid-summer. Position in sun or partial shade, planted in a soil-based or soil-less compost. *See also pages 136, 149, 155, 167, 171, 177; illustrations pages 90, 91, 92, 96.*

ZINNIA
Zinnia 'Envy'
HALF-HARDY ANNUAL
Zinnias, among the most colourful of the summer-flowering annuals, are mainly sold as mixtures. The unique pale green of 'Envy' is, however, so exceptional that it has become readily available as seed. 'Envy' is a sturdy plant 60cm (2ft) tall and belongs to the dahlia-flowered double zinnias with tiered blooms.
*See also page **155**; illustration page 33.*

AUTUMN AND WINTER

CROCUS
Crocus
CORM   ZONE 5
Like the other small crocuses of late winter, the yellows are best grown on their own in shallow pots; they can also be used as an underplanting to deciduous shrubs or in combination with rock-garden plants.
C. chrysanthus 'Gipsy Girl' has small golden flowers with bronze feathering on the outside. 'E. P. Bowles' has larger flowers combining yellow and bronze markings. 'Zwanenburg Bronze' (*right*) is remarkable for its rich colouring: satiny purple-brown outer petals clasp a cup of orange-yellow. All these crocuses have flowers that stand about 8–10cm (3–4in) high.
*See also pages 128, 137, **138**, 149, 166, 171, 177; illustration page 125.*

DWARF IRIS
Iris danfordiae
BULB   ZONE 5
This astonishing little bulb is one of the brightest flowers of mid- to late winter. No more than 10cm (4in) high, its

Iris *Iris danfordiae*

leaves develop fully only after flowering. The lemon-yellow of its sturdy blooms (*above*) catches the eye, but closer inspection reveals an orange crest and greenish spotting. It makes an attractive underplanting to deciduous shrubs or a first instalment in a mixture of spring bulbs. For the purist it is best planted thickly on its own in a simple pot.

Plant in autumn at a depth of 5–8cm (2–3in) in gritty, soil-based compost. Deep planting may discourage bulbs from splitting into small bulblets after

Crocus chrysanthus 'Zwanenburg Bronze'

Daffodil *Narcissus bulbocodium*

flowering, but does not ensure success. Bulblets need to be grown for several years to reach flowering size. Container gardeners replace iris bulbs annually. *See also pages 171, 177; illustration page 124.*

DAFFODIL, NARCISSUS
Narcissus
BULB   ZONE 4
A few dwarf daffodil species flower reliably in late winter, and they are among the loveliest bulbs to combine with rock-garden plants or, even better, to grow in shallow pots on their own.

Two are outstanding for their distinctive flower shape. The hoop petticoat daffodil, *N. bulbocodium* (Zone 6), has a funnel-shaped 'petticoat', the petals being relatively insignificant (*above*). This delightful little plant, 8–15cm (3–6in) high, ranges in colour from strong yellow to pale primrose.

Flowering a week or two earlier is *N. cyclamineus* (Zone 6), the delicate-looking parent of many elegant short-growing hybrids. It is 10–20cm (4–8in) tall, with uniform rich gold flowers. The trumpet has an unevenly flared rim, and the petals sweep sharply back.

One of the earliest trumpet daffodils to flower is the bright yellow 'Rijnveld's Early Sensation', at 25cm (10in) tall.

Plant all these daffodils in autumn, using gritty, soil-based compost. Set bulbs close but not touching, 2.5–5cm (1–2in) deep. They like reasonably moist conditions during the growing season. *See also pages 129, **138–9**, 145.*

APRICOT TO ORANGE FLOWERS

The geniality and warmth of orange flowers, especially when tempered by green or grey-green foliage, can be a great asset in the container garden. More subtle but still warm-toned are the apricots, softer shades of orange that are deliciously flushed with pink.

SPRING

WALLFLOWER

Erysimum

BIENNIAL   ZONE 7

Wallflowers, sometimes listed as *Cheiranthus*, bloom in mid- to late spring and are usually grown as biennials. Their warm colours and delicious fragrance give a hint of summer. Tall cultivars, up to 50cm (20in) high and dwarf ones, 30cm (12in) high, are generally sold as mixtures that include shades of apricot and orange-brown, a colour that looks lovely on their velvet-textured petals. A limited range of separate colours is available. 'Fire King Improved', a tall cultivar, has bright orange-red flowers. The vivid *E. × allionii* 'Orange Bedder' makes sturdy, compact plants 30cm (12in) high.
*See also pages **138**, 150.*

DAFFODIL, NARCISSUS, JONQUIL

Narcissus

BULB   ZONE 5

'Jetfire', which flowers in early to mid-spring, is one of the most richly coloured dwarf Cyclamineus daffodils. The swept-back petals are a deep yellow, while the frilly-edged trumpet is orange. Usually less than 30cm (12in) high, it is a good choice for window boxes. 'Suzy' (Zone 4) is an orange-cupped jonquil for mid-spring, with three to five large, sweetly scented flowers per stem. It grows to 38cm (15in). The Tazetta narcissi, renowned for their fragrance and with several flowers per stem, bloom in mid- to late spring. They include 'Geranium' and 'Cragford', both with tangerine cups surrounded by white petals and 40–45cm (16–18in) high. The more tender 'Soleil d'Or', with yellow petals, is mainly used for forcing.
*See also pages 129, **138**, 144; illustration page 48.*

RHODODENDRON, AZALEA

Rhododendron

SHRUB   ZONE 5

The Knap Hill hybrid rhododendrons, 1.5–2.2m (5–7ft) in height when grown in containers, carry trumpet-shaped flowers in a wide range of colours that includes strong oranges. A good example of this group, which flowers in late spring, is 'Gibralter'. Dark red buds open to reveal crinkled petals of blazing orange with a yellow flash, and the foliage colours well in autumn. 'Ginger' is a mixture of brilliant orange and rich yellow.

The members of another group, the Mollis azaleas, are about 1.5m (5ft) high and bear scentless flowers, usually of intense colour, in mid- to late spring. 'Spek's Orange' is deep orange in bud and opens slightly paler, with a green flash. 'Koningen Emma' ('Queen Emma') is a very deep orange lightened by a touch of pink. It is large flowered for a Mollis and its upper petals have a richer tone than the rest.
*See also pages 129, 139, 142, 148, 150, **156–7**, 167, 173.*

TULIP

Tulipa

BULB   ZONE 5

Several of the wild tulips have contributed warm, even fiery colours to the hybrids that are such a welcome and conspicuous feature of the spring garden. Selection and breeding have provided a fine gradation in colour from soft apricot to flaming orange.

The Batalinii Group of the dwarf *T. linifolia* are among the earliest tulips to flower and only 15cm (6in) high. 'Bright Gem' could be listed as yellow, but the reverse of the petals is brushed with orange. In 'Apricot Jewel' the outside of the petals shades from apricot through to orange-red.

'Prinses Irene' ('Princess Irene') is an unusual tulip for early to mid-spring: it grows to 35cm (14in) and the orange flowers have purple flames streaking from the base (*right*).

Mid-season tulips include 'Apricot Beauty', one of the loveliest in this range. It grows to 40cm (16in) and its flowers shade from peachy pink to cream. Another mid-spring beauty, 'Generaal de Wet', is remarkable for

the strength of the scent from its cupped, golden-orange flowers; it grows to 35cm (14in) high.

'Temple of Beauty', one of the late tulips, is also one of the tallest, growing to 65cm (26in) and therefore not suitable for an exposed position. Apricot-orange flowers stand above lightly mottled leaves.
*See also pages 129–30, 140, **150–51**, 157, 167; illustration page 23.*

SUMMER

AFRICAN DAISY

Arctotis

HALF-HARDY ANNUAL

Hybrid mixtures of African daisies are available as seed and provide a colourful range, including purple and crimson as well as many shades from cream to orange. In addition there are several hybrids (Zone 10) named for their colour, including 'Apricot' and the vibrant 'Flame'. If deadheaded regularly they produce a long succession of daisies over deeply cut, grey foliage on stems 40cm (16in) high.

These named hybrids must be propagated from cuttings, which can be overwintered under glass. All African daisies must be grown in full sun.
See also page 130; illustrations pages 9, 119.

Tulip *Tulipa* 'Prinses Irene'

Datura *Brugmansia* × *candida* 'Grand Marnier'

DATURA, ANGEL'S TRUMPET

Brugmansia × *candida* 'Grand Marnier'
EVERGREEN SHRUB   ZONE 9
POISONOUS

Daturas are spectacular exotics for a small garden or patio, but are large plants to overwinter where they need protection from frost. In containers they grow to 2.5m (8ft). They are remarkable for their impressive flared-trumpet flowers, in many cases wonderfully fragrant, which hang among large leaves in summer. The trumpets of *B.* × *c.* 'Grand Marnier' (*above*) are pale green flaring to soft peach, with gracefully upturned points.

Plant singly, using soil-based compost. Grow either as a bush or as a standard trained on a stem to a height of about 1.2m (4ft). Water generously during summer but sparingly at other times. In frost-prone climates, move to a frost-free greenhouse or conservatory from autumn to late spring. Plants can be pruned hard in early spring.
See illustration page 7.

POT MARIGOLD

Calendula officinalis
HARDY ANNUAL

The aromatic pot marigold is widely available in numerous mixtures as well as a few single colours (*right*). Fiesta Gitana Mixed are dwarf bushy plants, with a height and spread of 30cm (12in), bearing a long succession of double flowers in the full colour spectrum, from creamy yellow to glowing orange. A more subtle range of colours can be found in the taller Art Shades Mixed, which includes cream and apricot. In 'Apricot Bon Bon', the double flowers have a soft, warm tone.

Raise from seed, sowing in spring in the container where plants are to flower, and thin the seedlings after germination. Use gritty, soil-based compost. Pinch back the growing tips to encourage bushy growth and deadhead regularly for a long flowering season.
See also page 141.

CIGAR PLANT

Cuphea ignea
EVERGREEN SUB-SHRUB   ZONE 9

The Mexican cigar plant is a useful sub-shrub in mixed plantings based on warm and hot colour schemes in sunny spots. On a bush about 30cm (12in) in height and spread, orange-red, narrowly tubular flowers, 2.5cm (1in) long, flash among mid-green leaves. The mouth of the tube is curiously finished with a purplish-black band and white ring. The plant blooms from spring to autumn, and in ideal conditions throughout the year.

In frost-prone areas the cigar plant is commonly treated as an annual and planted in late spring. Cuttings taken during the growing season can be overwintered under glass. Grow in any soil-based or soil-less compost.
See also page 168; illustrations pages 25, 119.

Pot marigold *Calendula officinalis* 'Orange Gitana'

BLANKET FLOWER

Gaillardia
ANNUAL/PERENNIAL   ZONE 3

The perennial blanket flowers tend to be short-lived and are often used like annuals for summer displays. Their daisy-like flowers are in arresting combinations such as orange and flame-red or yellow and maroon. The short-growing 'Kobold' ('Goblin'), up to 30cm (12in) high, with flowers combining yellow and rusty orange, is useful in pots.

Buy nursery-raised stock and plant out in spring, using either soil-less or soil-based compost. Apply liquid fertilizer every two weeks, starting three to four weeks after planting.
See illustration page 121.

SUN ROSE

Helianthemum
EVERGREEN SHRUB   ZONE 6

Some of the sun rose cultivars in the orange range are exceptionally vivid. The incandescent orange-scarlet of 'Fire Dragon' demands attention, even though the plant itself is usually under 30cm (12in) high, with a spread of 45cm (18in). Its foliage is grey-green.
See also pages 133, 141, 161.

EVERLASTING FLOWER

Helichrysum bracteatum
ANNUAL

Usually grown for cutting and drying, *H. bracteatum* (syn. *Bracteantha bracteata*) has a height and spread of 30cm (12in). It requires free-draining compost and sun. 'Hot Bikini' has flowers in shades of orange, red, yellow and pink.
See illustration page 120.

IMPATIENS, BUSY LIZZY

Impatiens
HALF-HARDY ANNUAL

These tender perennials, normally grown as annuals, include some of the most strongly coloured plants for containers. One of the most startling is 'Mega Orange Star'. Although only 25cm (10in) high and wide, it is eye-catching all summer, with vivid orange flowers overlaid by a white star.

The New Guinea hybrid impatiens bear large flowers of dazzling colour against attractive, sometimes variegated foliage. In 'Tango' the searing orange of the flowers is set against dark green leaves on a plant with a height and spread of 60cm (2ft).
See also pages 161–2.

Lily *Lilium* 'Enchantment'

Coral gem *Lotus berthelotii* × *maculatus*

LILY
Lilium

BULB ZONE 5 POISONOUS

Among the most vivid of the lily species and hybrids are some of orange colouring, while those in softer shadings are highly unusual.

One of the most strongly coloured is 'Enchantment', a stem-rooting hybrid that blooms in early summer (*above*). The fiery orange-red flowers, borne clustered at the end of stems 90cm (3ft) high, are cup-shaped and outward-facing.

'African Queen', also stem-rooting and blooming in mid- to late summer, is spectacular. Stems, which can be more than 1.5m (5ft) tall, bear large fragrant trumpets that flare widely to show their orange interiors; the outsides of the petals are mahogany and yellow.

Much quieter than either of these is the Nankeen lily (*L.* × *testaceum*), which flowers in mid-summer. This is an old basal-rooting hybrid, with stems 1.2–1.8m (4–6ft) high, bearing hanging flowers in an unusual shade of pale apricot. These scented blooms carry a few reddish spots, and the pollen sacs are a conspicuous bright red. *L. henryi*, with pale apricot flowers spotted red, flowers a little later. This stem-rooting species may reach 2.5m (8ft), has lance-shaped leaves and bears numerous downward-facing flowers with petals that curve outwards.

*See also pages **134**, 142, 153, 162.*

CORAL GEM
Lotus berthelotii

SEMI-EVERGREEN PERENNIAL ZONE 9

This trailing perennial has beautiful foliage and unusual flowers, making it a splendid addition to a hanging basket of mixed sun-loving plants. It looks lovely, too, grown on its own in a tall pot or basket. The stems, which may be 60–90cm (2–3ft) long, trail needle-like but soft, grey-green leaves and in summer bear clusters of dark orange, claw-like flowers. The similar hybrid *L. b.* × *maculatus* has yellow flowers with orange-brown shading (*above*).

Plant in mid- to late spring, using a gritty, soil-based potting compost. These plants are frequently grown as annuals and discarded in autumn, but rooted cuttings are easily overwintered in frost-free conditions under glass.

See also illustration page 97.

MIMULUS, MONKEY FLOWER
Mimulus

HALF-HARDY ANNUAL

The modern mimulus hybrids, perennials that are quick to flower when grown from seed, are usually treated as annuals. Provided they receive adequate water, these moisture-loving plants thrive in sun or partial shade, producing flowers throughout the summer, and are well suited to both window boxes and hanging baskets. Their flowers are a pretty snapdragon shape, each flared trumpet having two upper and three lower lobes. Mimulus

is available not only in a range of bright flower colours including orange, red and yellow, but also as pastel shades such as apricot, salmon and cream and as bicolours too. Many flowers produce arresting rusty blotches and dots. Stock bought as young plants can often be selected for colour, but seed is usually sold as mixtures. In Malibu Mixed, 15cm (6in) high and with a spread of 30cm (12in), the flowers are mainly single colours in orange, red and yellow. Calypso Mixed (*below*), up to 23cm (9in) high, has a wider colour range.

If raising from seed, sow under glass in late winter or early spring in frost-prone areas. Buy young plants in late spring or early summer. Do not plant until there is negligible risk of frost. Use either a soil-based or soil-less potting compost.

See also illustration page 96.

PELARGONIUM, GERANIUM
Pelargonium

EVERGREEN PERENNIAL ZONE 9

Among the many modern hybrids, especially of Zonal and Regal pelargoniums, there are several in the apricot to orange range. 'Springtime' ('Springtime Irene') has short-jointed stems, making a bushy plant about 45cm (18in) high, and the salmon-pink flowers, like those of all the Irene Zonals, are semi-double.

Less conventional is *P. frutetorum* 'The Boar'. This trailing cultivar is ideal for hanging baskets, with a height and

Monkey flower *Mimulus* Calypso Mixed

spread of 60cm (2ft); clusters of single flowers in soft salmon-orange are carried on long stems above dark green leaves with a central brown blotch.

Salmon and orange are also available in the hybrid pelargoniums that are raised from seed annually. Mixtures such as the Orbit Series include orange, but there is an endless stream of new introductions in single colours.

The Regal pelargoniums can make attractive pot plants outdoors provided they are protected from rough weather and rain. 'Sunrise' is salmon-orange with red-brown markings and a white throat. 'Valenciana' is deep apricot. Both grow to 60–90cm (2–3ft).
See also pages 135, 153–4, 163, 170, 181–2, 187, 190, 194.

RHODODENDRON, AZALEA
Rhododendron
SHRUB   ZONE 5
The late-flowering rhododendrons and azaleas are useful for bridging the gap between spring and summer. Several hybrids have flowers in shades of scarlet to orange. 'Gloria Mundi' (Zone 3), a twiggy deciduous azalea, is typical of the Ghent hybrids in having fragrant honeysuckle-like flowers. Its frilled blooms, of intense orange with a yellow flare, appear in early summer.
See also pages 129, 139, 142, 145, 150, 156–7, 167, 173.

RUDBECKIA
Rudbeckia hirta
ANNUAL
The rudbeckias are familiar as components of sunny borders in the second half of summer and early autumn. The purplish-brown cones of their flowers make a dark centre to ray petals in a variety of vibrant shades of yellow, orange and rust.

The short-lived perennial *R. hirta* is usually grown as an annual and it has compact cultivars that make radiant additions to hot colour schemes. Rustic Dwarfs, generally less than 60cm (2ft) high, are a particularly good choice. The almost black cones make a telling contrast to petals in shades of bronze, mahogany, yellow and gold.

Plant in spring, using either a soil-less or a soil-based compost. As the first flush of flowers fades, cut back plants and apply a liquid fertilizer to encourage another flush of blooms.
See illustrations pages 55, 120.

DESERT MALLOW
Sphaeralcea ambigua
EVERGREEN SUB-SHRUB   ZONE 7
The mallow family includes a number of long-flowering although often short-lived and sometimes coarse ornamentals. The desert mallow is a softly hairy, shrubby perennial that is remarkable for the unusual warm coral of its silky, funnel-shaped flowers, which are borne throughout summer and into autumn. Pinching back the growing tips of young plants will encourage bushy growth. In containers plants are usually less than 90cm (3ft) high.

Another sub-shrubby mallow is *Malvastrum lateritium*, with beautifully formed flowers in a rare shade of apricot. Up to 45cm (18in) tall, it may have a spread of more than 1.2m (4ft).

Plant in spring, using gritty, soil-based compost and position in full sun. Good drainage is essential. These plants may tolerate low temperatures but they dislike cool, damp conditions. They, or rooted cuttings, should be over wintered under glass and kept well ventilated.
See illustration page 118.

MARIGOLD
Tagetes
HALF-HARDY ANNUAL
Bright colours and reliable, summer-long flowering have made marigolds popular annuals for flower beds and containers positioned in full sun. There are three main types. The African marigolds (usually listed under *T. erecta*) are upright plants with deeply cut, dark green, aromatic leaves, many cultivars being 60–90cm (2–3ft) high, although there are also smaller varieties 30–45cm (12–18in) high. The cultivars have double flowers 8cm (3in) across, in yellows and oranges.

The French marigolds (*T. patula*) have similar foliage but are more compact, being 15–45cm (6–18in) in height, and their smaller flowers are yellow to orange, often combined with shades of red-brown. Vigorous, compact crosses between these two groups are known as Triploid marigolds.

Cultivars of the signet marigold (*T. tenuifolia* var. *pumila*) make up the third main group. These are bushy plants, 15–30cm (6–12in) high, bearing masses of small single flowers.

A mammoth African marigold in deep orange is 'Toreador'. Growing 75cm (30in) high, it has ball-shaped,

Black-eyed susan *Thunbergia alata*

ruffled flowers 10cm (4in) or so across. The many mixtures of African types in yellow and orange include several, such as the Inca Hybrids, that are more compact. These grow to 30cm (12in).

Double French marigolds include 'Honeycomb', 30cm (12in) high, with orange-brown petals edged yellow. The Boy-o-Boy Series is only 15cm (6in) high, and the double flowers in this mixture include orange, red-brown and yellow. The Disco Series has a wide colour range with masses of large single flowers on plants 30cm (12in) high.

The profusion of small flowers produced by signet marigolds offers a charming alternative to the clotted density of some African and French types. 'Paprika' has daisy-like, single, red flowers with gold centres and edging. The Gem Series, 20in (8in) high, includes a vibrant orange as well as lemon and gold. The Starfire Hybrids are slightly more compact, individual flowers including mixtures of colours.

Raise all these marigolds from seed sown under glass in early to mid-spring. Once they have been hardened, plant seedlings and bought stock outdoors in late spring or early summer. Use any soil-based or soil-less compost.
See also pages 143, 146; illustration page 103.

BLACK-EYED SUSAN
Thunbergia alata
ANNUAL CLIMBER

In cool temperate regions, position these twining climbers in a warm, sheltered spot outdoors; with suitable supports they can grow to 3m (10ft). All summer soft orange, tubular flowers, with five lobes surrounding a chocolate centre, nestle among the heart-shaped leaves (*left*).

Raise from seed in early spring, and keep them at a temperature of 16–18°C (61–65°F) until they germinate. Thin and pot up the plants before hardening and planting outdoors. Place containers so that plants can climb up netting or wires fitted to walls. Alternatively, use a wigwam of bamboo stems to provide support.

NASTURTIUM
Tropaeolum majus
HALF-HARDY ANNUAL

The common and easily pleased nasturtium thrives in containers. Spurred flowers in bright colours are carried profusely over attractive, rounded, blue-green leaves. Orange is a conspicuous flower colour in all the mixtures. Vigorous versions such as

Nasturtium *Tropaeolum majus* Alaska Mixed

Tall Mixed climb or trail 2.5m (8ft) or more. More compact, semi-trailing mixtures such as the Gleam Hybrids have a height and spread of 30cm (12in) and are well suited to hanging baskets; they carry semi-double flowers in orange, scarlet and yellow. There is a bright colour range, too, in Alaska Mixed, attractive for the cream marbling of the foliage on plants 23cm (9in) high (*below left*).

Of the few separate colours sometimes available, 'Peach Melba', a dwarf selection 23cm (9in) high, carries pink flowers that are flushed orange. The vigorous 'Hermine Grashoff', with double bright orange flowers, must be propagated from cuttings.

When growing nasturtiums from seed, sow thinly in the container in mid-spring and later thin out the seedlings. Alternatively, sow under glass in late winter or early spring to provide early displays. Grow in any soil-based or soil-less compost but do not fertilize generously, because this will encourage foliage at the expense of flowers. Plants bloom most freely in full sun, but the foliage can look extremely attractive in partial shade.
See also pages 143, 155; illustration page 97.

VERBENA
Verbena 'Peaches and Cream'
HALF-HARDY ANNUAL

The mixture of orange, apricot and cream in the flowers of this cultivar (*below right*) is a welcome development in verbenas. Another appealing feature is that the flower heads may display all shades at the same time. These rather stiff plants, with a height of 23cm (9in) and a spread of 30cm (12in), are suitable for hanging baskets and other containers positioned in full sun.
See also pages 136, 155, 165, 171, 176–7; illustrations pages 106, 118.

VIOLA, PANSY
Viola
ANNUAL/BIENNIAL

Many of the mixtures of violas and pansies include plants with amber, apricot and rusty orange tints in the flowers. These shades are often found, for example, in the pansies Roggli Giants, a seed strain with large flowers, which can be as much as 10cm (4in) across, on plants with a height and spread of up to 20cm (8in). The intensity of the orange in 'Padparadja'

is exceptional. This hybrid, with a height and spread of 15cm (6in), has medium-sized, rounded flowers of almost uniform, eye-catching incandescence. Less attention-seeking is the viola 'Chantreyland', which grows to 20cm (8in). Its small flowers are a pretty soft apricot suffused with tangerine.

All these are short-lived perennials that are almost invariably raised from seed as biennials or annuals, or bought as bedding plants when they appear in garden centres in late spring.
*See also pages 136, **143–4**, 155, 167, 171, 177.*

AUTUMN AND WINTER

CROCUS
Crocus
CORM   ZONE 5

Many of the small crocuses that flower in late winter have remarkably intense colour, creating an impact out of all proportion to their size. A plant of astonishing brilliance is *C. ancyrensis* (sometimes listed as 'Golden Bunch'). Each corm produces five or more honey-scented flowers of vibrant orange with a three-tongued style that is deep orange-red. This diminutive species is less than 8cm (3in) high. A cheerful new cultivar of *C. chrysanthus*, 'Brass Band', has bronzed gold flowers and an orange tongue. It grows to a height of about 8cm (3in) and blooms in mid- to late winter. Crocuses look best planted densely on their own in shallow pots.
*See also pages 128, 137, **138**, 144, 166, 171, 177.*

Verbena *Verbena* 'Peaches and Cream'

RED FLOWERS

Reds include some of the most eye-catching, extrovert, even aggressive colours in the gardener's palette. But there are cooler reds, too, and flowers of astonishingly deep and rich colour in which the velvet texture of petals seems to intensify an inner glow.

SPRING

CAMELLIA

Camellia japonica
EVERGREEN SHRUB   ZONE 7

Many camellias are surprisingly tough, but early-flowering ones may have their magnificent blooms damaged by frost. A striking old cultivar with semi-double red flowers up to 13cm (5in) across is 'Adolphe Audusson': gold stamens stand out against the deep red of the petals. 'Bob Hope' is a more recent semi-double, with blood-red flowers and yellow stamens. In containers both will grow to about 1.8m (6ft), with a spread of 1.2m (4ft).
*See also pages 128, **156**.*

WALLFLOWER

Erysimum
PERENNIAL   ZONE 7

Most wallflower mixtures (sometimes listed under *Cheiranthus*) include rich colours in the red range, and several cultivars in separate colours are also available. 'Blood Red' carries velvety flowers drenched in a wonderfully deep hue, and is a tall wallflower, as is 'Vulcan', 30–38cm (12–15in) high, with deep crimson blooms. Dwarf cultivars suitable for window boxes include mixtures such as the Tom Thumb Series and 'Scarlet Bedder', all under 30cm (12in) high.
*See also pages **138**, 145; illustration page 8.*

HYACINTH

Hyacinthus orientalis
BULB   ZONE 5

In mid- to late spring red hyacinths produce spikes 20cm (8in) high so densely packed with heavily scented, waxy flowers that they form a column of highly concentrated colour. 'Jan Bos' has white centres to its carmine-red flowers, while 'Hollyhock' is slightly deeper in colour and its double flowers strengthen the effect of the red

Hyacinth *Hyacinthus orientalis* 'Hollyhock'

colouring even more (*above*). Both these hyacinths flower early.
*See also pages 129, 138, 156, **172**.*

RHODODENDRON, AZALEA

Rhododendron
SHRUB   ZONE 5

Compact rhododendrons and azaleas include some of the best flowering shrubs for containers, and there exists a wide choice of red-flowered hybrids. The evergreen rhododendron May Day, which makes a spreading dome under 1.5m (5ft) high, bears loose clusters of scarlet-red flowers in late spring. The underside of the leaves is pale and felted. The *R. yakushimanum* hybrid 'Dopey' (Zone 4) is an evergreen spreading shrub that grows up to 1.2m (4ft) high, and produces its red flowers from late spring into summer.

The popular 'Hinodegiri' (Zone 7), an evergreen azalea, grows to about 75cm (30in) but has a wider spread. It bears small crimson flowers in great profusion in mid- to late spring.

Many deciduous azaleas have flowers in strong reds and oranges, most blooming in mid- to late spring. The trumpet-shaped flowers of 'Royal Lodge' are vermilion, turning crimson as they age; in a container this variety is usually less than 1.8m (6ft) tall.
*See also pages 129, 139, 142, 145, 148, **156–7**, 167, 173.*

TULIP

Tulipa
BULB   ZONE 4

Centuries of breeding have provided an astonishing range of colour among modern tulips, and the vivid reds of several species have been passed on to some of the showiest hybrids. All the following are easily grown in containers and, according to the selection, provide splashes of eye-catching colour between early and late spring.

Kauffmanniana tulips are among the first to flower and, being less than 25cm (10in) high, are ideal for window boxes. Their leaves have attractive purple stripes. The pointed petals of 'Alfred Cortot' are deep scarlet, radiating from a central black blotch.

The single tulips that flower in early spring are a taller group, most being about 35cm (14in) high. 'Couleur Cardinal' is a splendid crimson tinged with purple. A double with the same flowering season is the long-lasting, vivid scarlet 'Carlton', 25cm (10in) high.

Several early tulips are derived from the spectacular *T. fosteriana* and of these one of the most brilliant is 'Madame Lefeber' ('Red Emperor'). It is sheeny scarlet-red with a yellow base and grows to 38cm (15in).

Sturdy tulips for mid- to late spring include 'Bing Crosby' (*below*), with long-lasting, lustrous, scarlet flowers on stems 40cm (16in) high. Quite different

Tulip *Tulipa* 'Bing Crosby'

in character is the species *T. linifolia*. At a height of 10–15cm (4–6in) this can be grown with rock-garden plants. The flowers open wide over narrow, wavy leaves to show a silky scarlet interior with a centre of dark purple.

T. greigii is a parent of numerous, brilliantly coloured, late-flowering, dwarf tulips, most being less than 30cm (12in) high. To many of its offspring, it has passed on magnificent red flowers and purple-brown striping of the foliage. The scarlet 'Red Riding Hood', for example, is deservedly popular.

Plant tulips in late autumn, preferably in a soil-based compost (they thrive in alkaline conditions). Large-flowered hybrids should be covered by at least 10cm (4in) of compost. Plant small species such as *T. linifolia* at a depth of 5–10cm (2–4in). Planting closely and in two layers will create a dense display, but do not allow bulbs to touch one another.

Remove flower heads as soon as the petals begin to drop, but leave stems and leaves to die down before lifting, drying and storing bulbs. If containers are needed for other plants, lift tulips after flowering and replant in autumn. For containers it is worth buying fresh stock annually.
See also pages 129–30, 140, 145, 157, 167; illustrations pages 8, 49, 92.

SUMMER

LOVE-LIES-BLEEDING
Amaranthus caudatus
HALF-HARDY ANNUAL
This tropical annual, much prized in gardens of the 17th century, is worth growing in pots, as it often was then, to make a handsome curiosity for decorating steps, paths and patios. Up to 1.2m (4ft) tall, it bears crimson tassels of dangling flowers between mid-summer and early autumn. The individual flowers are minute, but the rope-like stems of clustered blooms are up to 45cm (18in) long.

Raise these plants from seed sown in warmth in early spring. Plant hardened seedlings and bought stock in a sunny position outdoors in late spring. Use any soil-based or soil-less compost, preferably enriched with organic matter, because love-lies-bleeding thrives on a rich diet. Apply liquid fertilizer generously.

Snapdragon *Antirrhinum majus* 'Black Prince'

SNAPDRAGON
Antirrhinum majus
HALF-HARDY ANNUAL
The snapdragons, perennials that are usually grown as annuals, are available as tall, intermediate and dwarf cultivars in a wide range of colours, including various shades of red, and with several variations on the flower type. All have erect, densely packed flower stems, creating an impact throughout summer when planted in groups; they are also attractive as vertical accents in mixtures of other flowers.

Tall snapdragons such as Madame Butterfly, a mixture 60–90cm (2–3ft) high with lance-shaped leaves and spikes of double flowers superficially resembling azaleas, are suitable only for containers in sheltered spots.

Monarch, an intermediate, rust-resistant and sturdy series that grows to a height of 45cm (18in), is readily available in single colours. 'Scarlet Monarch' produces brilliant scarlet flowers. Plants form several lateral spikes, giving a long season.

'Black Prince' (*above*) is one of the darkest snapdragons available as a separate colour. Growing to 45cm (18in), it has deep crimson flowers and bronze foliage.

Dwarf snapdragons, particularly good in window boxes, include the rust-resistant Royal Carpet, a mixture up to 30cm (12in) high.

Raise from seed in late winter or early spring, sowing under glass in frost-prone areas. Plant hardened seedlings and bought stock outdoors in late spring or early summer. Use any soil-based or soil-less compost.

Pinch back the growing points of young plants to encourage bushy growth, and remove side shoots to produce impressive flower spikes. Snap off the spikes when the blooms fade in order to prolong the flowering season. *See also pages 130, 140, 158, 167.*

THRIFT, SEA PINK
Armeria maritima
EVERGREEN PERENNIAL   ZONE 3
Grassy evergreen hummocks, thickly studded in the first half of summer (and often later) with tightly packed flower heads, make the thrifts an attractive addition to rock-garden collections grown in full sun. Although wild plants are usually pink or white, cultivars are deeper coloured: rose-red 'Vindictive' and crimson-magenta 'Düsseldorfer Stolz' ('Dusseldorf Pride') are both under 15cm (6in) in height, with a spread of 25–45cm (10–18in).

Plant between autumn and mid-spring, using a gritty, soil-based potting compost.

ASTILBE
Astilbe × arendsii
PERENNIAL   ZONE 5
Hybrids of the moisture-loving astilbes, producing feathery sprays of long-lasting flowers over attractive divided foliage, include some strong reds.

The short-growing 'Fanal', up to 60cm (2ft) high, carries deep crimson-red flowers in early summer. 'Red Sentinel' blooms at the same time and is of similar colour, but its plumes are more open and may be 90cm (3ft) tall. 'Feuer' ('Fire') attains the same height but produces its feathery coral-red plumes in mid- to late summer. The beautifully bronzed young leaves of all these astilbes are dark green with a hint of red throughout summer. *See also page 158–9.*

BEGONIA
Begonia × tuberhybrida
TUBER ZONE 10
Tuberous begonias are often sold in flamboyant mixtures that include reds, such as the erect Nonstop Series and

the trailing kinds of the Pendula group. In addition there are numerous named cultivars in red: 'Allan Langdon', for example, is an erect bush, 30–60cm (12–24in) high, bearing large double flowers of cardinal-red from mid-summer to early autumn.

BOUGAINVILLEA
Bougainvillea × buttiana
EVERGREEN CLIMBER   ZONE 10

In California, the Mediterranean region, and many other parts of the world where the climate is hot, bougainvillea is a widely grown scrambler that may reach a height of 4.5m (15ft) or more outdoors. In cool-temperate regions, however, it needs to be grown in a greenhouse or sunroom.

Its profuse flowers are surrounded by attractive and flamboyantly coloured papery bracts. Many cultivars of the hybrid *B.* × *buttiana* are magenta, scarlet, orange or yellow: 'Scarlett O'Hara' ('San Diego Red'), for example, has magenta-red bracts; those of 'Scarlet Queen' are, predictably, scarlet.

Plant in a soil-based compost and position in full sun. Tie growths into supports. In early spring prune the previous season's growth, leaving spurs with one or two buds.

CHOCOLATE COSMOS
Cosmos atrosanguineus
PERENNIAL   ZONE 9

In late summer this slightly tender perennial, which grows to a height of 60cm (2ft), produces numerous small dahlia-like flowers of an exceptionally rich maroon (*below*). What is rather surprising is that there is a chocolate-like fragrance to match.

In late winter, plant the tubers individually 15cm (6in) deep, using a soil-based compost to which leaf mould or other humus has been added. Keep frost-free until the container is moved outdoors in early summer. Water generously in the growing season and apply a liquid fertilizer every two weeks, starting two to three weeks after growth begins to show in late spring. Overwinter in a frost-free environment and repot annually.
See also pages 132, 159–60.

DAHLIA
Dahlia
HALF-HARDY ANNUAL/
TUBEROUS PERENNIAL   ZONE 8

Modern hybrid dahlias are among the best plants to give the container garden a lift in the second half of summer and early autumn. All need a sunny, open

spot. Dahlias are grown from tubers, which are planted and lifted annually, or, in the case of the bedding dahlias, raised from seed each year. Many of those grown from tubers are too large for containers. However, the bushy 'Bishop of Llandaff', which grows to 1m (40in), is manageable and is an appealing plant with dark foliage and semi-double scarlet flowers.

The shorter-growing bedding dahlias raised from seed are generally the most suitable for tubs and even window boxes. They are usually sold as mixtures in which red is an important constituent. Bambino Mixed, for example, grows to 45cm (18in) and their small, semi-double flowers cover a wide colour range. In Coltness Mixed, which grows to 60cm (2ft), the flowers are single, while the dark bronzy foliage of Redskin, under 40cm (16in) in height, makes a good foil for double flowers in a mixture of vivid colours.

Grow all dahlias in a fertile, soil-based or soil-less compost. Plant unsprouted tubers in mid-spring, sprouted tubers in late spring, at a depth of 10cm (4in). Pinch back growing tips to encourage bushy plants and provide stakes for large ones, tying in as stems develop. Lift tubers in autumn and store in a frost-free place.

Sow seed of bedding dahlias under glass in late winter or early spring. Plant hardened seedlings or bought stock outdoors during late spring.
See also page 168.

PINK
Dianthus
PERENNIAL   ZONE 3

Dwarf pinks are among the loveliest summer-flowering rock-garden plants. The alpine pink (*D. alpinus*), only 10cm (4in) high, is variable in colour, ranging from pink to purple, and flowers in early summer. The rose-red flowers of 'Joan's Blood' have red-purple centres. The maiden pink (*D. deltoides*) is 15–23cm (6–9in) high, with masses of small flowers. Several named selections, including 'Leuchtfunk' ('Flashing Light') and 'Samos', have crimson flowers. All bloom in early to mid-summer.

Old-fashioned and modern hybrid pinks grow 30cm (12in) tall. 'Brympton Red', with its single fragrant flowers of bright crimson overlaid with a deeper shade, has all the charm of the old

Chocolate cosmos *Cosmos atrosanguineus*

hybrids. 'Ian', a modern pink with flowers of deep velvet red, darker at the petal edges, blooms in early to mid-summer and sometimes again in late summer or autumn.
*See also pages 132, **160***.

FUCHSIA
Fuchsia
DECIDUOUS SHRUB   ZONE 10
All the following fuchsias have red petals. 'Marinka', a long-standing favourite among trailing fuchsias, has almost-uniform red flowers. So too does 'Golden Marinka', with golden foliage. Another trailing hybrid with almost-uniform red flowers is 'Red Spider', with its long sepals that surround the petals. In 'Cascade' the white sepals curve back, fully exposing the carmine petals. The trailing stems of all of these may easily grow 90cm (3ft) long.

Most of the upright hybrids form bushes up to 90cm (3ft) high. 'Rufus' (Zone 8), which has small flowers of almost-uniform red, is also suitable for training as a standard. 'Garten-meister Bonstedt' has red-brown petals and sepals. 'Thalia' is a bushy plant with velvety foliage. Throughout summer it bears slender flowers with red sepals and orange-scarlet petals.
*See also pages 132–3, 160–1, **168**; illustrations pages 8, 97, 115, 116.*

LILY
Lilium
BULB   ZONE 4   POISONOUS
Among the numerous hybrid lilies – an outstanding group of summer flowers – are some that produce strong reds. The richly fragrant 'Star Gazer', for example, blooms in mid- to late summer: it grows to 90cm (3ft) and bears large, outward-facing flowers, the broad crimson petals, curving back at the tips, edged with white, and heavily spotted maroon. Similarly coloured and also strongly scented is *L. speciosum* var. *rubrum*, a variety of a stem-rooting species that needs a warm position to thrive. Stems may be more than 1.2m (4ft) high and bear many nodding waxy flowers in late summer.

Very different in character is the short-stemmed 'Red Carpet'. It is 30cm (12in) high, with yellow buds opening in mid-summer to upward-facing flowers of intense scarlet.
*See also pages **134**, 142, 147, 162.*

LOBELIA
Lobelia erinus
HALF-HARDY ANNUAL   POISONOUS
Variations on the familiar blue and purple lobelias make a welcome change. The Fountain Series, often sold as a mixture, includes 'Rose Fountain', 15cm (6in) or so high, with long, slender stems bearing masses of small rose-red flowers. Plants in the Cascade Series are also trailing: 'Red Cascade' produces purple-red flowers with white eyes and 'Rosamund' has wine-red flowers with white eyes.
*See also pages 135, 169, **175–6**.*

SCARLET TRUMPET HONEYSUCKLE
Lonicera × brownii
CLIMBER   ZONE 3
The scarlet trumpet honeysuckle, which grows to 3.7m (12ft), is a beautiful hybrid, with blue-green leaves showing off clusters of scarlet flowers. These have two lips opening to an orange throat. There are several cultivars, 'Dropmore Scarlet' (*right*) being richly coloured and flowering throughout most of summer.

Plant in autumn or early spring, using a soil-based compost. Provide supports. Prune lightly and top-dress with fresh compost in spring.

NEMESIA
Nemesia strumosa
HALF-HARDY ANNUAL
Much of the charm of nemesias lies in the pretty form of the flowers, funnel-shaped and pouched, and in the bright colours of the seed mixtures in which they are generally sold. Carnival, with large flowers, and Tapestry, which includes many subtle shades, both mixtures under 30cm (12in) high, draw on a range that covers crimson, scarlet, pink, orange, yellow, cream and blue. Markings in the throat often add a cheering dash. The unusual bicolour 'Mello Red and White' combines two colours with dazzling effect.

Raise from seed, sowing under glass in early spring in frost-prone areas. Plant hardened seedlings or bought stock outdoors in late spring, using any soil-based or soil-less compost. Nemesias need sun – they are especially lovely in sunny window boxes and hanging baskets – but do not flower for long in hot weather.
See also pages 169–70, 176.

Scarlet trumpet honeysuckle *Lonicera × brownii* 'Dropmore Scarlet'

WATER LILY
Nymphaea 'Laydekeri Purpurata'
PERENNIAL
Many of the small water lily hybrids may be grown in 30–60cm (12–24in) of water, making them suitable for tubs and other small containers. The tulip-shaped flowers of *N.* 'Laydekeri Purpurata', deep pink to wine-red with orange stamens, are produced freely throughout summer. Its small leaves are purple on the undersides and occasionally blotched maroon.
*See also page **142**.*

PELARGONIUM, GERANIUM
Pelargonium
EVERGREEN PERENNIAL   ZONE 9
Pelargoniums are mainstays of the container garden, justly popular for being easy plants that tolerate more neglect than most while producing bright flowers over a long season, provided they are grown in sun. In frost-free areas they will flower almost the whole year round. Elsewhere, they are commonly grown as annuals, though they may be overwintered under cover (*see page 85*). There are four main groups of pelargonium.

The scented-leaved kinds are grown for their aromatic foliage. The Regals (sometimes listed under *P.* × *domesticum*) have large, showy flowers, but only a few of them are robust enough to be cultivated outdoors. 'Dubonnet', with repeating wine-red flowers, and 'Grand Slam', scarlet with red markings, are worth trying in sunny, sheltered spots. Both of these grow to about 60cm (2ft).

The two most important groups for the container gardener are the Zonal and the Ivy-leaved pelargoniums. The Zonals are shrubby plants, usually less than 90cm (3ft) high, and often show a distinctive dark zone on the leaf. Their single, semi-double or double flowers are borne in dense clusters, usually well above the foliage. Their wide colour range includes many dashing reds: 'Irene', a parent of many other good Zonals, is semi-double and rich crimson; also semi-double is the scarlet 'Gustav Emich', while 'Madame Dubarry' is a resplendent coral-red single and 'Paul Crampel' (*below*), a bright scarlet single. There are miniatures, too, usually less than 20cm (8in) in height: 'Caligula' has double crimson flowers. The seed strains available, such as the Pulsar Series, are

generally mixtures that include reds.

Ivy-leaved pelargoniums, derived from *P. peltatum*, have flowers similar to those of the Zonals, but the plants are trailing, sometimes having a spread of 1.2m (4ft) or more, and their somewhat fleshy leaves are similar in shape to ivy foliage. 'Rote Mini-Cascade' is a short-jointed example with single red flowers. Others include 'Mexican Beauty' and 'Yale', both deep crimson semi-doubles, and 'Tavira', also semi-double but light crimson. A few seed strains are available.

Plant in soil-based or soil-less compost, and prune plants that have flowered in summer before over-wintering them. Take cuttings in early autumn, or, if raising from seed, sow in late winter at a temperature of 61–64°F (16–18°C). Keep overwintered plants just moist until they are started into growth in spring. Pelargoniums are usually bought for planting in late spring, when overwintered stock should also be planted outdoors. Deadhead regularly to keep plants flowering.
See also pages 135, 147–8, 163, 170, 181–2, 187, 190, 194; illustrations pages 8, 9, 21, 25, 111, 115.

Pelargonium 'Paul Crampel'

PETUNIA
Petunia
HALF-HARDY ANNUAL
Most mixtures available as seed contain reds, including the extravagant Fluffy Ruffles Mixed (veined and splashed flowers that are waved and ruffled) and the bright but more sober Super Cascade Series, which is ideal for hanging baskets.

The range of separate colours available as seed is limited, although occasionally an unusual shade is picked out. 'Flame Carpet', a dwarf single usually less than 30cm (12in) high, produces yellow-throated flowers of vibrant coral. Colour selections are more readily available in young plants.
*See also pages 136, 142, 163, 170, **176**.*

ROSE
Rosa
DECIDUOUS SHRUB   ZONE 4
Among the hundreds of rose hybrids with red blooms are many that may be grown in containers. Most suitable as container plants are the Cluster-flowered bush roses (Floribundas) and their dwarf forms, the so-called Patio roses. 'Red Rascal', 45cm (18in) high, is a double with scarlet-crimson blooms.

Smaller still, and better in containers than in the open garden, are Miniature roses, which rarely exceed 30cm (12in). 'Red Ace' is a tested cultivar with semi-double flowers in deep red. It repeats well but has little scent.

Ground-cover roses, too, are useful for growing in pots and tubs. 'Scarlet Meidiland', for example, which makes a mound up to 1.2m (4ft) high with an ultimate spread of 1.8m (6ft), bears large clusters of small but double scarlet flowers in several flushes.

Plant roses between autumn and early spring, using soil-based compost. Feed with a liquid fertilizer every two weeks. Deadhead regularly and prune in late winter, Cluster-flowered and Large-flowered bush roses hard, others lightly. Repot every second year; top-dress in alternate springs.
See also pages 136, 142, 164, 170, 203.

SALVIA
Salvia
ANNUAL
One of the most vivid of all bedding plants is *S. splendens*. This tender perennial, usually grown as a half-hardy annual, has spikes 30–60cm (12–24in)

Salvia *Salvia splendens*

Mixed dwarf zinnias *Zinnia* Miniature Pompon

high, densely packed with scarlet flowers surrounded by long-lasting bracts of the same colour (*above*). There are also white, pink and purple forms. The cardinal sage (*S. fulgens*) is a perennial with spikes of vivid red flowers 60cm (2ft) high.

The evergreen shrub *S. microphylla* (Zone 9) needs frost-free conditions. Growing to 1.2m (4ft) high, from mid-summer to mid-autumn it carries small crimson or scarlet flowers.
See also pages 170, 176; illustration page 111.

NASTURTIUM
Tropaeolum majus
HALF-HARDY ANNUAL
Climbing, semi-trailing and compact nasturtiums are commonly sold as mixtures in which reds feature prominently. The range of separate colours sold as seed is limited, but 'Empress of India', a long-standing favourite of compact growth, is often listed. It has a height and spread of 23cm (9in) and produces a long succession of deep crimson, single flowers set among blue-green leaves.
See also pages 143, 149; illustrations pages 97, 103.

VERBENA
Verbena
HALF-HARDY ANNUAL
Most colour mixtures of verbena include reds. Separate colours are often available as bedding plants and a limited

range also as seed. 'Blaze' is a compact hybrid, 23cm (9in) high, carrying the characteristic tight clusters of tubular flowers, in this case scarlet. 'Valentine' makes a larger plant, up to 38cm (15in) high, a white eye giving a sprightly touch to the clear red florets. Verbenas that do not come true from seed, and which therefore must be propagated from cuttings, include the scarlet perennial 'Lawrence Johnston' (Zone 9).

These versatile verbenas combine well with other plants, especially in window boxes and hanging baskets.
See also pages 136, 149, 165, 171, 176–7.

VIOLA, PANSY
Viola
ANNUAL/BIENNIAL
These invaluable plants flower recklessly over a long period, especially in areas where the summers are on the cool side. They are charming whether grown on their own or combined with other plants. Dusty, velvety and rich reds feature prominently in many viola and pansy seed mixtures. Colour selections are often best made from nurseries and garden centres in late spring, when plants are sold as they come into bloom. From time to time, seed is also available of violas and pansies with names, such as 'Alpen Fire' and 'Flame Princess', that suggest their colour range.
See also Pansy, right, and pages 136, 143–4, 149, 167, 171, 177.

ZINNIA
Zinnia
HALF-HARDY ANNUAL
Among the most colourful of the summer-flowering annuals, zinnias stand up well to heat and drought, but the large-flowered forms may be damaged by rain. They are mainly sold as mixtures in which there are often several shades of red as well as pink, purple, maroon, orange, yellow and white. Cactus-flowered and dahlia-flowered hybrids produce large blooms as much as 15cm (6in) across, the former shaggy, the latter dense and neat. Plants grow to 75cm (30in). There are also more compact hybrids such as Persian Carpet, under 30cm (12in), with semi-double and double flowers, and Miniature Pompon (*left*), up to 23cm (9in) high.

Sow seed in warmth in early spring. Plant hardened seedlings outdoors in late spring. Use soil-based or soil-less compost. Deadhead regularly to keep plants flowering.
See also page 144.

AUTUMN AND WINTER

WINTER HEATH
Erica carnea
EVERGREEN SHRUB   ZONE 6
Numerous cultivars of the winter heath are available. This dwarf evergreen shrub has needle-like leaves. In the flowering season, stems are tipped with clusters of small bells in pink, white or red. The nearest to a deep red is 'Vivellii', which flowers from mid-winter to early spring. The dark green foliage takes on a pleasing bronze tint during winter.
See also pages 137, 165, 171, 183.

PANSY
Viola
ANNUAL/ BIENNIAL
Shades of red are found in a few named selections of winter-flowering pansy and one of the most valuable is the 'Redwing', which brings cheer to containers and window boxes through the bleakest season. The two upper petals are rich rust, and there are touches of the same colour as well as a dark mask on the yellow of the other petals. It grows to around 15cm (6in).
See also Viola, left, and pages 136, 143–4, 149, 167, 171, 177.

155

Many pinks, especially those associated with traditional flowers, are soft pastels, which have a fresh delicacy. At the other extreme, the vividness of some pinks can be shocking. Being combined with grey foliage helps almost all pinks; the more aggressive shades are subdued, while the pale ones appear brighter and more intense.

SPRING

DAISY

Bellis perennis
BIENNIAL
Before the range of ornamentals was dramatically increased by successive waves of plant introductions, double forms of familiar flowers such as the common daisy held a special place in the affection of gardeners. 'Dresden China', which some claim dates from the 18th century, has flowers that are densely packed pink pompons. Although small, they are in scale with the 10cm (4in) high plant, making it a perfect companion for dwarf spring bulbs such as blue grape hyacinths (*Muscari*) and scillas.

Seed mixtures in a range covering pink, red and white include several small-flowered doubles, such as 'Pomponette', and others with blooms more than 5cm (2in) across, such as Goliath Mixed (*below*) and Habanera Mixed. The large-flowered cultivars are up to 20cm (8in) high.

'Dresden China', which does not

Daisy *Bellis perennis*
Goliath Mixed

produce seed, is propagated by division. To raise other kinds from seed, sow in early summer and grow until ready to plant out in autumn in soil-based or soil-less compost. Daisies are suited to window boxes and low containers in sunny spots.
See illustrations pages 41, 89, 93.

CAMELLIA

Camellia
EVERGREEN SHRUB   ZONE 7
Camellias are outstanding container shrubs, beautiful on account of their polished dark green leaves as well as their elegant flowers, which open in late winter and spring. The flower colour is predominantly pink or red, but there is considerable variation in shape, elaborately categorized by specialists, from single to fully double. In containers, most of the numerous cultivars of *C. japonica* and its hybrids grow up to 1.8m (6ft) high, with a spread of 1.2m (4ft).

'Hagoromo', also listed as 'Magnoliiflora', is a beautiful semi-double cultivar of *C. japonica*, with pale pink, magnolia-like flowers. The much darker 'Elegans' ('Chandleri Elegans') is an anemone-centred double.

The various hybrids listed under *C. × williamsii* often start flowering in winter, and they have an advantage over *C. japonica* cultivars in that their blooms drop as they fade, before turning brown. The free-flowering 'Donation' is a bright pink semi-double, and 'J. C. Williams' is a lighter pink and single.

Plant camellias singly in large pots or tubs, using a neutral or ericaceous compost like those suitable for rhododendrons. Camellias like a cool, moist root run, but their compost should not be soggy. Place containers in partial shade or even in the unrelieved shade cast by a wall. In frost-prone areas, do not place plants where flowers will be exposed to early morning sun. To reduce the risk of blooms being damaged by frost, give plants overhead protection or, in the case of those flowering very early, bring them under cover. Prune after flowering, but only to cut out diseased or damaged wood and to maintain a good shape.
See also pages 128, 150.

CLEMATIS

Clematis macropetala
CLIMBER   ZONE 5   POISONOUS
Among the most beautiful of the spring-flowering species is the delicate *C. macropetala*. The cultivar 'Markham's Pink' grows to 3.7m (12ft), its nodding flowers a soft but rich shade of pink.
*See also pages 128, **131–2**, 159, 167, 174; illustration page 75.*

LENTEN ROSE

Helleborus orientalis
EVERGREEN PERENNIAL   ZONE 4
The Lenten roses sometimes ignore their name and flower in winter but they are usually at their peak in early spring. Stems up to 60cm (2ft) high carry several saucer-shaped flowers above the old foliage, which is soon replaced by glossy, dark green leaves. Flower colour ranges from greenish white to deep purple, the interior often beautifully speckled. The richest colours have a grape-like bloom.

The Lenten roses do well in full or partial shade. Plant individually in mid-autumn, using a soil-based compost to which leaf mould has been added. Plants resent root disturbance, so should be repotted only when this is absolutely essential.
See illustration page 88.

HYACINTH

Hyacinthus orientalis
BULB   ZONE 3
The Dutch hyacinths are among the most highly bred of all spring bulbs, with fragrant waxy flowers clustered in dense spikes from mid- to late spring. Pinks are represented in a broad colour range. One of the deepest, 'Pink Pearl', is tinged with carmine. Paler pinks include 'Anna Marie' and 'Lady Derby' – the latter has larger flowers carried less stiffly than the others and blooms slightly later. All are approximately 20cm (8in) in height.
*See also pages 129, 138, 150, **172**; illustration page 88.*

RHODODENDRON, AZALEA

Rhododendron
SHRUB   ZONE 5
The vast genus *Rhododendron*, which also includes deciduous and evergreen azaleas, contains many outstanding

Rhododendron *Rhododendron*
'Bow Bells'

flowering shrubs that are suitable for containers. Their preference for shade makes them an ideal choice for large pots in small shady spots. The broad colour range includes many pinks.

A superb evergreen species, *R. williamsianum* (Zone 7), makes a dome 1.2–1.5m (4–5ft) high with bronze young leaves turning to deep green. The bell-shaped flowers, borne in small clusters or singly in mid-spring, are carmine in bud but on opening fade to soft pink. A popular, more compact species, *R. yakushimanum*, up to 75cm (30in) high but spreading, flowers in late spring, as do most of its outstanding hybrids. Its leathery leaves, silvery when young, are felted brown on the underside. Upright flower trusses are deep pink in bud, but the blooms are an apple-blossom mixture on opening and then pure white.

One of the earliest spring-flowering hybrid rhododendrons is 'Cilpinense' (Zone 6). This semi-evergreen, generally less than 1.2m (4ft) in height and spread when grown in a container, bears masses of pink buds that open to near-white flowers with rose spots. 'Bow Bells' (Zone 6), slightly later to flower, is similarly compact; its blooms are borne in loose clusters, deep pink in bud but opening to show a soft pink interior, and the young leaves are copper coloured (*above*). 'Anna Baldsiefen', less than 75cm (30in) high, and a vivid

pink, also flowers early. Its leaves are bronzed in winter. 'Temple Belle' (Zone 6), under 1.5m (5ft) in height and spread, flowers in mid- to late spring, the open bunches of clear pink blooms attractive against rounded leaves that are grey-green on the underside.

Many of the hybrid evergreen azaleas have been introduced from Japan. 'Hinomayo' is a tall example of the group known as the Kurume azaleas, most of which are under 1.2m (4ft) in height but with a spread of about 1.5m (5ft). The vivid pink, funnel-shaped flowers are borne in mid- to late spring.

There are also numerous pink-flowering deciduous hybrids. 'Homebush', under 1.5m (5ft) in height and spread, produces dense clusters of semi-double flowers in late spring. They are purplish pink with paler shading. Few of the hybrid azaleas can match the beauty of *R. schlippenbachii*, a deciduous species up to 1.8m (6ft) high. The soft pink flowers bloom profusely between mid- and late spring, preceding the leaves, which are purplish red when young and colour well in autumn.

Plant single specimens of azaleas and rhododendrons in large pots or tubs using ericaceous compost. Little pruning is needed except to tidy straggly growth, but faded flowers should be removed to prevent seed production. The blooms of even hardy rhododendrons and azaleas, especially of those that flower early, may be spoilt by frost. Overhead protection from trees or an overhanging roof will reduce the risk of damage.
See also pages *129, 139, 142, 145, 148, 150, 167, 173; illustration page 45.*

SAXIFRAGE
Saxifraga
EVERGREEN PERENNIAL   ZONE 4
Many saxifrages are remarkably slow growing, with tight rosettes of small leaves gradually building up to domes or flatter mats. *S. × irvingii* 'Jenkinsiae' is a suitable one for adding to a collection of rock-garden plants in free-draining soil. It forms a cushion only 2.5cm (1in) high but as much as 30cm (12in) across. In early to mid-spring this saxifrage is covered with stemless pink flowers.

The mossy saxifrages make more substantial and denser hummocks of green leaves and require moist growing

conditions. The foliage of 'Peter Pan' stands 8cm (3in) high, with a spread of 30cm (12in), above which crimson stems carry pink flowers in early to mid-spring. *See also page* **140.**

TULIP
Tulipa
BULB   ZONE 5
The traditional association of pink tulips and blue forget-me-nots (*Myosotis*) remains one of the most pleasing and reliable standbys for spring gardens. The classic tulip for this combination is 'Clara Butt', 60cm (2ft) tall but with rather small, globular, rosy-pink flowers in late spring. Other single tulips flowering in late spring and about 50cm (20in) high include 'Palestrina', salmon-pink but with a green tinge to the outside of the petals, and 'China Pink', a Lily-flowered tulip with petals less markedly curved outward than many in the group. 'Garden Party', 45cm (18in) tall, has single flowers whose white petals are edged with a strong reddish pink; it blooms in mid-spring. Two fine doubles flowering in mid- to late spring are deep pink 'Peach Blossom' (*below*), 30cm (12in) high, and softer coloured 'Angélique', 40cm (16in) high.

Several multi-flowered pink tulips are also available. 'Toronto', which flowers in mid- to late spring, is 30cm (12in) high and has two or three long-lasting flowers of brilliant pink. 'Happy Family', slightly later to flower and a strong rose-pink, is 45cm (18in) high.
See also pages 129–30, 140, 145, **150–1,**

Tulip *Tulipa* 'Peach Blossom'

SUMMER

STONECRESS
Aethionema 'Warley Rose'
EVERGREEN PERENNIAL   ZONE 4
In early summer, this easy rock-garden plant produces many short spikes of deep pink flowers over grey-green foliage. It grows to 15cm (6in) high, but can have a spread of 38cm (15in), and is a suitable companion for other vigorous dwarf plants that like a free-draining soil and enjoy a position in full sun.

Plant between autumn and early spring, using gritty, soil-based compost. Trim off the faded flower stems in summer.

LILAC HIBISCUS
Alyogyne huegelii
EVERGREEN SUB-SHRUB   ZONE 9
From spring to autumn, furled buds open to flowers that, despite their name, are a satiny purple-pink. Sometimes more than 10cm (4in) across, they make a sensational display on an evergreen bush that in containers is usually under 1.5m (5ft). Plant in spring, using soil-based potting compost. Give the plant, or cuttings, winter protection.
See illustrations pages 10, 109.

ANISODONTEA
Anisodontea capensis
EVERGREEN SHRUB   ZONE 9
Dark veining intensifies the pink of the small flowers borne through summer on this sun-loving shrub (*below*). It grows to 90cm (3ft) but needs to have the tips of its shoots pinched out in order to encourage bushiness. Grow anisodontea as individual specimens or with other plants needing full sun.

Plant in spring, using soil-based compost, but do not place outdoors until there is negligible risk of frost.

Water generously throughout summer. Plants or rooted cuttings kept under glass during winter should be watered sparingly.
See illustration page 105.

SNAPDRAGON
Antirrhinum majus
HALF-HARDY ANNUAL
Separate colours of tall, intermediate, and dwarf snapdragons are often more readily available as young plants than as seed. The Monarch Series, being of intermediate height and rust-resistant, offers one of the best ranges of seed available in single colours. 'Coral Monarch', up to 45cm (18in) high, is a bright coral-pink.
*See also pages 130, 140, **151**, 167.*

MARGUERITE, PARIS DAISY
Argyranthemum
EVERGREEN PERENNIAL   ZONE 9
All the colour variations of the marguerite are worth trying, most sharing its easy-to-please, free-flowering ways. There are several good pinks: 'Petite Pink' ('Pink Delight') and 'Pink Australian' are pretty singles and 'Vancouver' and 'Mary Wootton' are good doubles, the former being strongly coloured, and with anemone-centres. Plants are 30–60cm (12–24in) in height, and they can be trained successfully as standards.
*See also pages **130–1**, 140; illustrations pages 98, 109, 115.*

ASTILBE
Astilbe
PERENNIAL   ZONE 5
Astilbes are among the loveliest perennials for containers provided their compost is kept moist. Their beautiful ferny foliage is often deeply bronzed or copper, especially when young, and their long-lasting flower plumes remain attractive even in their dry state during winter. Most astilbes thrive in partial shade as well as full sun, but it is easier to keep container-grown plants adequately watered if they are grown in shade.

The species and hybrids include many good pinks. The dwarf *A. chinensis* 'Pumila' sends up stiff spikes, 45cm (18in) high, of mauve-pink flowers in late summer and early autumn. *A.* 'Bronce Elegans', which rarely exceeds 30cm (12in), has looser spikes of tiny pink and cream flowers,

Anisodontea *Anisodontea capensis*

spikes of tiny pink and cream flowers, also produced late in the season, arching over handsomely bronzed foliage.

A much larger plant than either of these and flowering in early to mid-summer is *A.* 'Straussenfeder' ('Ostrich Plume'). This grows to 90cm (3ft), bearing graceful, coral-pink plumes.

Plant between autumn and early spring, using soil-based compost to which leaf mould has been added. Keep the compost moist. Flower spikes retained through the winter should be cut down in early spring.
See also page 151.

HEATHER, LING
Calluna vulgaris
EVERGREEN SHRUB   ZONE 5
Many cultivars of ling have pink flowers, which usually bloom in late summer and often well into autumn. Most are 30–45cm (12–18in) in height, but several useful cultivars are shorter. 'County Wicklow', for example, rarely exceeds 23cm (9in) but has a spread of 35cm (14in) or more. Its flowers are double and pale pink. The salmon-pink 'J. H. Hamilton' is also compact. Plant in spring or summer, using an ericaceous potting compost. Trim plants in spring and top-dress with fresh compost.
See also pages 131, 183.

GODETIA
Clarkia amoena
HARDY ANNUAL
The satin-textured, frilled flowers of godetias, borne profusely in sunny spots, are full of charm. The seed of these plants, now listed under *Clarkia*,

is normally bought as mixtures in which pink is the predominant colour. Some mixtures are dwarf, under 30cm (12in) high, while the tallest are as much as 60–90cm (2–3ft) high. Among intermediates are the Azalea-flowered Mixed, which grow to 38cm (15in) high, with semi-double flowers.

Several colour selections are available. One of the prettiest is the dwarf 'Salmon Princess', in which an overall pink colour is warmed by a peachy tone (*below left*).

The best results are achieved by sowing seed direct in the container, using soil-based or soil-less compost, and then thinning to leave plants 10–15cm (4–6in) apart. Avoid excessive feeding, which will encourage leafy growth at the expense of flowers.

CLARKIA
Clarkia unguiculata
HARDY ANNUAL
This clarkia (sometimes listed as *C. elegans*) is a bushy plant about 60cm (2ft) in height, and in seed mixtures is usually available with double flowers closely clustered on slender stems. Double Mixed, for example, covers a range of pink shades but also includes scarlet, purple, salmon and white.

Sow seed thinly in the container in early spring, thinning subsequently to leave plants 15cm (6in) apart. Pinch back the tips of shoots to encourage bushy growth. In sheltered areas, sow in early autumn for a display in early summer.

CLEMATIS
Clematis
CLIMBER   ZONE 3   POISONOUS
Many large-flowered hybrid clematis bloom at various times in summer in shades of pink. When grown as climbers, for which supports are needed, the following may reach a height of 3.7m (12ft). They are also beautiful when allowed to trail from a tall container.

'Bees' Jubilee' flowers in early summer and may repeat later in the season. The mauve-pink of the single flowers is made vivid by carmine shading down the centre of the sepals, which surround creamy stamens. Grow this plant in light shade to avoid the risk of the flowers bleaching. Cut out a proportion of the old wood in spring.

A very prolific flowerer in late summer is 'Comtesse de Bouchaud',

with its bright pink single flowers tinted mauve with cream stamens. 'Hagley Hybrid', also late flowering, has single mauve-pink blooms, up to 10cm (4in) wide, with purple-red anthers. Cut both hybrids hard back in spring.
*See also pages 128, **131–2**, 156, 167, 174.*

SPIDER FLOWER
Cleome hassleriana
HALF-HARDY ANNUAL
The fast-growing spider flower (*below*), sometimes listed as *C. spinosa*, needs full sun and heat to reach 1.2m (4ft). From mid-summer to early autumn, it carries large heads of unusual flowers, with narrow petals and conspicuous protruding stamens. The normal colour is white with a pink flush, but there are mixtures including pure white, purple, carmine and strong pinks. 'Rose Queen', a deep pink, is one of several separate colours available.

Raise from seed, in frost-prone areas starting under glass in early spring. Harden off before planting outdoors in late spring, using a soil-based or soil-less compost. Deadhead faded flowers throughout the summer.

COSMOS
Cosmos bipinnatus
HALF-HARDY ANNUAL
Cosmos is an easy and rewarding annual for full sun, providing an airy display of dahlia-like flowers, usually single, over finely cut leaves in summer and autumn. They are most commonly grown as mixtures of pink, red and white flowers. *C. bipinnatus* Sonata Mixed is especially useful for containers. The plants, up to 50cm (20in) in height, bear masses of

Godetia *Clarkia amoena* 'Salmon Princess'

Spider flower *Cleome hassleriana*

159

Cosmos *Cosmos* Sea Shells

pink. Most cosmos grow to 90cm (3ft) and when grown in containers usually need staking. 'Daydream' produces striking white flowers with a strong pink stain around the yellow centre. The flowers of Sea Shells, also in a mixture, with pink predominating, have curiously fluted rays (*above*).

Raise from seed, sowing under glass in early spring in frost-prone areas. Plant in groups for maximum effect, using soil-based or soil-less compost. Avoid excessive feeding, which will encourage foliage at the expense of flowers. Deadhead regularly to keep the plants flowering over a long period. *See also pages 132, 152.*

PINK
Dianthus
PERENNIAL   ZONE 4
With their grey-green, grass-like foliage, neat flowers that are often beautifully patterned, and, in some cases, a deliciously spicy scent, pinks have been an inspiration to gardeners for centuries. They are not difficult to grow, and are remarkably tolerant of drought, but need full sun to do well.

A traditional way of growing the larger pinks is in terracotta pots with hooped stakes inserted around the edge to prevent the plants from flopping.

There are true species and numerous hybrid alpine pinks suitable for growing in troughs with other rock-garden

plants. 'Inshriach Dazzler' makes a tight mound of foliage studded with carmine-pink flowers in summer. 'Pike's Pink' has semi-double flowers with a strong colour. Both are typically no more than 10cm (4in) high. Taller than these is the Cheddar pink (*D. gratianopolitanus* Zone 5), which can grow to 30cm (12in). It bears single fringed flowers, fragrant and fresh pink, from late spring to mid-summer.

The old-fashioned pinks, usually 30cm (12in) or so tall, flower only in early summer. They include singles and doubles, most with a ravishing scent. 'Inchmery' is a pretty pale pink double.

The modern pinks are faster growing than the old-fashioned kinds, although similar in height. The main flowering season of these hybrids is early to mid-summer but they often flower again in autumn. Not all are scented but 'Doris', a pale salmon-pink semi-double, is very fragrant (*below*).

Grow pinks in gritty, soil-based compost. Modern pinks need to be propagated every two or three years and old-fashioned pinks every four or five years. This is easily done from cuttings taken in the first half of summer. To encourage well-branched pinks, pinch back young plants, especially modern pinks, in mid- to late spring. Snap off the main shoot just above a joint.
See also pages 132, 152–3.

Pink *Dianthus* 'Doris'

DIASCIA
Diascia
PERENNIAL   ZONE 8
The perennial diascias are full-sun plants that produce masses of small, more-or-less tubular flowers over a long period in summer. They are often treated as annuals, but rooted cuttings of all the following diascias can be overwintered under glass.

The stiff stems of *D. rigescens* initially sprawl before growing upwards, to 30cm (12in), and displaying dense spikes of salmon-pink flowers over a long summer season. From mid- to late summer 'Ruby Field', a smaller plant up to 15cm (6in) high, carries flowers of the same colour but in open sprays. Two more that bloom in the second half of summer are *D. vigilis* (Zone 7), with spires up to 45cm (18in), loosely clustered with pale pink flowers that have a dark eye, and *D. cordata*, 20cm (8in) tall, with bright pink flowers.

Plant in mid- to late spring, using soil-based compost. If plants are retained for the following season, cut out old stems in mid-spring.
See illustrations pages 22, 101, 104, 105.

DICENTRA, BLEEDING HEART
Dicentra
PERENNIAL   ZONE 4
There are several compact dicentras with beautifully divided leaves and dangling lockets of mauve or pink flowers in late spring and early summer. 'Stuart Boothman' makes a fern-like clump of blue-grey, 45cm (18in) high and with a spread of 30cm (12in), and the flowers are soft pink. It thrives in partial shade.

Plant in autumn or early spring, using a soil-based compost.
See illustration page 89.

FUCHSIA
Fuchsia
SHRUB   ZONE 10
A few hybrid fuchsias produce flowers of uniform pink, but an attractive feature of many is the contrast between the colour of the petals and that of the tube and sepals.

The trailing 'Pink Galore' has double flowers that are soft pink all over, whereas 'Lena' (Zone 8), also trailing, is a semi-double with the tube and sepals flesh-pink and much darker petals. In 'Pink Marshmallow', another trailing double, it is the tube and sepals that are pink, while the petals are white. 'Jack Shahan' (Zone 9) is a trailing fuchsia with large, single flowers, the petals deep pink and the sepals paler. All four grow to 45cm (18in) but can have a spread of more than 90cm (3ft).

'Brilliant' (Zone 8), a small upright shrub, has rose-scarlet petals and purplish-pink sepals. 'Other Fellow' is another upright hybrid, growing 60–90cm (2–3ft) in a season. Its small single flowers have pink petals beneath the white tube and sepals. 'Leonora', a more vigorous hybrid that is eminently suitable for training as a standard, is a pink single with green-tinged sepals. *See also pages 132–3, 153, **168**; illustrations pages 87, 114.*

Cranesbill *Geranium cinereum* 'Ballerina'

CRANESBILL

Geranium

PERENNIAL   ZONE 4

Several of the smaller cranesbills are attractive among rock-garden plants. One of the most free-flowering is *G. cinereum* 'Ballerina' (*above*). A long succession of cup-shaped mauve-pink flowers, with purple veins running to a dark eye, is carried on lax stems over its 10cm (4in) mound of decorative grey-green leaves.

Another dwarf cranesbill, *G. sanguineum* var. *striatum* (*G. s.* var. *lancastrense*), up to 13cm (5in) high, can also be grown on its own but is especially useful as an underplanting for shrubs. The flowers are pale pink with crimson veining.

Plant between autumn and mid-spring, using gritty, soil-based compost. Cut back plants after flowering to encourage a second flush of blooms. *See also page 168.*

SUN ROSE

Helianthemum 'Rhodanthe Carneum'

EVERGREEN SHRUB   ZONE 5

This sun rose, perhaps better known as 'Wisley Pink', is free-flowering over a long season provided it has full sun and is grown in free-draining compost. It makes a grey-green mound, 30cm (12in) in height and spread, covered in small, soft pink saucers of flowers with orange-yellow centres. *See also pages 133, **141**, 146.*

HYDRANGEA

Hydrangea

SHRUB   ZONE 6

In neutral or alkaline composts, the mophead hydrangeas or hortensias, cultivars of *H. macrophylla*, are pink or red. In these conditions 'Générale Vicomtesse de Vibraye', pale blue in acid soils, is soft pink. It comes into flower in mid-summer. 'Mariesii', also pink or blue according to the compost in which it is grown, is a lacecap hybrid in which the mixture of sterile and fertile flowers creates a light effect overall.

Another mophead hydrangea, *H.* 'Preziosa', has foliage that colours well in autumn. In early summer the flowers are deep pink but they take on red tones as they age; they are also attractive as dried flowers.

All of these make bushy plants that grow to 90–120cm (3–4ft) high in containers and their flowering season continues into the autumn. *See also pages 133, 175.*

IMPATIENS, BUSY LIZZY

Impatiens

HALF-HARDY ANNUAL

These tender perennials, usually grown as half-hardy annuals, come in a wide range of eye-catching colours (*below*). Seed is available as mixtures that feature many shades of pink, some of them shocking. Accent Mixed is a luminously dazzling selection up to 15cm (6in) high with a spread of 20cm (8in). Super Elfin Mixed has bushy plants up to 30cm (12in) high carrying large blooms in a range of vibrant colours. Intermediate in height between these is Eye-Eye Mixed, the pastel colours of the flowers being intensified by a bright eye.

The New Guinea hybrids are invaluable for the container gardener, their large flowers in arresting colours being presented against dark or variegated foliage. These plants grow to a height of 35cm (14in) and have a spread of up to 45cm (18in). They are usually bought as plants in mid- to late spring, but are available as seed.

Sow seed of impatiens in spring, starting plants under glass in frost-prone areas. Harden off before planting outdoors in late spring, using soil-based or soil-less compost. The New Guinea

Mixed impatiens *Impatiens* hybrids

hybrids do well in full sun, but other kinds are better in partial shade. Water regularly. Apply a liquid fertilizer every two weeks, starting three or four weeks after planting.

See also page 146; illustrations pages 53–4, 110.

CHILEAN BELLFLOWER

Lapageria rosea

EVERGREEN CLIMBER   ZONE 9

The Chilean bellflower is a twining climber of sublime beauty, usually less than 3.7m (12ft) high, that is often grown as a greenhouse plant in temperate regions. It can also be planted outdoors in a warm, sheltered spot in the shade. This attractive climber produces dangling, waxy, deep pink bells in the second half of summer and into autumn.

Plant singly in spring, using ericaceous compost such as that formulated for rhododendrons, adding organic material such as leaf mould. Provide supports. Water generously during the growing season and feed with weak liquid fertilizer every two weeks.

SWEET PEA

Lathyrus odoratus

HARDY ANNUAL/BIENNIAL CLIMBER
POISONOUS

Their fragrance and butterfly appeal make sweet peas favourites for summer floral arrangements (the more they are cut, the more they flower). These highly ornamental annuals climb using tendrils and can reach a height of 3m (10ft). They can be grown successfully in the container garden if trained up sunny walls or fences to which netting has been fixed. Another option is a large tub or similar container, with its own wigwam of canes, positioned in a sunny, sheltered spot.

Seed is commonly available as colour mixtures, including a good range of pastel shades – pinks and mauves featuring prominently – and dark reds and purples. The large-flowered Spencer sweet peas are the most commonly grown, while Antique Fantasy is a mixture of old-fashioned kinds, smaller in flower but strongly scented. There are also dwarf mixtures: Knee Hi Mixed and Jet Set Mixed, up to 90cm (3ft) in height, provide a good colour range of compact plants which require minimal support.

New additions appear every year among large-flowered sweet peas.

Good examples include: 'Memories', with white petals flushed a warm shade of rose-pink, and 'Mrs Bernard Jones', with large, reddish-pink, frilled flowers.

Sow seed in autumn or early spring, pinching back the growing tips of seedlings when they are 10cm (4in) high. Plant in pots between mid- and late spring, in soil-based or soil-less compost. Feed well in the growing season and guide young plants on to supports. Cut flowers or deadhead regularly to prolong flowering.

See also pages 133, 169, 175.

MALLOW

Lavatera trimestris

HARDY ANNUAL

The annual mallow forms an upright bush, 50–90cm (20–36in) high, that in summer to autumn bears large, satiny flowers with a wide, funnel shape. These plants need full sun, and tall cultivars should be planted in sheltered positions.

'Sunset' ('Loveliness'), with flowers of deep pink, is 75cm (30in) or more tall. Even more useful in a planter is the compact 'Silver Cup', up to 60cm (2ft) high, with glowing pink flowers (*below*).

Sow seed in spring in the container, using soil-based or soil-less compost. Thin by early summer so that plants are about 15cm (6in) apart. Avoid excessive feeding, which will encourage foliage at the expense of flowers.

See also page 133.

LILY

Lilium

BULB   ZONE 3   POISONOUS

Almost all of the pink lilies make excellent container plants. Outstanding is the stem-rooting 'Pink Perfection', whose strong stem, 1.2–1.5m (4–5ft) high, carries up to 20 highly scented, trumpet-shaped, dusty pink blooms, 15cm (6in) across, in mid- to late summer. The spectacular 'Journey's End' is another very fragrant lily, which flowers slightly later. Stems 90–120cm (3–4ft) high carry large, star-shaped blooms with deep pink midribs; maroon spotting intensifies the colour but the recurved tips and wavy edges of the petals are pale pink.

By comparison, 'Joy' (syn. 'Le Rêve') is lightly scented; its soft pink, mauve-tinged, funnel-shaped flowers, blooming on strong stems 90cm (3ft) high, make it one of the most enchanting hybrid lilies for mid-summer. 'Cote d'Azur', also flowering in mid-summer, is a useful compact hybrid, the upward-facing flowers of rich pink carried on stems about 60cm (2ft) high.

*See also pages **134, 142, 147, 153**.*

ALYSSUM

Lobularia maritima

HARDY ANNUAL

Several good selections of alyssum are available, providing a colour range in addition to the familiar white that is

Mallow *Lavatera trimestris* 'Silver Cup'

useful when choosing an edging plant for a container. One of the loveliest is 'Rosie O'Day', which bears clusters of fragrant deep-pink flowers over a long season. It is under 15cm (6in) in height and has a spread of 30cm (12in).
See also page 135.

Oleander *Nerium oleander*

OLEANDER
Nerium oleander
EVERGREEN SHRUB   ZONE 9
POISONOUS
The leathery evergreen leaves give a clue to the drought- and heat-tolerance of the oleander, one of the most familiar shrubs of Mediterranean-type gardens (*above*). Pink-flowered oleanders are common, but there are numerous single and double cultivars in red, yellow and white, as well as intermediate shades. The propeller shape of the five-petaled singles is particularly appealing. These plants have an exceptionally long flowering season in summer and autumn.

Plant singly in late spring, using soil-based compost. Cut back the tips of shoots on young plants to encourage bushy growth. Water freely during the growing season but sparingly from autumn to mid-spring.

TOBACCO PLANT
Nicotiana
HALF-HARDY ANNUAL   POISONOUS
Pink flowers are conspicuous in many tobacco plant mixtures, while in the limited range of separate colours 'Domino Salmon Pink' stands out as an unusual warm shade. Bushy plants grow to 30cm (12in), and the flowers are open all day rather than (as with many tobacco plants) just in the evening.
See also pages 135, 142.

PELARGONIUM, GERANIUM
Pelargonium
EVERGREEN PERENNIAL   ZONE 9
There is a good range of pinks to choose from in all categories of pelargonium, especially among the Ivy-leaved and Zonal kinds.

Good Ivy-leaved examples include 'The Crocodile', a semi-double with cream-variegated leaves, 'Hederinum Variegatum' ('Duke of Edinburgh') (*below*), a single pink with silvery foliage, 'Madame Crousse', a semi-double with pale pink flowers, and 'Galilee', a double with bright pink flowers. These can trail from hanging baskets with stems 75cm (30in) or more in length.

'Rio', one of numerous single pink Zonals, has bright pink flowers, each petal marked by a crimson dot. 'Party Dress' is a semi-double with more delicate colouring. Most Zonals reach 90cm (3ft) high, but there are also Dwarf and Miniature kinds: 'Bridesmaid', a fancy-leaved double with soft pink flowers, has a height and spread of only 23cm (9in).

An impressive Regal pelargonium for sheltered positions is 'Aztec', whose large pink blooms have brown markings.
See also pages 135, 147–8, 153–4, 170, 181–2; illustrations pages 115, 119.

Pelargonium *Pelargonium* 'Hederinum Variegatum'

PETUNIA
Petunia
HALF-HARDY ANNUAL
Almost all petunia mixtures include a range of pinks, from soft peachy colours to more assertive shades that are near magenta, while a limited range of single colours is also available. 'Pastel Salmon' is an unusual colour, the flowers looking particularly beautiful set against the silver foliage.
See also pages 136, 142, 154, 170, 176.

MOSS PHLOX
Phlox subulata
EVERGREEN PERENNIAL   ZONE 3
In mid- to late spring, the moss phlox is a mound of flat, starry flowers, mainly in pinks, mauves and reds. The mat of small linear leaves obscured at this season is only 10cm (4in) high with a spread more than twice this. 'Alexander's Surprise', a fine pink, makes a lovely addition to a collection of rock-garden plants.

Grow in gritty, soil-based compost in full sun. Trim plants after flowering to keep them compact.
See also page 129.

RANUNCULUS
Ranunculus asiaticus
PERENNIAL   ZONE 5   POISONOUS
When grown as a perennial, this is usually considered a flower of early summer. However, the magnificent doubles, with layers of tissue-paper petals in white and shades of red, orange, yellow and pink are raised in quantity by nurserymen for the spring trade. In their relatively short season, few flowers are more showy (*below*).

For extravagant spring displays it is advisable to buy plants as the buds are

Ranunculus *Ranunculus asiaticus*

Rose *Rosa* 'The Fairy'

Schizanthus pinnatus

HALF-HARDY ANNUAL

The butterfly flower is often grown in containers to provide spring displays in a cool greenhouse, but it can also be effective placed outdoors for flowering in summer. Usually available in pink-dominated mixtures, its orchid-like flowers have contrasting markings and conspicuous veining in the throat. Tall cultivars grow to 90cm (3ft) or more, while the shorter ones are more suitable for containers. The Disco mixture grows to 38cm (15in), the compact plants covered with prettily marked flowers for weeks on end.

Raise from seed sown in warmth in early spring. Plant outdoors in late spring, in soil-based or soil-less compost, placing the container in a sunny, sheltered spot. Water regularly and feed with a liquid fertilizer every two weeks, starting in early summer. Pinch back the tips of shoots on young plants to encourage bushy growth. *See illustration page 13.*

STONECROP, SEDUM

Sedum 'Herbstfreude'

PERENNIAL   ZONES 3–9

Several of the fleshy-leaved stonecrops carry tightly packed heads of small flowers in late summer or early autumn. 'Herbstfreude' (*below*), also known as

opening, so that you can choose the colours. Plant in soil-based or soil-less compost and keep well watered. Feed with a liquid fertilizer about two weeks after planting. These highly bred plants are rather prone to disease, so take off flowers as they fade and discard the plants when they have finished blooming.
See illustrations pages 13, 89.

ROSE

Rosa

SHRUB   ZONE 4

Within the range of modern Patio roses, 'Gentle Touch' is one of the most free-flowering. Lightly scented, double, pale pink flowers, like a Hybrid Tea rose in shape, bloom all summer long on bushes with a height and spread of 38cm (15in).

Several much older roses are also suitable for containers. The 19th-century 'Cécile Brünner', sometimes known as the sweetheart rose, forms a twiggy bush up to 75cm (30in) high. The pale pink double flowers, only lightly scented, are exquisite miniature Hybrid Teas in bud, although untidy on opening. Long established but more modern in style is 'Mevrouw Nathalie Nypels', a Polyantha rose with lightly scented, semi-double, deep pink flowers, which grows to 75cm (30in) high. Larger than these is the Hybrid Musk 'Ballerina', up to 1.2m (4ft) in height and spread, bearing large sprays of single flowers in an apple-blossom mixture of pink and white. Again, unfortunately, they have little scent. 'The Fairy', 60–90cm (2–3ft) in both height and spread, is a Polyantha that comes into flower rather late but bears masses of small double flowers in pretty sprays (*above*).
*See also pages 136, 142, **154**, 170, 203.*

Stonecrop *Sedum* 'Herbstfreude'

'Herbstfreude' (*below*), also known as 'Autumn Joy', forms a clump of grey-green foliage, topped in late summer by pink flowers that take on bronze and copper tints as they age. When in bloom, the plant has a height and spread of 60cm (2ft). The dead flowers are attractive all winter, and especially beautiful when covered with frost.

Plant between early autumn and mid-spring, using soil-based compost. Place containers in a sunny spot. Avoid excessive watering and feeding as this will result in lax growth, and the stems will then flop.

VERBENA
Verbena
HALF-HARDY ANNUAL
Many of the verbenas are useful trailing plants, those with pink blooms looking especially beautiful when combined with blue flowers and grey foliage.

The seed mixtures of brightly coloured bedding verbenas usually include pinks. There are also good verbenas that do not breed true from seed. 'Silver Anne', spreading to 75cm (30in) but with stiff stems to a height of 45cm (18in), has clusters of large flowers that are deep pink on opening and fade to near-white. 'Sissinghurst' (*below*) has rounded heads of bright pink flowers on plants up to 20cm (8in) in height with a spread of 45cm (18in).
*See also pages 136, 149, 155, **171**, 176–7; illustrations pages 22, 27, 98, 101, 105.*

Verbena *Verbena* 'Sissinghurst'

AUTUMN AND WINTER

CYCLAMEN
Cyclamen
TUBER   ZONE 5   POISONOUS
The cyclamen are remarkably consistent in appearance and in their pink, white and red colour range. The large-flowered cyclamen, giant forms of *C. persicum* (Zone 8), are mainly used as houseplants, but where the climate is mild enough they can give an outdoor display lasting four to eight weeks from mid-winter to early spring. They are usually 23–35cm (9–14in) high.

Two dwarf species make lovely additions to rock-garden mixtures. The flowers of *C. hederifolium* (syn. *C. neapolitanum*) are borne from late summer to early winter over marbled leaves. The plant is 13cm (5in) high with a spread of 25cm (10in). The leaves of *C. coum* (*below*) are rounded, and some selections have a variegation that gives them a pewter-like finish. Plants are rarely more than 8cm (3in) high, and the pink, carmine or white flowers appear from early winter to early spring.

Plant tubers when cyclamen are dormant, using a soil-based compost with added leaf mould. Barely cover the tubers of the dwarf species, but set the large-flowered cyclamen so that the tubers are just bedded into the compost. Water regularly when

Cyclamen *Cyclamen coum*

cyclamen are in growth and feed with a weak liquid fertilizer every two weeks after the leaves start to show. Stop watering and fertilizing completely as the leaves begin to die down.
See also page 137.

WINTER HEATH
Erica carnea
EVERGREEN SHRUB   ZONE 5
Most of the numerous cultivars of the winter heath (*below*) are 15–30cm (6–12in) high but may have a spread of more than 60cm (2ft). They flower between early winter and late spring. 'Pink Spangles' is one of many with pink flowers. Although all winter heaths prefer acid soil and so are useful companions for other acid-loving plants, they do tolerate alkaline conditions and, because they stand light shade, can be used to underplant a wide range of taller shrubs.

Plant in autumn, using a soil-based compost. Trim the shrub all over once it has finished flowering.
*See also pages **137**, 155, 171, 183.*

Mixed winter heaths *Erica carnea*

HEATH
Erica × darleyensis
EVERGREEN SHRUB   ZONE 6
The many cultivars of this hybrid can be used in much the same way as those of *E. carnea*, also preferring acid soil but generally tolerating alkaline ones.

'Arthur Johnson' grows to about 60cm (2ft) but usually has a wider spread. It flowers through winter into spring, when the cream-pink tips of the young shoots are an attractive feature. Plant in autumn, using a soil-based compost. Trim the shrub all over after flowering.
See also page 137.

Mauve covers an important bracket in the colour range in which shades of blue are modified by pink or red. At the other extreme are imperial and ecclesiastical purples. Most shades in the mauve and purple range mix well with other colours in sophisticated schemes.

SPRING

AUBRIETA

Aubrieta
PERENNIAL   ZONE 5
The aubrietas, more or less evergreen, are good with other vigorous rock-garden plants. They are usually less than 15cm (6in) high with a spread of 45cm (18in) or more, and the masses of flowers borne through spring and into summer are predominantly in purple shades. 'Royal Red' is purplish red and 'Doctor Mules' purplish blue.

Plant in autumn or spring, using soil-based compost. Trim after flowering and top-dress with fresh compost in spring.

CROCUS

Crocus vernus
CORM   ZONE 3
Some of the best large-flowered Dutch crocuses are in the mauve to purple range. 'Vanguard' (*below*) sometimes starts flowering in late winter, its silvery outer petals embracing inner petals of pale purple. More globular in flower shape are 'Purpureus Grandiflorus', a

sheeny and intense bluish purple, and the paler 'Remembrance'.
*See also pages 128, 137, **138**, 144, 149, 171, 177; illustration page 51.*

FRITILLARY

Fritillaria
BULB   ZONE 5   POISONOUS
Several fritillaries have flowers of purplish red and deep plum. The snake's-head fritillary (*F. meleagris*) has one or two prettily chequered, drooping bells per 30cm (12in) stem, borne in mid-spring. The pendent flowers of *F. michailovskyi*, up to five on a stem 20cm (8in) high in early to mid-spring, are of brown-purple with a grey bloom relieved by a yellow rim.

Plant in autumn, setting the bulbs at 8–10cm (3–4in) depth. Use standard soil-based compost for *F. meleagris*, but *F. michailovskyi* needs added grit.
See also page 128.

PRIMROSE

Primula 'Miss Indigo'
EVERGREEN PERENNIAL   ZONE 4
Of the many colour variants among primroses, 'Miss Indigo' (*below*) is one of the most unusual, the double inky blue flowers only lightly relieved by touches of white at the edges. At 15cm (6in) high, it makes an attractive contrast to the familiar yellow primrose and also works well with early-flowering spring bulbs.
*See also page **139**.*

Pasque flower *Pulsatilla vulgaris*

PASQUE FLOWER, PULSATILLA

Pulsatilla vulgaris
PERENNIAL   ZONE 5
The beauty of the Pasque flower (*above*) is greatly enhanced by the silky fine hairs that cover the buds, flowers and seed heads, as well as the finely cut leaves. The ferny foliage clumps are topped in early spring by cupped flowers filled with bright golden stamens. Mauve is the basic flower colour, but there are also reddish and purplish variations.

Plant between autumn and early spring in a large container with other rock-garden plants, using gritty, soil-based compost.

Crocus *Crocus vernus* 'Vanguard'

Primrose *Primula* 'Miss Indigo'

RHODODENDRON, AZALEA

Rhododendron

SHRUB ZONE 5

Several compact rhododendrons and azaleas with mauve or purplish-blue flowers make unusual container shrubs. An appealing species, *R. russatum* (Zone 7) makes a shrub 90–120cm (3–4ft) in height and spread that is covered in spring in purplish-blue flowers with white throats. The hybrid rhododendron 'Blue Diamond', much the same size, flowers in mid-spring; its blooms are more mauve than the name suggests. The flowers of 'Blue Danube', borne in mid-spring, are a rich purplish blue.
*See also pages 129, 139, 142, 145, 148, 150, **156–7**, 173.*

TULIP

Tulipa

BULB ZONE 5

The few tulips that are available in the mauve to purple range are valuable for extending the decorative possibilities of a major group of spring bulbs. All the following are single, about 60cm (2ft) in height, and flower in late spring. 'Bleu Aimable' is rich pink-mauve and 'Demeter', slightly taller than the others in this group, is reddish purple. 'Blue Parrot' has large blue-purple blooms, while the Lily-flowered 'Burgundy' is another strong purple. Darkest of all is the glamorous 'Queen of the Night', with long-lasting, rounded flowers in a dense, silky-sheened purple that is almost black.
*See also pages 129–30, 140, 145, **150–1**, 157.*

VIOLET

Viola

PERENNIAL ZONE 5

Many cultivars and hybrids of the sweet violet (*V. odorata*), which bloom from late winter to mid-spring, were formerly grown commercially on a large scale for floral arrangements. One of the survivors is 'Czar', which has rich purple, fragrant flowers on long stems. Plants are up to 15cm (6in) high, with a spread of 30cm (12in). Slightly shorter but spreading more freely is *V. riviniana* Purpurea Group (*V. labradorica* 'Purpurea'). Its scentless mauve flowers are borne profusely between mid- and late spring among deep purple foliage. Less vigorous, but of much the same height, is *V. sororia* 'Freckles' (*right*), which blooms in early spring.

Plant these violets in autumn or early spring, using a soil-based compost. Tolerant of partial shade, they are suitable as an underplanting to shrubs, provided that the compost is kept moist. Trim back plants when they have finished flowering, to keep them tidy.
*See also pages 136, **143–4**, 149, 155, 171, 177.*

SUMMER

FLOSSFLOWER

Ageratum houstonianum 'Pacific'

HALF-HARDY ANNUAL

The hybrid 'Pacific' makes a useful variation on the familiar blue of the flossflower. It grows quickly to form a dome 20cm (8in) high, packed with deep mauve pompons, which is attractive in window boxes and as an edging to larger plants.
*See also page **173**.*

SNAPDRAGON

Antirrhinum majus

HALF-HARDY ANNUAL

Warm colours dominate snapdragon seed mixtures, but a few selections in the mauve to purple range provide material for cool mixed plantings. 'Lavender Monarch', for example, has pale purple flowers. More unusual is 'Popette', a large-flowered bicolour in which the reddish-purple lip contrasts well with the white. Both grow to about 45cm (18in).
*See also pages 130, 140, **151**, 158.*

Violet *Viola sororia* 'Freckles'

COLUMBINE

Aquilegia flabellata var. *pumila*

PERENNIAL ZONE 4 POISONOUS

Several dwarf columbines that are suitable for container planting have all the charm of their larger relatives. *A. f.* var. *pumila* is less demanding than many columbines, and in late spring and early summer it freely bears pinkish-mauve flowers over grey-green, ferny leaves.

Plant between autumn and early spring, using gritty, soil-based compost. Deadhead to prevent plants producing copious seed.
See illustration page 121.

CLEMATIS

Clematis

CLIMBER ZONE 3 POISONOUS

In this colour range, clematis includes the large-flowered 'Jackmanii', one of the most widely planted climbers. It is at its best in mid-summer, when it bears masses of velvety blue-purple flowers with four petal-like sepals surrounding the creamy stamens. 'Gipsy Queen' is a splendid alternative, also flowering from mid-summer onwards, the dark anthers encircled by six rounded 'petals' of rich blue-purple.

The second half of summer is the season for the cultivars and hybrids of the small flowered *C. viticella*. The dusty purple, double flowers of 'Purpurea Plena Elegans' are borne profusely over a long season, and there is a strong blue tinge to the purple of 'Etoile Violette', which has single flowers with a cluster of creamy stamens.
*See also pages 128, **131–2**, 156, 159, 174.*

CUP-AND-SAUCER PLANT

Cobaea scandens

ANNUAL/PERENNIAL CLIMBER ZONE 9

Although this vigorous climber is an evergreen perennial, in temperate gardens it is treated as an annual. It attaches itself to supports with tendrils and in a single growing season is capable of reaching a height of 5m (16ft). The nodding flowers, borne one to a stem, have a purple 'cup' but the 'saucer', the calyx at the base of the bell, is green. Specimens grown as perennials flower from spring to early winter, those grown as annuals from late summer to autumn.

To raise from seed, sow in warmth in early to mid-spring. Harden off

before planting out singly in late spring or early summer. Use any soil-based or soil-less compost in a container at least 30cm (12in) deep. Avoid excessive feeding because this will encourage foliage at the expense of flowers. To encourage plants to branch, pinch back the tips of growing shoots.
See also page 132.

FALSE HEATHER
Cuphea hyssopifolia
EVERGREEN SHRUB   ZONE 8
The heather-like *Cuphea hyssopifolia* is commonly grown as an annual. In summer and early autumn, a thick scattering of small mauve to purple or white flowers covers these bushes, which grow up to 45cm (18in) high.
See also page 146.

DAHLIA
Dahlia 'Fascination'
TUBER   ZONE 9
The bedding dahlias are underused as container plants, despite being available in a wide range of colours that can brighten patios and gardens in the second half of summer. One of the many dwarf hybrids is 'Fascination', 45cm (18in) in height and spread, with single flowers of an unusual light purple colour.
See also page 152.

FUCHSIA
Fuchsia
SHRUB   ZONE 10
Fuchsias are among the most popular container plants, since they are easy to grow in sun or light shade and produce a long succession of pretty ballerina flowers that dangle attractively. The pistil and stamens characteristically protrude well below the petals of the single, semi-double or double flowers. There are numerous hybrids, many of them bicoloured, with the tube and four waxy sepals of one colour and the petal skirt of another. These hybrids show considerable variations in hardiness, but even those hardy enough to grow outdoors in the garden in temperate areas need to be over-wintered under glass when grown as pot plants. Fuchsias take readily from cuttings, which are more convenient to overwinter than the parent plant .

Many hardy fuchsias form upright bushes. Strong-growing hybrids such as 'Riccartonii' (Zone 8) can be 1.5m

(5ft) high, with a spread of 1.2m (4ft). Their small single flowers have a red tube and sepals above purple petals. More typical hybrids grow 60–90cm (2–3ft) in a season and have larger flowers. 'Mrs Popple' (Zone 7), for example, a single, has deep blue-purple petals beneath scarlet sepals and tube. 'Dollar Princess' (Zone 9) has double flowers, the petals rich purple and the tube and sepals bright cerise. More tender bushy fuchsias include the double 'Voodoo', dark red except for the blue-purple petals, and 'Tom Woods', single-flowered, with petals violet-purple and the tube and sepals waxy white.

Dwarf hardy fuchsias, which have a height and spread of about 45cm (18in), include 'Papoose' (Zone 9), a bright red semi-double with deep purple petals, and 'Tom Thumb' (Zone 8), carmine with mauve petals veined purple-red (*below*).

Fuchsias that trail are particularly useful in hanging baskets and many other containers. Although normally less that 45cm (18in) in height, they can have a spread of 90cm (3ft) or more. 'Dark Eyes' (Zone 9) is an attractive double, with petals of deep blue-purple protruding beneath the deep red sepals and tube.

Plant fuchsias in pots and containers outdoors in late spring or early summer. Either a soil-based or a soil-less compost can be used for all fuchsias except large specimens to be

Fuchsia *Fuchsia* 'Tom Thumb'

grown through the winter and for standards; for these, use soil-based compost. Overwinter standards in a frost-free greenhouse; rooted cuttings may be grown on a window sill, preferably in full light.
See also pages 132–3, 153, 160–1; illustrations pages 87, 114.

CRANESBILL
Geranium cinereum var. *subcaulescens*
PERENNIAL   ZONE 4
G. cinereum var. *subcaulescens* is one of the most arresting of all the small cranesbills, and looks attractive when planted in a mixture of rock-garden plants. It has dark-eyed flowers of a purple-tinged cerise up to 2.5cm (1in) across, and produced intermittently throughout the summer. They are highly conspicuous on a mound of grey-green foliage about 15cm (6in) high, with a spread of 30cm (12in).
See also page 161.

GLOBE AMARANTH
Gomphrena globosa
HALF-HARDY ANNUAL
The upright bushy plants of globe amaranth are decorated in the second half of summer and autumn by clover-like flower heads. The long-lasting tiny flowers, hidden by the bracts, make this plant popular for drying. Seed is commonly sold as mixtures, the colour range including white and shades of yellow, orange and pink as well as purple. Plants are up to 20cm (8in) high. 'Buddy', only 15cm (6in) high, has flowers of royal purple.

Sow in warmth in early to mid-spring, using any soil-based or soil-less compost; harden off and plant out in late spring or early summer. Feed with a liquid fertilizer every two weeks, starting three weeks after planting out.

HEBE
Hebe 'Youngii'
EVERGREEN SHRUB   ZONE 8
Better known as 'Carl Teschner', this hybrid is one of several dwarf hebes that can be combined in a container with rock-garden plants or used as an edging with a larger shrub. Dark stems carry a dense cover of grey-green leaves forming a mound 30cm (12in) high with a spread of up to 60cm (2ft). For weeks in early to mid-summer, clusters of small flowers create a haze of purplish blue.

Plant in autumn or early spring, using a soil-based compost, and position containers in full sun. To keep the plant looking tidy, deadhead flowers once they have faded.

HELIOTROPE
Heliotropium
ANNUAL

This sub-tropical evergreen shrub, usually grown as an annual, makes a fragrant addition to the container garden. Small mauve to deep purple flowers are borne in dense clusters over deep green, corrugated leaves right through the summer. Selections that come true from seed include 'Marine', a bushy compact plant up to 45cm (18in) high with deep purple flowers. Several cultivars, including the purplish-blue 'Princess Marina' (*below*), need to be propagated from cuttings. *H.* 'Chatsworth' is also in the purple range.

To raise from seed, sow in warmth during late winter. Cuttings taken in summer or early autumn, and specimens being trained as standards, can be overwintered under glass. Standards, which can be trained to a height of 60–90cm (2–3ft), usually need the support of a cane. Large specimens making bushy plants that are more than 60cm (2ft) high also benefit from staking. The prompt removal of dead blooms will help keep plants flowering over a long season.
See illustrations pages 104, 109.

Heliotrope *Heliotropium* 'Princess Marina'

Sweet pea *Lathyrus odoratus*

SWEET PEA
Lathyrus odoratus
HARDY ANNUAL/
BIENNIAL CLIMBER   POISONOUS

There are frequent new additions to the mauve and purple range of sweet peas (*above*), most of which are fragrant to some extent, some deliciously so. 'Leamington' is an old favourite, with winged flowers of deep lilac. 'Pageantry' has large purple-red flowers. Most of the named cultivars of sweet pea are capable of growing to 3m (10ft).
See also pages 133, 162, 175; illustration page 74.

LAVENDER
Lavandula
EVERGREEN SHRUB   ZONE 5

Lavenders are easy sun-loving shrubs with aromatic foliage and spikes of small, fragrant flowers that are mostly grey-blue or purple-blue in colour, although there are white forms. One of the most richly coloured is *L. angustifolia* 'Hidcote' (Zone 6), the deep purple flower spikes in late summer covering a grey-green bush that is about 60cm (2ft) high. Another interesting lavender of much the same size is *L. stoechas* subsp. *pedunculata* (*right*), a more tender plant (Zone 8). This has attractive grey foliage and in mid-summer the purple flower spikes, on long stiff stems, are topped by ear-like bracts.

Grow lavenders singly or with other plants that do well in free-draining conditions, using gritty, soil-based compost. Trim off dead flowers in early

autumn. To keep the plants compact, clip over in spring.
See also page 133; illustrations pages 16, 34, 69.

TRAILING LOBELIA
Lobelia erinus
HALF-HARDY ANNUAL   POISONOUS

Several cultivars of trailing lobelia have purple-red flowers, providing scope for a broad range of colour effects. The slender stems of 'Red Cascade', 30cm (12in) or more long, trail numerous small, white-eyed flowers. Similar but less purplish is 'Ruby Cascade'.
*See also pages 135, 153, **175–6**; illustration page 23.*

NEMESIA
Nemesia caerulea
HALF-HARDY ANNUAL

The long-flowering season and subtle colouring of its flowers make this short-lived perennial, usually grown as an annual, a choice addition to quiet schemes or a lovely plant to show off in its own container. Named cultivars and seed-raised plants carry spikes of miniature snapdragon flowers in shades of violet-blue, dusty mauve or purple-pink, brightened by cream or yellow markings. 'Joan Wilder', a compact plant up to 25cm (10in) high, is in the lavender range.

Plant in spring in soil-based compost and grow in full sun. When plants become lax and untidy in the second half of summer, cut them back and feed with a liquid fertilizer. They will soon

Lavender *Lavandula stoechas* subsp. *pedunculata*

produce fresh flower spikes. *N. caerulea* is short-lived, but can be propagated from cuttings taken in late summer. *See also pages 153, 176; illustrations pages 10, 101.*

PELARGONIUM, GERANIUM
Pelargonium
EVERGREEN PERENNIAL   ZONE 9
The numerous Ivy-leaved and Zonal pelargoniums include examples with mauve and light purple flowers, but rich shades in this range are uncommon. Justly popular among the Ivy-leaved pelargoniums is 'L'Elégante', with its single flowers of palest mauve. The foliage is beautiful, the dark green leaves variegated cream and sometimes edged purplish pink. In the same group the free-flowering, semi-double 'La France' is a deeper mauve; 'Amethyst', also semi-double, is even darker. They all have a spread of up to 90cm (3ft).

Zonals with mauve or purple flowers include 'Dove', which has large, single, mauve flowers. This hybrid grows to a height of about 15cm (6in) and looks pretty in pots or window boxes. Of similar height are 'Frau Emma Hössle', mauve-pink, and 'Keepsake', purple-pink, which have double flowers.

The Unique pelargoniums are grown mainly for their scented leaves. Even though the bold foliage of 'Purple Unique' is strongly aromatic, it is the single flowers, purple with crimson feathering, that catch the eye. This vigorous hybrid can have a height and spread of more than 90cm (3ft).

Among the Regal pelargoniums are a few with flowers of sumptuous funereal shades. 'Lord Bute', for example, bears flowers of majestic purple-black, although these are relieved by a wine-red edge. This splendid plant, up to 60cm (2ft) tall, stands up to bad weather better than most Regals. Another worth trying is the more compact 'Pompeii', 45cm (18in) high, in which the near-black petals are outlined in pink-white. *See also pages 135, 147–8, **153–4**, 163, 181–2, 187, 190, 194; illustrations pages 104, 115.*

PETUNIA
Petunia
HALF-HARDY ANNUAL
Soft mauves and rich purples are shown off to perfection by the velvet-textured flowers (*right*) that are featured

Rhodochiton *Rhodochiton atrosanguineus*

in many petunia seed mixtures. A selection of single colours can often be made when buying young plants and a few separate colours are also available as seed. An impressive example is 'Plum Purple', which boasts an overlay of crimson on pink-mauve darkened by purple veining radiating from a deep-coloured, velvety throat. It grows to 23cm (9in) high. *See also pages 136, 142, 154, 163, **176**; illustrations pages 94, 102, 109, 112.*

Purple petunia *Petunia* hybrid

RHODOCHITON
Rhodochiton atrosanguineus
ANNUAL CLIMBER
This unusual evergreen perennial, sometimes listed as *R. volubilis*, uses its leafstalks as tendrils (*left*). Grown from seed as an annual to make a short climber 1.5–1.8m (5–6ft) high, it is best trained on a wigwam of canes or a wire circle to show off the intriguing form of its dangling flowers. A pinkish-purple five-pointed bell, the calyx, forms a cap beneath which hangs a long reddish-purple tube with five rounded lobes at the opening. The flowers are borne over a long season.

Sow seed in warmth in early spring, using soil-based compost. Harden off plants before moving them outdoors in late spring.

ROSE
Rosa
SHRUB   ZONE 4
Modern roses in this colour range seem to hark back to old-fashioned kinds, as is indicated by the name of the Polyantha 'Yesterday'. This has fragrant semi-double, mauve-pink flowers on a bush that is 90cm (3ft) or so in height and spread. Much deeper is the royal purple of 'The Prince', one of the English roses that have been bred in the style of the large-flowered old roses. It provides a long season of scented double blooms on bushes 1.2m (4ft) high. *See also pages 136, 142, **154**, 164, 203.*

ANNUAL CLARY
Salvia viridis
HALF-HARDY ANNUAL
Although the flowers of this annual salvia, often listed as *S. horminum* (*right*), are insignificant, the bracts surrounding them are long-lasting and bright and hold their colour when dried. Mixtures such as the compact Claryssa, sometimes sold as separate colours, include pink, greenish white and purple. 'Blue Beard' has bracts of an exceptionally rich blue-purple. Most of these salvias grow to a height of about 45cm (18in).

Sow in warmth in early to mid-spring, planting out after hardening off in late spring in a container placed in full sun. When plants are about 8cm (3in) high, pinch back the growing tips to encourage bushy growth. *See also pages 154, **176**.*

VERBENA

Verbena

HALF-HARDY ANNUAL

The species and hybrid verbenas, perennials that are grown as annuals, flower over a long season in summer and are colourful plants to use as fillers in container plantings. Upright kinds can grow to 40cm (16in), but some of the most useful are trailing, with stems 45cm (18in) or more long. There are many colours to choose from – mauves and purples are well represented.

The upright *V. rigida* (*V. venosa*), of which there are named cultivars, carries scented purple flowers on wiry stems. *V. tenuisecta*, with purplish-mauve flowers, many having lax trailing stems, is very useful as an edging plant. Several of the hybrid verbenas, including the small-flowered and trailing 'Hidcote Purple', must be propagated by cuttings.

Sow seed strains such as the mixture Showtime in warmth between early and mid-spring; plant out after hardening off in late spring, using soil-based or soil-less compost. Plant bought stock and plants raised from cuttings at this time also. Pinch back the tips of young plants to encourage bushy growth. Feed with a liquid fertilizer every two weeks, starting three weeks after planting; deadhead regularly.
See also pages 136, 149, 155, 165, 176–7; illustrations pages 10, 100.

Viola *Viola* hybrid

Annual clary *Salvia viridis*

VIOLA, PANSY

Viola

ANNUAL/BIENNIAL/PERENNIAL ZONE 5

Mauve and purple feature prominently in strains of violas (*above*) and pansies such as Viola Bambini Mixed and Majestic Giants Mixed. There are also named selections of pansies and violas in this colour range. The viola 'Prince Henry' is easily raised from seed. It grows about 10cm (4in) high and produces masses of blue-purple flowers over a long season, starting in late spring. Pansies propagated from cuttings include the silvery mauve and sweetly scented 'Maggie Mott' and 'Gustav Wermig', with darker mauve flowers; both grow to about 15cm (6in).
*See also pages 136, **143–4**, 149, 155, 167, 177; illustrations pages 66, 90.*

AUTUMN AND WINTER

CROCUS

Crocus

CORM ZONE 3

The many cultivars of *C. chrysanthus* provide an extensive choice of colours for late winter. 'Lady Killer', for example, is a dashing combination of white interior and velvety-mauve exterior. *C. sieberi* 'Violet Queen' has rounded flowers of deep mauve with yellow centres. Both grow to a height of 8cm (3in).
*See also pages 128, 137, **138**, 144, 149, 166, 177.*

WINTER HEATH

Erica carnea

EVERGREEN SHRUB ZONE 5

There is often a purplish tinge to the many pink cultivars of the winter heath that flower between late autumn and early spring. In 'Loughrigg', the purplish tone is more pronounced, although in bud the flowers appear pink. In winter, the dark foliage of this cultivar produces extremely attractive bronze tints.
*See also pages **137**, 155, 165, 183.*

DWARF IRIS

Iris

BULB ZONE 5

The dwarf irises surprise by their apparently fragile appearance and defiance of late-winter weather. The best known, *I. reticulata*, is under 20cm (8in) high when in bloom, but later the narrow leaves grow longer. Its velvety blue-purple flowers, brightened by gold markings, are up to 8cm (3in) across and deliciously scented. There are also many dwarf cultivars and hybrids, one of the most unusual being 'J. S. Dijt', which is a deep reddish purple. All these bulbs look lovely grown thickly in a pot on their own, mixed with other early bulbs such as snowdrops, or combined with rock-garden plants.

Plant the bulbs in autumn at a depth of 5–8cm (2–3in) in gritty, soil-based potting compost.
*See also pages **144**, 177.*

In flowers the range extends from misty or metallic grey-blues, through pale but clear and intense bright blues, to shades of purple. Hints of green, pink and red add variety.

SPRING

GLORY-OF-THE-SNOW
Chionodoxa
BULB   ZONE 4

In its native mountains, glory-of-the-snow, a small group of bulbs with starry blue flowers, makes a dazzling display as the snow retreats. Among the loveliest of the short-growing bulbs that flower in early to mid-spring, they are attractive grown in pots on their own but look their best planted among other spring flowers or as an under-planting to shrubs. They will grow in sun or partial shade.

The most widely grown is *C. forbesii* (often listed as *C. luciliae*), with lax stems up to 20cm (8in) high, often with more than one stem per bulb. Each stem may bear up to 10 white-centred flowers of mauve-blue. The larger flowers of *C. luciliae* Gigantea Group are generally less bright and borne on slightly shorter stems. The most intense blue of the group is found in *C. sardensis*. Its flowers have a small white eye, and it is rarely more than 15cm (6in) high.

Plant in early autumn, setting the bulbs at a depth of 5–8cm (2–3in) in gritty, soil-based compost.

CORYDALIS
Corydalis flexuosa
PERENNIAL   ZONE 5

This is an exquisite woodland plant, thriving in moist, cool conditions, but also growing happily in full sun. Seed-raised stock and named cultivars show variations in height and spread of 15–30cm (6–12in). All are perennials of great refinement, producing masses of curiously tilted flowers throughout spring and even sometimes in summer. These are light to greenish-blue in colour and seem to float over ferny foliage that is grey-green or darker, with red-brown markings (*right*).

Plant in autumn or spring, using a soil-based compost, preferably with some added leaf mould. Keep well watered and apply liquid fertilizer every two weeks from mid-spring. Maintain plants in their containers, or plant them out in the open garden after the spring display.
See illustrations pages 64, 66, 90.

HYACINTH
Hyacinthus orientalis
BULB   ZONE 5

Breeders of modern hyacinths have concentrated on producing fat, uniform spikes of waxy flowers in a wide colour range that includes many blues. The resulting plants are not elegant, but their dense solidity makes them good for group planting, most growing to a height of about 20cm (8in). They have, miraculously, retained their powerful sweet scent.

The popular 'Delft Blue' has flowers of soft, porcelain refinement, while 'Blue Jacket' is much darker, with a purple stripe, and 'Ostara' has a blue base to the flowers, but the flared petals are deep purplish blue.

Plant in early autumn, setting the bulbs about 8cm (3in) deep in soil-based or soil-less compost. Use fresh bulbs each year for containers, while bulbs that have flowered are worth moving to the open garden. Allow the foliage to die down naturally, then lift and replant the bulbs.
See also pages 129, 138, 150, 156.

Corydalis *Corydalis flexuosa*

Grape hyacinth *Muscari armeniacum*

GRAPE HYACINTH
Muscari
BULB   ZONE 4

Several grape hyacinths are easy spring bulbs, producing tapering spikes crowded with small bell-shaped flowers that are pinched at the mouth. They are mostly in shades of blue.

One of the loveliest, *M. armeniacum* (*above*) flowers in mid- to late spring, producing spikes up to 25cm (10in) high packed with scented, deep blue bells that are white at the rim. 'Blue Spike' is a light-blue, long-lasting, double form.

Equally lovely is *M. aucheri* (*M. tubergenianum*), with slightly shorter spikes, remarkable for the contrast between the deep blue of the topmost bells and the paler blue of those below. All these grape hyacinths make an attractive dense planting on their own, but are also successful when mixed with other short-growing spring flowers that enjoy full sun.

Plant in early to mid-autumn, setting bulbs about 8cm (3in) deep – and close together but not touching – in soil-based or soil-less compost. Use fresh bulbs annually in containers. Grape hyacinths that have finished flowering can be planted in the open garden; after flowering, allow the foliage to die down naturally, then lift the bulbs and plant them out.

FORGET-ME-NOT
Myosotis
HARDY ANNUAL

The forget-me-nots, so successful at providing a romantic blue haze in the open garden, are also versatile companion plants for mid- to late spring flowers, especially bulbs, in the container garden. Although so often repeated, the combination with tulips never fails.

Dwarf cultivars include 'Blue Ball', only 15cm (6in) high and with bright blue flowers. 'Royal Blue', 30cm (12in) high, bears masses of indigo-blue flowers and is useful because of its early flowering.

To raise from seed, sow outdoors in a seed bed in early summer. Plant in containers in early to mid-autumn or even just before flowering, if plants are available. Discard plants when they have finished flowering.

RHODODENDRON, AZALEA
Rhododendron
SHRUB   ZONE 5

Although there are a few blue-flowered rhododendron species, this colour is somewhat unusual among the numerous rhododendron and azalea hybrids. The three evergreen rhododendrons listed below bloom in mid- to late spring.

'Bluebird', with a height and spread of 90cm (3ft), makes a neat shrub bearing compact clusters of mauve-blue flowers that deepen to violet as they age. The small flowers clustered at the tips of stems on 'Blue Tit', a hybrid of much the same size, are lavender-blue, deepening in colour as they age. The densely bushy 'Saint Tudy', 90–120cm (3–4ft) high, bears masses of purple-blue flowers.
See also pages 129, 139, 142, 145, 148, 150, 156–7, 167.

SQUILL
Scilla
BULB   ZONE 3

The Siberian squill (*S. siberica*) provides one of the most intense blues in early spring, with lax stems up to 15cm (6in) high carrying up to five nodding flowers of broad bell shape. Each bulb produces several stems, ensuring a display over several weeks. The similar *S. mischtschenkoana* (*S. tubergeniana*), which sometimes starts flowering in late winter, is slightly shorter and its flowers are pale blue with dark blue

lines. Both these bulbs are beautiful among other low-growing early spring flowers in sun or partial shade.

Plant 5–8cm (2–3in) deep in early to mid-autumn, using soil-based or soil-less compost. Keep well watered while plants are in growth. After flowering, allow foliage to die down, then plant the bulbs in the open garden.

SUMMER

AFRICAN LILY
Agapanthus
PERENNIAL   ZONE 8

Well-grown African lilies make handsome plants grown singly in large containers. In late summer, tall stems hold the rounded blue heads of funnel-shaped flowers well above an impressive base of linear leaves (*right*). Evergreen African lilies such as *A. africanus*, with its deep blue flowers on stems up to 90cm (3ft) high, are generally less hardy than the deciduous kinds. These include *A. campanulatus*, with grey-green leaves and stems up to 1.2m (4ft) high bearing heads of pale or darker blue flowers.

Many of the numerous hybrid African lilies are individually named. The Headbourne hybrids are valued for their hardiness. Most Headbourne hybrids grow 60–75cm (24–30in) high, with flowers varying in the intensity of their blue.

Plant in mid- to late spring, using soil-based compost incorporating slow-release fertilizer, and setting the crown of fleshy roots at a depth of about 5cm (2in). Water well in the growing season. When flowers have faded, cut off stems as low as possible. In cold areas, move containers to a frost-free greenhouse or conservatory from mid-autumn and keep just moist until growth starts again in spring. It is not necessary to move plants to a larger container as soon as they have out-grown the current one; pot-bound plants usually flower well. However, top-dress with fresh compost in spring. Divide in mid-spring.
See also page 130.

FLOSSFLOWER
Ageratum houstonianum
HALF-HARDY ANNUAL

This popular bedding plant, with its fluffy clusters of pompon flowers from

African lily *Agapanthus* hybrid

early summer to autumn, is best known for its compact, blue-flowered cultivars, which are useful in window boxes and for edging larger containers. The hybrid 'Blue Danube', with its mauve-blue flowers, makes neat plants up to 20cm (8in) high, while 'Blue Mink', with its powder-blue flowers, and 'Southern Cross', a bicolour with a blue halo surrounding a white centre, grow to 30cm (12in).

To raise from seed, sow in warmth in early to mid-spring. Harden off and plant outdoors in late spring or early summer, using a soil based or soil-less compost. Keep well watered and feed with a liquid fertilizer every two weeks, starting approximately three to four weeks after planting.
See also page 167; illustration page 100.

BRACHYSCOME
Brachyscome
HALF-HARDY ANNUAL

Throughout summer and into autumn, *B. iberidifolia*, the Swan River daisy, and the similar *B. multifida* are covered with slightly fragrant daisies in blue, mauve-pink and white. These wispy Australian natives reach about 30cm (12in) in height. Both are commonly available as mixtures, and single colours are also to be found, mainly in white or shades of blue and purple. Provided they are grown in sun, they are good for softening the edges of containers.

To raise from seed, sow in warmth in early to mid-spring. Pinch back young shoots to encourage bushy growth. Harden off and plant outdoors in late spring, using soil-based or soil-less compost. Apply liquid fertilizer every two weeks, starting three to four weeks after planting.
See also illustrations pages 22, 113, 119.

BROWALLIA
Browallia
HALF-HARDY ANNUAL/
PERENNIAL   ZONE 9
The browallias are tropical perennials that are usually grown as annuals. The most widely cultivated are compact cultivars such as 'Blue Troll', which makes a ball-shaped plant, 25cm (10in) high, carrying masses of white-eyed, violet-blue flowers. It can flower at almost any season and is often used in hanging baskets for winter display in conservatories and greenhouses. Grown outdoors in a sunny sheltered position, it will flower throughout summer and into autumn.

To raise from seed for outdoor display, sow under glass in early to mid-spring. Plant outdoors in late spring, using a soil-based or soil-less compost. Keep well watered during the flowering season and apply liquid fertilizer every two weeks, starting three to four weeks after planting.
See also page 131.

BELLFLOWER
Campanula
PERENNIAL   ZONE 4
Blue is the predominant colour of bellflowers, including the numerous low-growing species that are especially attractive when mixed in troughs and similar containers with other rock-garden plants that thrive in sun or partial shade. Bellflowers are invaluable because most bloom after the spring flowering season of many rock-garden plants.

All forms of *C. carpatica* are worth growing for their generous display of saucer-shaped flowers. Most have a height and spread of 20–30cm (8–12in). Particularly beautiful is the compact *C. c.* 'Blaue Clips', with its violet-blue flowers, while 'Birch Hybrid', only 10cm (4in) high but producing a long succession of purple-blue flowers, is a pretty bellflower to combine with very dwarf rock-garden plants. Also long-

flowering is *C. poscharskyana* 'Stella' (Zone 3), rarely more than 15cm (6in) high but making a spreading plant that is covered for weeks in star-shaped dark blue flowers.

More tender than these and often grown as a biennial for indoor decoration is the Italian bellflower (*C. isophylla,* Zone 9). Its trailing stems, 30cm (12in) or so long and massed with star-shaped blue flowers, are delightful in a hanging basket.

With the exception of the Italian bellflower, which needs frost-free conditions in winter and a warm position outdoors in summer, plant between mid-autumn and mid-spring, using gritty, soil-based compost. Apply weak liquid fertilizer two or three times during the growing season.
See also page 131.

CLEMATIS
Clematis
CLIMBER   ZONE 5   POISONOUS
Although the blue of clematis is usually tinged with mauve or purple, this does not lessen the splendour of some of the large-flowered hybrids. One of the most spectacular of those that flower in early summer and then repeat later, with smaller flowers, is 'Lasurstern'. The blooms, with seven to nine 'petals' and creamy stamens, are blue-purple at first, fading to blue-mauve. (The flowers are bleached by strong sunlight.) 'Perle d'Azur', which flowers lavishly in the second half of summer, usually has six pale blue 'petals' that show a hint of mauve around the greenish stamens.
See also pages 128, 131–2, 156, 159, 167.

CONVOLVULUS
Convolvulus sabatius
ANNUAL/PERENNIAL   ZONE 9
The tumbling growth and long succession of purplish-blue trumpet flowers through summer and into autumn make *C. sabatius* (also known as *C. mauritanicus*) an exceptionally valuable container plant (*above right*). *C. sabatius* rarely stands more than 20cm (8in) high, but the slender trailing stems can be 45cm (18in) or more long. It needs a sunny position and, because it is tender, in temperate regions it is generally treated as an annual. Cuttings can be overwintered under glass.

Plant in late spring, using either soil-based or soil-less compost. Feed with a

Convolvulus *Convolvulus sabatius*

liquid fertilizer every two weeks, starting approximately three to four weeks after planting.
See illustration page 108.

WATER HYACINTH
Eichhornia crassipes
PERENNIAL
The water hyacinth, a tropical free-floating aquatic, is a slender plant that in temperate areas needs to spend the winter under glass in frost-free and well-lit conditions in shallow water. However, it can be moved to a sunny spot in an outdoor container pool for the summer once risk of frost has passed.

The stems of its glossy evergreen leaves act as buoys, keeping afloat plants that produce spikes about 10cm (4in) high of mauve-blue flowers with a yellow eye. Thin the plants if they increase too vigorously.

BLUE MARGUERITE
Felicia
EVERGREEN SHRUB   ZONE 9
In temperate regions, these small-flowered blue daisies are usually treated as annuals and discarded in autumn, although rooted cuttings taken in summer are easily overwintered under glass. They produce a long display in summer and autumn, provided they have sun and well-drained compost.

The compact *F. amoena* (also known as *F. pappei*) has narrow leaves. The large-flowered 'Santa Anita', which grows to 60cm (24in), is a widely available selection of the bushy

Blue marguerite *Felicia amelloides*

F. amelloides (*above*). There are variegated forms of both species and cultivar.

Plant in late spring, using free-draining soil-based or soil-less compost. During the growing season, trim plants if they become untidy and apply liquid fertilizer every two weeks, starting three to four weeks after planting.
See illustration page 10.

HYDRANGEA
Hydrangea
SHRUB   ZONE 6

Hortensias or mophead hydrangeas, which are cultivars of *H. macrophylla,* produce blue or pink flower heads up to 20cm (8in) across. Their colour is also influenced by the soil or compost in which these cultivars are grown – blue is intensified on acid or neutral soil, while in alkaline soils flowers have a pink or red colouring. Proprietary preparations can be applied to the growing medium to bring out the blue colouring. 'La France' and 'Générale Vicomtesse de Vibraye' (*right*) are capable of producing good blues.

In the lacecap hydrangeas, also cultivars of *H. macrophylla*, the flower heads consist of small fertile florets in the centre surrounded by large sterile florets. Their colour is also affected by the chemistry of the soil. 'Blue Wave' is outstanding in an ericaceous compost.

Most container-grown hydrangeas reach 90–150cm (3–5ft) with a spread of 60–120cm (2–4 ft). They flower from mid-summer to early autumn.
See also pages 133, 161.

MORNING GLORY
Ipomoea tricolour 'Heavenly Blue'
ANNUAL/PERENNIAL CLIMBER
ZONE 8   POISONOUS

This fast-growing, twining perennial, usually grown as an annual, can attain 2.5m (8ft) or more, provided it has a suitable support and is grown in a sheltered sunny spot. The cultivar 'Heavenly Blue' deserves its name – the white-throated, trumpet flowers, as much as 13cm (5in) across, being a clear sky-blue.

To raise from seed, sow in warmth in early spring. Plant outdoors in late spring or early summer, using soil-based or soil-less compost. Apply liquid fertilizer every two weeks.

SWEET PEA
Lathyrus odoratus
HARDY ANNUAL CLIMBER   POISONOUS

Pastel and dark blues are an attractive component of many sweet pea mixtures, and there are also numerous named selections in this colour range, to which new additions are constantly being made. Established examples include 'Blue Danube', with prettily waved, mid-blue flowers, and the richly fragrant 'North Shore', which combines a navy blue standard with paler wings.
See also pages 133, **162***, 169.*

LOBELIA
Lobelia erinus
HALF-HARDY ANNUAL   POISONOUS

Lobelia is one of the most familiar of all container plants. This perennial, usually treated as an annual, is easy to grow. It produces quantities of neat little flowers over a long season and, because it tolerates light shade, is suitable as an underplanting. Trailing forms are especially useful for softening the edge of a container and are good fillers in a hanging basket.

Compact lobelias, making neat rounded plants about 6in (15cm) high, include 'Cambridge Blue' with sky-blue flowers, 'Crystal Palace Compacta' with

Hydrangea *Hydrangea* 'Générale Vicomtesse de Vibraye'

dark blue flowers and bronze foliage, and 'Mrs Clibran Improved', which has dark blue flowers with a white eye. Trailers, with slender stems about 30cm (12in) long, include 'Sapphire', with white-eyed flowers of deep blue, and the Fountain Series, available as mixed seed and in separate colours that range from blue or white to pink and red.

To raise from seed, sow in warmth in early to mid-spring. Harden off and plant outdoors in late spring. Use soil-based or soil-less compost and apply liquid fertilizer every two weeks, starting three weeks after planting. *See also pages 135, 153, 169; illustration page 116.*

NEMESIA
Nemesia
HALF-HARDY ANNUAL
In addition to the familiar range of yellow, orange, red, and cream from mixed seed, there is also an attractive sky-blue nemesia, 'Blue Gem'. The compact plant, 20cm (8in) high, grows quickly and bears prettily formed flowers with white touches at the centre. They are smaller than the flowers of other annual nemesias but are borne in great profusion.
See also pages 153, 169–70.

CATMINT
Nepeta
PERENNIAL   ZONE 5
The catmints, aromatic plants with grey-green foliage and sprays of soft mauve-blue flowers, are ardent sun-lovers and tolerate dry conditions. They have a long main flowering season in early summer and, if plants are cut back lightly in mid-summer, there is usually a second good flush. The compact *N. × faassenii* has a height and spread of 45cm (18in) and the slightly hardier *N.* 'Six Hills Giant' can grow to 90cm (3ft). Both can be used in tubs and other large containers as part of a semi-permanent planting of perennials and shrubs that like sun and good drainage.
Plant in mid-spring, using a gritty, soil-based compost. Cut plants back in early to mid-autumn.

PETUNIA
Petunia
HALF-HARDY ANNUAL
Plant breeders have produced such an astonishing variety of long-flowering,

rain-resistant hybrid petunias in a range of colours that these plants have become one of the first choices for the container garden. Two broad groups of petunias have been recognized: the Grandifloras, with large flowers, sometimes more than 10cm (4in) across; and the Multifloras, which produce a large number of smaller flowers. The availability of F_1 hybrids, doubles, ruffled flowers and cascading kinds has opened up even wider choices. Plants usually have a height and spread of about 30cm (12in), while dwarf cultivars are more compact and cascading petunias have a wider spread.

There are shades of blue in most of the mixtures, and separate seed is available for some blue selections. 'Blue Daddy' is a single Grandiflora with flowers 10cm (4in) across that are light blue with heavy violet veining. 'Blue Skies' is another single with slightly smaller pale blue flowers.

To raise from seed, sow in warmth in early spring. Plant outdoors in late spring or early summer, using soil-based or soil-less compost. Excess moisture or heavy feeding and shade will encourage foliage at the expense of flowers. Deadhead regularly.
See also pages 136, 142, 154,163, 170.

SALVIA
Salvia
ANNUAL/PERENNIAL   ZONE 9
Among the salvias are several blue-flowered species that are tender perennials commonly grown as annuals in sunny sheltered spots. One of the loveliest is the slender *S. patens*, which grows to 60cm (2ft) and in late summer produces widely spaced, eye-catching, bright blue flowers. *S. p.* 'Cambridge Blue' (*above right*) is similar, but has flowers of a paler blue. Another perennial almost invariably grown as an annual is *S. farinacea*. Its numerous stems grow to a height of 50cm (20in) – the upper part, like the flowers, furry and richly coloured. *S. f.* 'Victoria' is midnight-blue. Of even darker blue are the flowers of *S. discolor*, which make a startling contrast with the white backs of the leaves. The plants have a height and spread of about 45cm (18in).

To raise from seed, sow in warmth in early spring. Harden off and plant outdoors in late spring or early summer, using a soil-based or a soil-less compost. Apply liquid fertilizer

Salvia *Salvia patens* 'Cambridge Blue'

every two weeks, starting three to four weeks after planting.
See also pages 154, 170; illustrations pages 22, 87, 97, 100, 114.

FAN FLOWER
Scaevola aemula
ANNUAL/PERENNIAL   ZONE 10
This drought-resistant, trailing plant from coastal regions of Australia has proved a useful container plant. Stiff stems, clothed with coarsely toothed, dark green leaves, carry clusters of purplish-blue, fan-shaped flowers from early summer to early autumn. Plants can have a spread of 90cm (3ft) or more, yet, unless stems seek support by working their way up through other plants, their height is usually less than 40cm (16in). 'Blue Wonder' and 'Blue Fan' are two good named selections.

Plant in late spring, using a soil-based compost. Do not feed generously, since this will encourage leafy growth at the expense of flowers. Overwinter rooted cuttings under glass.
See illustration page 112.

VERBENA
Verbena
HALF-HARDY ANNUAL
Among the hybrid verbenas, which are usually grown as annuals, there are several good blues. 'Amethyst', one of the best, has a height and spread of 30cm (12in) and bears clusters of white-eyed, cobalt-blue flowers. The more compact 'Blue Lagoon' has a

height and spread of 23cm (9in); there is no eye to the violet-blue flowers. *See also pages 136, 149, 155, 165, **171**.*

VIOLA, PANSY
Viola
ANNUAL/BIENNIAL/PERENNIAL
ZONE 5

Although the violas and pansies are short-lived perennials, most are grown as biennials or annuals. The reliably perennial horned or tufted viola (*V. cornuta*), evergreen and up to 30cm (12in) high, produces masses of spurred blue flowers in early summer and again later, if cut back. Several violas are as near black as is found in any flower, but the poise and shape of the flower dispel any sinister hint. *V.* 'Mollie Sanderson' has mat black flowers 2.5cm (1in) across, which are brightened by a yellow eye. 'Penny Black' (*below*) has smaller flowers of darkest blue-black velvet. Both grow to 15cm (6in).

Many of the large-flowered pansies, most 15–25cm (6–10in) high, have blue or partly blue flowers. The striking 'Ullswater Blue' has a yellow eye and a blue-black mask imposed on sky-blue petals. It can be raised from seed, as can the blue-flowered violet 'Baby Lucia', only 10–13cm (4–5in) high.
*See also Pansy, below, and pages 136, **143–4**, 149, 155, 167, 171.*

Viola 'Penny Black'

WISTERIA
Wisteria
DECIDUOUS CLIMBER   ZONE 5

All wisterias are vigorous climbers. When grown in open ground and given the support of a pergola or a stout tree, the Chinese wisteria (*W. sinensis*) is capable of extending 30m (100ft). It bears drooping clusters of fragrant mauve-blue flowers in early summer, sometimes with a lesser display in late summer. The Japanese wisteria (*W. floribunda*) is less rampant but also a strong climber, and in beauty its scented flowers almost match those of its Chinese cousin. Wisterias grown in containers do not make the phenomenal growth of plants in the open garden, and in any event are best restricted. They can be kept to almost any size by pruning and training and are frequently grown as standards.

Between mid-autumn and early spring, plant in a large container at least 50cm (20in) deep, using soil-based compost incorporating slow-release fertilizer. Insert a cane to support the climber. To control growth and promote the development of short stems that will produce flowers, cut back shoots in late summer, leaving stubs about 5cm (2in) long extending from the framework of main stems. More pruning may be needed in winter. Top-dress with fresh mix in mid-spring.

Reticulata iris

AUTUMN AND WINTER

CROCUS
Crocus chrysanthus
CORM   ZONE 4

The most versatile of the crocuses flowering in late winter, *C. chrysanthus* is available in a wide range of colours, including shades of blue. A popular selection, 'Blue Pearl', is pale blue with a bronze-yellow base and conspicuous orange stigmas. As with other cultivars, the leaves appear with the flowers, which stand about 8cm (3in) high.
*See also pages 128, 137, **138**, 144, 149, 166, 171.*

DWARF IRIS
Iris
BULB   ZONE 5

There are many blue selections of the exquisite Reticulata iris (*below left*), which are easy bulbs to grow and particularly valuable on account of their early flowering season, in mid- to late winter. Good examples include: 'Cantab', pale blue with an orange blotch on the falls; 'Clairette', with pale blue standards and a dark blue blotch at the tip; and 'Harmony', sky-blue with deeper blue falls and conspicuous golden markings. All grow to about 15cm (6in) high.

I. histrioides 'Major' belongs to the same broad group of dwarf irises. Usually only 10cm (4in) high, its sturdy build and its intense blue, with a paler area around the orange crest, make it one of the most arresting small flowers of late winter.
*See also pages **144**, 171; illustration page 125.*

PANSY
Viola
ANNUAL/BIENNIAL

The winter-flowering pansies are sown in late spring or early summer to flower in winter and early spring. Sown in late winter they will flower in spring and summer. They are commonly sold as mixtures. Universal Mixed includes a wide range of clear and blotched colours, with several shades of blue, all 6–8in (15–20cm) high. Separate colours include 'Beaconsfield', a bicolour with upper petals of pale blue and lower petals of rich purple-blue, and 'True Blue', a clear mid-blue.
*See also Viola, above, and pages 136, **143–4**, 149, 155,167, 171; illustrations pages 8, 13.*

GREEN FOLIAGE

In container gardening, foliage is the most frequently overlooked component. Many flowering plants have attractive green leaves, and there are many others that are outstanding for their foliage alone. In the vast range of green shades, some serve best as background or infill, preventing flower colours from appearing as a congested mass. Many foliage plants can be grown successfully on their own. The evergreens are invaluable for providing continuity throughout the year.

JAPANESE MAPLE
Acer palmatum
SHRUB   ZONE 5
Few deciduous shrubs can match the variety of leaf shape and colour available in the numerous cultivars of the Japanese maple (*below*). Many have a moment of supreme beauty when the foliage colours in autumn; most have a

delicate charm as the leaves unfold in spring; and the summer mantle of all is exceptionally refined. Japanese maples can be grown either in sun or in partial shade, but they need shelter from wind. Most produce their best autumn colour in acid or neutral conditions.

The slow-growing *A. palmatum* var. *dissectum* does well in containers, building up a mound of intricate, weeping branches carrying finely dissected leaves. Those of the Dissectum Viride Group are the brightest green.

Plant between mid-autumn and early spring, using an ericaceous compost to which leaf mould or other humus has been added. Keep the compost moist. Repot in spring only if the roots are congested; otherwise, just top-dress with fresh compost annually in early to mid-spring.
See also pages 183, 188.

MAIDENHAIR FERN
Adiantum
EVERGREEN/DECIDUOUS FERN
ZONE 3
In temperate regions, the maidenhair fern (*A. capillus-veneris*, Zone 7) is usually grown indoors, where its elegantly lacy fronds, up to 25cm (10in) long, remain evergreen. It can reach 90cm (3ft) in height and spread. The hardier *A. pedatum* is deciduous and produces wiry black stems from which appear sprays of delicate fronds. This species, which rarely exceeds 45cm (18in) high, with a spread of 30cm (12in), needs full or partial shade.

Plant *A. pedatum* in mid-spring, using a soil-based compost to which leaf mould or other humus has been added. Set the rootstock at a depth of about 2.5cm (1in). Keep plants well watered during the growing season and remove fronds as they fade.

LADY'S MANTLE
Alchemilla mollis
PERENNIAL   ZONE 3
All through the long summer season lady's mantle (*below*) bears sprays of tiny yellow-green flowers on plants with a height and spread of about 40cm (16in). It is also a superb foliage plant: when fanned open, the downy leaves hold bead-like droplets of water. Suitable for sun or shade in a wide range of conditions, it is excellent grown under shrubs.

Japanese maple *Acer palmatum*

Lady's mantle *Alchemilla mollis*

Plant between mid-autumn and early spring, using soil-based compost. Remove the flower heads as they fade; if left, plants self-seed freely. Lift and divide every two years, and in other years top-dress with fresh compost.

HART'S-TONGUE FERN
Asplenium scolopendrium
EVERGREEN FERN   ZONE 4
The hart's-tongue fern (*below*) produces a bold shuttlecock of evergreen strap-shaped leaves that makes a good background to flowers. The Crispum Group has fronds that are crested and waved, while in the Undulatum Group the waviness of the leaf edges is very pronounced. All are about 50cm (20in) in height with a spread of 38cm (15in).

Plant these ferns in early to mid-spring, using a soil-based compost to which leaf mould or other humus and lime have been added. Place in full or partial shade and keep well watered during the growing season.
See illustrations pages 52–3, 110.

LADY FERN
Athyrium filix-femina
DECIDUOUS FERN   ZONE 4
The lady fern has lacy, fresh green fronds up to 90cm (3ft) high, giving it a light elegance. Although it tolerates fairly dry soil, its delicately refined beauty lasts longer in moist conditions.

Plant in early to mid-spring, using a soil-based compost to which leaf mould or other humus has been added. Place plants in full or partial shade and water well during the growing season.

Hart's-tongue fern *Asplenium scolopendrium*

Box *Buxus sempervirens*

BERGENIA
Bergenia
EVERGREEN PERENNIAL   ZONE 3
The foliage of some bergenias is more remarkable for its purple and red tints in winter than for its solid greens in summer. One that remains more or less green throughout the year, however, is *B. cordifolia*, a useful underplanting to shrubs as well as being attractive planted on its own. Growing to 60cm (2ft), it bears sprays of pinkish-mauve flowers in spring, and its large, rounded leaves have wavy edges.

Plant between mid-autumn and early spring, using a soil-based compost. Cut down flower stems when the blooms have faded. Lift and divide plants every two years and top-dress in spring in other years.
See also page 189.

BOX, COMMON BOX
Buxus sempervirens
EVERGREEN SHRUB   ZONE 6
This small-leaved, glossy evergreen (*above*) has long been cultivated and valued for the ease with which it can be trimmed into dense shapes, either geometric or fanciful representations. Although capable of eventually reaching a height of 3m (10ft) or more, this slow-growing shrub is generally restricted to a height of 90cm (3ft) when grown in a container. The pale green flowers, which appear in mid-spring, are inconspicuous. The dwarf form 'Suffruticosa', often used as an edging plant, can easily be kept at a height of 5–8cm (2–3in).

Plant in mid-autumn or early to mid-spring, using soil-based compost into which slow-release fertilizer is incorporated. Cut back in mid-spring to promote bushy growth and trim established bushes in late summer or early autumn. Top-dress in mid-spring.
See also page 186; illustrations pages 13, 17, 19, 20, 70, 82, 95.

CYPRESS
Chamaecyparis obtusa 'Nana Gracilis'
EVERGREEN CONIFER   ZONE 3
Although eventually reaching a height of 1.8m (6ft) or more, this slow-growing, semi-dwarf conifer is most commonly seen as a dense cone with a height and spread at the base of less than 3ft (90cm). The foliage is an exceptionally rich dark green, arranged in upright sprays.

Plant in mid-spring, using soil-based compost. Top-dress annually in early to mid-spring. Repot, in mid-spring, if the roots are congested.
See also page 183.

CORDYLINE, CABBAGE TREE
Cordyline australis
EVERGREEN TREE   ZONE 9
In cold areas this palm-like member of the lily family is often grown under glass, but where the climate is mild enough its spiky head makes a bold centrepiece to a large planting. Plants used for this purpose are normally about 90–120cm (3–4ft) high, but are insufficiently mature to flower. Cordylines are useful near the sea, for they stand up well to wind and salt spray.

Cordyline *Cordyline australis*

Plant cordyline (*above*) in mid- to late spring, using soil-based compost with a slow-release fertilizer added. Top-dress with fresh compost in mid-spring. *See also page 189; illustrations pages 21, 111.*

MALE FERN
Dryopteris filix-mas
DECIDUOUS FERN   ZONE 4

The male fern is one of the easiest ferns to grow, tolerating a wide range of conditions and forming a graceful clump of much-divided fronds above stalks that are covered with rust-coloured scales (*right*). It can grow to 90cm (3ft) or more, and in very mild conditions may be semi-evergreen. There are several forms, usually more compact, with crested fronds.

Plant in early to mid-spring, using soil-based compost with added humus. Place in shade and water well.

BAMBOO
Fargesia
EVERGREEN BAMBOO   ZONE 4

The fountain-like effect of several clump-forming bamboos is well displayed when they are grown in containers. Among the most graceful of evergreens, bamboos are tall and airy, and give a patio or small garden an established, sub-tropical look.

Two of the best for this purpose

have recently undergone name changes. The bamboo now known as *F. nitida* (previously known as *Arundinaria nitida* or *Sinarundinaria nitida*) has purplish stems up to 3m (10ft) high that arch with the plentiful mass of small leaves. The slender stems, up to 2.5m (8ft) high, and the larger leaves of *F. murieliae* (*Arundinaria murieliae*, *A. spathacea*, *Thamnocalamus spathaceus*) create a more pronounced arching clump that sways in even a light breeze.

Plant in tubs or in other large containers during the second half of spring, using a soil-based compost, which should be kept moist at all times. These bamboos (*right*) can be grown in sun or partial shade, but need shelter from cold winds. Top-dress with fresh compost in mid-spring. *See illustration page 23.*

FATSHEDERA
× *Fatshedera lizei*
EVERGREEN SHRUB   ZONE 7

Although often grown as an indoor plant, this hybrid between *Fatsia* and an ivy makes a handsome foliage plant for growing outdoors in containers and will thrive in sun or shade. Growing to 1.5m (5ft) or more high, its leathery, five-lobed leaves are dark green and glossy. The pale green flowers, which appear in autumn, are rarely significant

Male fern *Dryopteris filix-mas*

Bamboo *Fargesia*

on specimens grown outdoors.

Plant in autumn or early to mid-spring, using soil-based compost. Fatshederas (*below right*) tend to flop if unsupported, so insert a cane when planting and tie in the leading shoot as it develops. Top-dress annually in early to mid-spring.

FATSIA
Fatsia japonica
EVERGREEN SHRUB   ZONE 7

The large, glossy, fingered leaves of the fatsia suggest sub-tropical luxury, and indeed this upright plant is capable of exceeding 3m (10ft). Clusters of creamy, rounded flower heads appear in autumn and are followed in spring or early summer by bunches of black berries.

Plant in autumn or mid-spring, using a soil-based compost. In early spring, repot if the roots are congested; otherwise top-dress with fresh compost. Extensive pruning is not normally required, but cut back any weak or straggly growth in mid-spring. *See also page 186.*

IVY, COMMON IVY
Hedera helix
EVERGREEN CLIMBER   ZONE 5

Ivies are a very versatile group of evergreens, most flourishing in sun or shade. In containers they are sometimes used as climbers but more often as trailers. When allowed to climb, they cling to whatever surface is available by means of aerial roots and often pass through a long juvenile stage before producing the non-climbing shoots that carry flowers and berries. The small-leaved cultivars are the most suitable as trailers, and when grown in this way they normally do not flower.

Common ivy, whose green leaves have three or five lobes, has numerous cultivars, both green leaved and variegated. Green-leaved cultivars include: 'Duckfoot', with small leaves that have three rounded lobes; 'Green Ripple', with small leaves, coppery in winter, with three or five lobes elegantly pointing forward; 'Donerailensis', with three-lobed leaves of a sombre green with white veins in summer, which in winter turn copper with the veins showing green; 'Manda's Crested' ('Curly Locks'), with medium-sized leaves that take on a red tinge in winter; 'Spetchley', with very small leaves of dark green; and 'Triton' ('Green Feather'), with much dissected, dark green leaves.

Plant ivies between early autumn and early spring, using a soil-based compost. It may take several months before climbing ivies start to cling. To get them started, tie young shoots close to their support. To encourage trailing ivies to branch, pinch back the growing tips of stems. All ivies do better if given liquid fertilizer every three or four weeks during the growing season.
See also pages 184, 186; illustrations pages 55, 72–3, 88.

CORKSCREW RUSH
Juncus effusus 'Spiralis'
EVERGREEN PERENNIAL   ZONE 3
This curiosity is an aquatic perennial, suitable for the edges of a container pool. Tightly spiralling or more loosely twisted stems up to 45cm (18in) long make a muddled clump. The corkscrew rush bears inconspicuous clusters of brown flowers in early to mid-summer.

Plant in mid- to late spring, using an aquatic compost in a basket or perforated pot. Set in water at a depth of 5–8cm (2–3in). Tidy plants during the growing season and remove any straight leaves.

JUNIPER
Juniperus sabina 'Tamariscifolia'
EVERGREEN CONIFER   ZONE 4
Junipers provide a large number of dwarf or semi-dwarf evergreen shrubs that can be grown in containers. Many have grey-green or grey-blue foliage. The sprawling *J. s.* 'Tamariscifolia', which is green-leaved, makes a flat-topped bush 45cm (18in) high with horizontal branches 60–90cm (2–3ft) long.

Plant in mid-spring, using a soil-based compost. Repot only when the roots are congested; otherwise top-dress in early to mid-spring.
See also page 194.

OSTRICH FERN
Matteuccia struthiopteris
DECIDUOUS FERN   ZONE 2
A short stem supports a perfect shuttlecock 90–150cm (3–5ft) high, of yellow-green, sterile fronds surrounding a circle of shorter, dark brown fronds

that are fertile. The symmetry of the ostrich fern is appealing but it requires a regular supply of moisture to achieve perfection.

Plant in early to mid-spring, using a soil-based compost to which leaf mould or other humus has been added. Grow in full or partial shade and keep well watered. Cut down dead fronds in mid- to late autumn.

ROYAL FERN
Osmunda regalis
DECIDUOUS FERN   ZONE 4
This splendid fern lives up to its regal pretensions, since its copper-tinted fronds unfold with great elegance. Bright green and leathery in summer, when they sometimes attain a height of 1.8m (6ft), they turn bronze in autumn. Mature royal ferns can have a spread of over 1.2m (4ft). They will grow in sun or shade but require permanently moist conditions.

Plant in early to mid-spring, using a soil based compost, to which leaf mould or other humus has been added. Set the crowns so that their tops are level with the soil surface. Clear the foliage away in mid- to late autumn, and top-dress annually in early to mid-spring by replacing the top 5–8cm (2–3in) of compost.

PELARGONIUM, GERANIUM
Pelargonium
EVERGREEN PERENNIAL   ZONE 9
Many pelargoniums have attractive foliage, and in some cases the ornamental and aromatic qualities of the leaves count for more than the flowers. Those with scented leaves, pungent as well as sweet-smelling, will normally release their fragrance when lightly touched. These excellent pot plants deserve to be more widely grown for this reason alone.

One of the most splendid is the peppermint pelargonium (*P. tomentosum*), which can make a mound 1.2m (4ft) high and wide, with large, pale green, downy-soft leaves that release a powerful peppermint scent when bruised. This pelargonium is unusual because it prefers light shade. Its white flowers are inconspicuous.

The oak-leaved pelargonium (*P. quercifolium*), usually less than 90cm (3ft) high, has narrow, dark-veined, aromatic leaves, deeply lobed and with a serrated edge. The flowers, borne in

Fatshedera × *Fatshedera lizei*

181

late spring and summer, are pink with purple markings. 'Graveolens', with a height and spread of 60–90cm (2–3ft), has deeply lobed and toothed lemon-scented leaves. All through summer it carries pink flowers with purple spots on the upper petals. 'Radula' (*below*), of similar size, is a hybrid with maroon markings on its petals and rough-surfaced leaves smelling of rose and lemon. The more compact 'Prince of Orange', with darkly veined pink flowers, has leaves with the most delightful intense orange fragrance. *See also pages 170, 187, 190, 194; illustrations pages 104–5, 127.*

Pelargonium *Pelargonium* 'Radula'

PINE
Pinus
EVERGREEN CONIFER   ZONE 3
Many dwarf pines are easy to grow in containers and they are valuable for their striking evergreen needles. They are best placed in full sun on their own or combined with rock-garden plants.

The slow-growing mountain pine (*P. mugo*) may eventually exceed 1.8m (6ft) in height and spread while developing into an attractively gnarled specimen (*right*). Several dwarf forms are sold as grafted plants: 'Mops' makes a grey-green ball 60cm (2ft) high and wide.

Dwarf forms of the Scots pine (*P. sylvestris*) include 'Beuvronensis', with a height of 90cm (3ft) and slightly broader spread. Its short needles are grey-green and the buds have a red tinge in winter.

Plant in autumn or early spring, using a soil-based compost. Top-dress annually in early to mid-spring.

SHIELD FERN
Polystichum
EVERGREEN FERN   ZONE 5
The soft shield fern (*P. setiferum*) may form a sprawling clump 1.2m (4ft) wide, but has a more upright habit in cool, moist conditions. Light green fronds up to 90cm (3ft) high are soft in texture, and the stems are covered with grey-brown scales. The Acutilobum Group has particularly elegant, narrow fronds about 60cm (2ft) high. The hard shield fern (*P. aculeatum*) has leathery fronds, up to 90cm (3ft) high, with a glossy upper surface and mat underside. The Christmas or sword fern (*P. munitum*) has lustrous evergreen fronds that taper to a fine point. In containers this fern rarely exceeds 90cm (3ft) in height.

Plant in mid-spring in a soil-based compost to which leaf mould or other humus and lime have been added. Place in full or partial shade and keep well watered during the growing season.

PORTUGAL LAUREL
Prunus lusitanica
EVERGREEN SHRUB OR SMALL TREE
ZONE 7
The Portugal laurel is a sombre but beautiful shrub or small tree that is capable of reaching to more than 4.5m (15ft) but is easily restricted to 2.5m (8ft) or less. In a container it is best grown as a tree, on a single stem, with the head clipped to a rounded or

Pine *Pinus mugo*

domed shape. Unclipped bushes bear cream flowers in early summer, followed by strings of black fruit. The red stalks to the glossy dark leaves are also an attractive feature.

Plant in early autumn or mid-spring, using a soil-based compost to which a slow-release fertilizer has been added. Top-dress annually in mid-spring after removing the top 5–8cm (2–3in) of compost. Use secateurs to trim the foliage in late summer.

TELLIMA
Tellima grandiflora
SEMI-EVERGREEN PERENNIAL ZONE 4
The heart-shaped, purplish-green leaves of the clump-forming tellima make an interesting addition to a container planting, with the small, bell-shaped cream flowers, 60cm (24in) high, providing a late spring bonus.

Plant in autumn or early spring, in a soil-based compost.
See illustration page 96.

THUJA
Thuja occidentalis 'Holmstrup'
EVERGREEN CONIFER   ZONE 4
The species *T. occidentalis* is too large for containers, but numerous dwarf and compact forms are suitable. 'Holmstrup' makes a rich green pyramid, packed with upright sprays of foliage, that can eventually exceed 1.5m (5ft). It needs full sun and is best in a sheltered spot.

Plant in autumn or early to mid-spring, using soil-based compost. Top-dress annually in mid-spring.
See also page 185.

REEDMACE
Typha minima
PERENNIAL   ZONE 6
Reedmaces have a reputation for being invasive, yet the dwarf reedmace is a well-behaved waterside plant, suitable for small pools of any kind, including those in containers. Growing to a height of 45–60cm (18–24in), it has thin, grassy leaves and long stalks. The brown flower heads produced in mid- to late summer are succeeded by decorative seed heads.

Plant in spring in the container pool in a perforated pot or basket, using an aquatic compost. Set at a depth of 5–15cm (2–6in); such a covering of water reduces the risk of plants being killed by cold weather in winter.

GOLD TO CHARTREUSE FOLIAGE

There are numerous plants with greenish-yellow foliage or leaves that are variegated in shades ranging from cream to gold. They are plants to use with discretion, but the sunny warmth of their colouring can create a cheerful mood in the container garden just as it can on a larger scale. Yellow foliage is most pronounced when plants are grown in an open, sunny position, although some yellow foliage scorches under a fierce sun.

MAPLE
Acer
DECIDUOUS SHRUB   ZONE 5
The foliage of the golden-leaved maples is likely to be scorched by strong sun, yet it will lose its glow if plants are positioned in full shade. A sheltered position in partial shade is best.

The slow-growing *A. shirasawanum* f. *aureum* (often listed as *A. japonicum* 'Aureum') will eventually reach a height of 1.2–1.5m (4–5ft). Its yellow leaves, beautiful when unfolding at the same time as the clusters of red flowers are showing, turn rich crimson in autumn. Also slow growing is the golden form of the Japanese maple (*A. palmatum* 'Aureum'), which may exceed 1.8m (6ft) high, and has dense fan-shaped sprays of rich yellow-green foliage.
*See also pages **178**, **188**.*

SPOTTED LAUREL
Aucuba japonica 'Picturata'
EVERGREEN SHRUB   ZONE 7
Although the spotted laurel tolerates the most unpromising conditions, the variegated forms are worth growing in good compost in an open spot. Plants are either male or female, but only female plants bear berries. The male plant 'Picturata' can grow to more than 1.8m (6ft) and be as broad as it is high. Its large, leathery leaves are dark green with a central yellow splash. The female plant 'Crotonifolia' is a similar size. Its leaves are boldly splashed with yellow, and its scarlet berries often persist through winter and into spring.

Plant in early to mid-autumn or early to mid-spring, using a soil-based compost. Top-dress annually in spring with fresh compost; repot only when the roots are congested.
See also page 202.

HEATHER, LING
Calluna vulgaris
EVERGREEN SHRUB   ZONE 4
Among the many cultivars of heather there are several that have strongly coloured foliage. Its long-lasting ornamental value, however, is sometimes undermined by mismatched flower colours. Worthwhile exceptions include 'Gold Haze', which has bright gold foliage with white flowers. In spring the young growths of 'Orange Queen' are rich yellow, but in summer they age to deep orange. Both these cultivars grow to 60cm (2ft) and flower in late summer or early autumn.
See also pages 131, 159.

CYPRESS
Chamaecyparis
EVERGREEN CONIFER   ZONE 5
Numerous dwarf cultivars of *Chamaecyparis* species produce gold foliage. The Lawson cypress (*C. lawsoniana*) makes a large, vigorous, conical tree, yet the cultivar 'Aurea Densa' reaches its height of 1.8m (6ft) only slowly. The conical bush is packed with short, stiff sprays of golden foliage. More compact is a cultivar of the Hinoki cypress (*C. obtusa*) called 'Nana Aurea'. This plant makes a dome about 60cm (2ft) high of dense, fan-shaped sprays of rich yellow-green foliage.
*See also page **179**.*

WINTER HEATH
Erica carnea
EVERGREEN SHRUB   ZONE 5
The vivid yellow foliage of some heaths and heathers is highly ornamental. However, as with the golden-leaved heathers (*Calluna*), flower and foliage colour do not always go well together, which makes the exceptions even more valuable.

Among useful container heaths is 'Ann Sparkes': by winter, when the rose-pink flowers are borne, the golden foliage has turned to a rich bronze. 'Aurea' bears bright gold foliage in spring and summer, which changes to light green in winter, during the flowering season. Its flowers are pink, fading to near-white. These two cultivars grow 15–20cm (6–8in) high.
*See also pages **137**, 155, 165, 171.*

EUONYMUS
Euonymus
EVERGREEN SHRUB   ZONE 5
There is a surprising range of variegation among *E. fortunei* cultivars, most of which make useful small shrubs for containers, although the species itself can be semi-prostrate or even a self-clinging climber. One of the brightest cultivars is *E. f.* 'Emerald 'n' Gold', with its rich yellow edging to glossy green leaves, which assume a red tinge in winter. The leaves of the slightly more subdued 'Sunspot' (*below*) have a green edge and a cream or golden-yellow centre. Both make hummocks of foliage about 45cm (18in) high by 60cm (2ft) wide, and bear small sprays of greenish-white flowers from early to mid-summer.

Japanese spindle (*E. japonicus*, Zone 7) also has some good variegated forms. 'Ovatus Aureus' has glossy, dark green leaves with bold yellow edging. This useful shrub tolerates salt spray; it grows to 1.8m (6ft) or more.

Plant in early to mid-autumn or mid-spring, using soil-based compost. If necessary, plants can be shaped in late summer or early autumn. Top-dress with fresh compost in spring; repot when the roots are congested.
See also page 186.

Euonymus *Euonymus fortunei* 'Sunspot'

Hakonechloa *Hakonechloa macra* 'Aureola'

Ivy *Hedera helix* 'Buttercup'

HAKONECHLOA

Hakonechloa macra
EVERGREEN PERENNIAL GRASS   ZONE 6
The variegated forms of this Japanese, clump-forming genus are more widely grown than the green-leaved species itself. 'Alboaurea' makes a softly arching clump about 30cm (12in) high, the leaves variegated white and yellow and showing very little green. Even more striking is 'Aureola' (*above*), its ribbon-like, bright yellow leaves having only a few narrow lines of green. Both make lovely specimens planted on their own, positioned in an open or partially shaded spot.

Plant in mid-autumn or early to mid-spring, using a soil-based compost. The rhizomes spread slowly, but if necessary divide in spring; otherwise give an annual topdressing of fresh compost.

IVY, COMMON IVY

Hedera helix
EVERGREEN CLIMBER   ZONE 5
The sombre green of many common ivy cultivars is relieved by gold variegation, but in most cases the full richness of the variegation develops only when plants are grown in sun.

'Californian Gold' has medium-sized leaves with yellow blotches and speckles over green, while 'Midas Touch' bears yellow leaves with grey-green splashes and bright green speckling. 'Buttercup' has small to medium-sized leaves, which are bright greenish yellow (*above*). They tend to burn in full sun, yet lose their yellow tint if heavily shaded. One of the most popular in this group is 'Goldheart', which has small to medium-sized dark green leaves with a rich gold splash in the centre. Its variegation remains vivid even when the plant is grown in shade. Another ivy with sunny variegation is 'Golden Ingot', its yellow splashed with shades of green.
*See also pages **180–81**, 186; illustration page 124.*

HELICHRYSUM

Helichrysum petiolare 'Limelight'
EVERGREEN SHRUB   ZONE 9
This yellow-green, trailing shrub is as useful as the more familiar, grey-leaved helichrysum and, like it, is normally grown as an annual. Its felted leaves, covering a plant with a spread of 1.2m (4ft) or more, cool down hot colour schemes and fill out, but do not clutter, mixed plantings in hanging baskets, window boxes and other containers.
*See also page **193**; illustrations pages 106, 115.*

HOSTA

Hosta
PERENNIAL   ZONE 3
Hostas provide some of the finest foliage plants that can be grown in temperate gardens, and many make superb container plants – generally seen at their best when grown alone. The hosta cultivars cover a wide range of leaf shapes, sizes, and colours: gold, yellow and cream are found in both plain-leaved and variegated forms.

'Sum and Substance' has impressively large, heavily textured leaves that are greenish gold and stand 75cm (30in) high. *H. fortunei* 'Aurea' makes a clump of soft yellow leaves, 60cm (2ft) high, which gradually turn to green.

Of those with yellow edges to the leaves, *H. sieboldiana* 'Frances Williams' is outstanding. A quilted blue leaf standing up to 75cm (30in) tall is outlined by an irregular cream edge that deepens to yellow in autumn. In *H. fortunei* 'Aureomarginata', green leaves edged with yellow make a clump 60cm (2ft) high. Of the smaller hostas, one of the best is 'Golden Tiara'. It grows to 30cm (12in) and has gold edges to its heart-shaped green leaves.

In *H. fortunei* 'Gold Standard' it is the edge that is green, the centre of the leaf gradually changing from green to rich yellow. It makes a clump up to 75cm (30in) high.

The lily-like flowers of these hostas, an added attraction in summer, may be white, as with *H. sieboldiana* 'Frances Williams', or shades of lavender, mauve or purple.

Plant hostas in autumn or spring, using soil-based compost to which leaf mould or other humus has been added. Apply liquid fertilizer every two to three weeks during the growing season. Slugs and snails relish the foliage of hostas and need to be controlled. Top-dress hostas generously with fresh compost in spring.
See also pages 187, 193.

GOLDEN HOP

Humulus lupulus 'Aureus'
PERENNIAL CLIMBER   ZONE 5
Les vigorous than the common hop, but even so capable of climbing to 4.5m (15ft) or more, the golden hop makes unusual foliage for containers. The leaves, with three or five elegantly cut lobes, are a beautiful yellowish-green until mid-summer, when the green becomes more pronounced. The yellow is strongest in full sun.

Plant in autumn or spring, using a soil-based compost. Provide supports for the twining stems.
See illustration page 75.

DEAD-NETTLE

Lamium maculatum 'Aureum'

PERENNIAL   ZONE 4

Many dead-nettles have silvery foliage: in 'Aureum' the leaves are a strong yellow-green with a white stripe. It also carries pink flowers in early summer. Plants are 15cm (6in) high, and the stems, up to 50cm (20in) long, root as they spread. This slow-growing cultivar can make an attractive underplanting to a large shrub or as a filler in a mixture. Plant in spring, using a soil-based compost.

See also page 187.

CREEPING JENNY

Lysimachia nummularia 'Aurea'

PERENNIAL   ZONE 4

In summer this creeping perennial (*below*), only 5cm (2in) high but with trailing stems as long as 45cm (18in), happily combines bright yellow, cup-shaped flowers and greenish-yellow leaves, which are carried in neat pairs along the stems. It is best planted so that it spills over the edge of a pot.

Plant in spring, in soil-based or soil-less compost. Although moisture-loving, it will tolerate dry conditions. The foliage turns green in shade.

See illustration page 96.

OSMANTHUS

Osmanthus heterophyllus

EVERGREEN SHRUB   ZONE 79

This slow-growing, holly-like shrub, with inconspicuous but fragrant

flowers in autumn, has several variegated forms. 'Goshiki' has bold yellow mottling and its young growth is coloured a rosy bronze. Plant in spring, using soil-based compost.

See illustration page 124.

PHORMIUM, NEW ZEALAND FLAX

Phormium 'Yellow Wave'

EVERGREEN PERENNIAL   ZONE 9

Phormiums are grown mainly for their clumps of leathery, sword-shaped leaves, which are sometimes coloured with linear yellow variegation. Unlike some phormiums, 'Yellow Wave' has lax leaves, about 90cm (3ft) high, which are yellow, bordered by fine green edges.

See also page 190; illustration page 12.

BAMBOO

Pleioblastus auricomus

EVERGREEN BAMBOO   ZONE 5

This dwarf bamboo (sometimes listed as *P. viridistriatus*) is exceptionally beautiful when grown on its own and placed in full sun. In shade much of its golden radiance is lost. Growing to 75cm (30in), its downy, ribbon-like leaves are a rich gold that is unevenly striped with green (*below*).

Plant in mid-spring, using a soil-based compost. Cut out old stems in early spring to encourage fresh growth. Top-dress generously with fresh compost in spring; repot only if the roots become congested.

See also pages 180, 187.

PICK-A-BACK PLANT

Tolmiea menziesii 'Taff's Gold'

EVERGREEN PERENNIAL   ZONE 7

The common name of the species refers to the way plantlets develop where leaves join stems. This zestful characteristic is also found in the cultivar 'Taff's Gold', in which the leaves are prettily speckled green and soft yellow. This is a hearty filler for hanging baskets and other containers, forming a dense clump 30cm (12in) or more high, and trailing elegantly. There are spikes of tiny, green-brown flowers in spring.

Plant in early spring, using a soil-based compost. Renew plants every year or two, propagating from plantlets.

See illustration page 25.

THUJA

Thuja

EVERGREEN CONIFER   ZONE 3

One of the most widely grown of all golden-leaved conifers is the dwarf cultivar of the American thuja, *T. occidentalis* 'Rheingold'. This slowly forms a loose cone, eventually more than 90cm (3ft) in height, its old-gold richness standing out particularly well in the winter garden.

Among the many dwarf cultivars of the Chinese thuja (*T. orientalis*) is 'Aurea Nana', which makes a dense, globular bush, packed with sprays of yellow-green foliage.

See also page 182.

THYME

Thymus

EVERGREEN SHRUB   ZONE 4

Thymes are grown mainly as aromatic herbs, yet several also make attractive foliage plants. The golden thymes offer more showy alternatives to those such as *T. vulgaris* 'Silver Posie' with creamy variegation that creates a cool silvery effect. Lemon thyme (*T.* × *citriodorus*), for example, has cultivars with yellow foliage or gold variegation: 'Aureus' is a springy dwarf shrub, about 10–20cm (4–8in) high, forming a dense, spreading mat up to 45cm (18in) across of tiny, fragrant bright golden leaves and bearing lilac flowers in summer. Another attractive thyme, 'Doone Valley', only 8cm (3in) high, displays gold mottling running through dark green. *T. serpyllum* 'Goldstream' is a lighter green and yellow. Both have mauve flowers in late summer.

See also page 197; illustration page 125.

Creeping jenny *Lysimachia nummularia* 'Aurea'

Bamboo *Pleioblastus auricomus*

WHITE AND CREAM IN LEAVES

The detailed beauty of variegated foliage is often lost in the open garden. This is one reason for growing plants in a way that allows them to be seen close to. Variegated plants also add sparkle to ambitious planting schemes and introduce a light note to shady areas.

VARIEGATED GROUND ELDER

Aegopodium podagraria 'Variegatum'
PERENNIAL   ZONE 4
The variegated form of ground elder is less invasive than the plain green species, and the clumps of cream-splashed leaves, about 25cm (10in) high, are ornamental in shade. Plant in spring, using soil-based compost.
See illustration page 17.

ORNAMENTAL CABBAGE

Brassica oleracea Capitata Group
ANNUAL
As well as the edible cabbages, there are some that have been bred specifically for their ornamental value. Many have creamy white and green heads, and the leaves of the flower-like rosettes are often waved or crinkled (*below*). These biennials grown as annuals are most frequently used for long-lasting autumn and winter schemes. Most have a height and spread of 30–45cm (12–18in).

To raise from seed, sow outdoors in spring. Plant in containers in late summer or early autumn, using a soil-based compost with added lime.
See also page 189; illustration page 95.

BOX, COMMON BOX

Buxus sempervirens 'Elegantissima'
EVERGREEN SHRUB   ZONE 6
There are several variegated forms of box – the touches of white, cream or gold lightening the sombre green of these plants, especially those grown in shade. 'Elegantissima' is a slow-growing, dense, dome-shaped cultivar with creamy white edges to the leaves, which create a silvery effect. It rarely exceeds 1.2m (4ft).
See also page 179; illustration page 70.

EUONYMUS

Euonymus fortunei
EVERGREEN SHRUB   ZONE 5
Several cultivars of *E. fortunei* show white or cream variegation. 'Silver Queen' has young foliage that is yellow in spring but later changes to grey-green with a creamy white edge. This plant is up to 90cm (3ft) high but often wider. 'Emerald Gaiety', of similar dimensions, has rounded dark green leaves edged in startling white. Both of these cultivars grow in sun or shade.
See also page 183.

FATSIA

Fatsia japonica 'Variegata'
EVERGREEN SHRUB   ZONE 8
The plain-leaved fatsia is handsome, but the addition of random, creamy white splashes on the tips of the fingered leaves puts it in a higher class. It thrives in a sheltered, partially shaded spot.
See also page 180.

VARIEGATED GROUND IVY

Glechoma hederacea 'Variegata'
EVERGREEN PERENNIAL   ZONE 8
Trailing stems, which can be 90cm (3ft) or more long, and prettily variegated, heart-shaped leaves make ground ivy ideal for window boxes and hanging baskets. It grows well in sun or shade. Plant in spring, using any soil-based or soil-less compost. The ground ivy is often treated as an annual but it can be salvaged from summer displays, cut back and used the following year.
See illustrations pages 105, 115.

IVY

Hedera
EVERGREEN CLIMBER   ZONE 5
Several large-leaved, variegated ivies make impressive climbers, climbing to 4.5m (15ft) or more. They also look attractive trailing from a large container. One of the most widely grown is *H. canariensis* 'Gloire de Marengo' (Zone 9). Its handsome green leaves, usually unlobed, have grey mottling and a creamy white edge.

Although the white-variegated cultivars of common ivy (*H. helix*) are numerous, few match the cool beauty of 'Glacier', with three- or five-lobed leaves edged with creamy white and overlaid with patches of grey-green and silver-grey. Other good selections include 'Caecilia', with frilly, three-lobed leaves that are green and creamy white; 'Kolibri', which has small green leaves boldly splashed and speckled with white; and 'Little Diamond', bushy, with silvery leaves.
See also pages 180–81, 184.

HEUCHERA

Heuchera 'Snow Storm'
EVERGREEN PERENNIAL   ZONE 4
The fresh delicacy of *H.* 'Snow Storm' (*below*) creates a beautiful lightness among plants that enjoy dappled shade. Forming a clump with a height and

Ornamental cabbage *Brassica oleracea*

Heuchera *Heuchera* 'Snow Storm'

spread of 30cm (12in), it is composed of overlapping, heart-shaped leaves that have a scalloped, ruffled edge. While their base colour is ivory, the edges are green, as is the speckling, which varies in intensity from leaf to leaf. The leaf veins turn deep pink in winter. Red flower sprays appear in early summer.
*See also page **189-90**.*

Hosta *Hosta fortunei* 'Francee'

HOSTA
Hosta
PERENNIAL   ZONE 3
The crisp combination of white and green is found in a number of variegated hostas. A classic in this group is *H. undulata* var. *albomarginata* (*H.* 'Thomas Hogg'). This makes a clump 60cm (2ft) high of deeply veined, green leaves with a wavy white edge tapering to a fine point. Another good choice for containers is *H. fortunei* 'Francee', with its clump, 60cm (2ft) high, of large, rich green leaves edged in white (*above*). Both these hostas have mauve flowers in summer. In 'Sugar and Cream', the edge to the wavy leaves has a warmer tone. This hosta stands 60cm (2ft) high and bears fragrant white flowers in summer.
*See also pages **184**, 193; illustration page 23.*

HOLLY, COMMON HOLLY
Ilex aquifolium 'Argentea Marginata'
EVERGREEN SHRUB OR TREE   ZONE 7
Many hollies are grown simply for the beauty of their glossy, usually prickly and often variegated foliage. Male and female flowers normally bloom on separate bushes, and female plants produce berries only if there is a male plant nearby. One of the loveliest of the hollies is the white-variegated 'Argentea Marginata'. The white edge combined with the lustrous foliage creates a silvered effect that is beautiful in sun or shade. Mature plants can bear good crops of berries. When grown as container specimens, many hollies – even though slow growing – may need shaping to keep them to a height of 1.5–2.5m (5–8ft).

Plant hollies in mid- to late spring, using a soil-based compost. Clip topiary specimens in mid-summer. Top-dress with fresh potting compost annually in spring; repot only when the roots are congested.

DEAD-NETTLE
Lamium maculatum
SEMI-EVERGREEN PERENNIAL   ZONE 4
The adventurous habits of the dead-nettles have made them valued ground-cover plants, but they are also useful as trailing fillers in containers.

The foliage of 'Beacon Silver' has a metallic white, mauve-tinged variegation. This cultivar carries heads of small mauve flowers.
*See also page **185**.*

PELARGONIUM, GERANIUM
Pelargonium
EVERGREEN PERENNIAL   ZONE 9
Among the several handsome pelargoniums with white or cream variegation, 'Lady Plymouth' is an understated aristocrat. Elegantly cut, grey-green leaves that are sweetly aromatic have an irregular creamy margin. The lemon-scented *P. crispum* 'Variegatum' is more assertive, with upright stems carrying tightly crinkled leaves edged with cream. 'Atomic Snowflake' has rose-scented leaves of velvety, pale green edged with cream.
*See also pages 135, 147–8, **153–4**, 163, 170, 181, 190, 194; illustration page 104.*

GARDENER'S GARTERS
Phalaris arundinacea var. *picta*
EVERGREEN PERENNIAL   ZONE 4
This notoriously invasive grass is highly ornamental, with a cream and bright green variegation that runs the length of the narrow leaf blades. The flower panicles are a subsidiary feature but add to the plant's overall appeal. In a densely planted container, the spreading tendencies are to some extent controlled, and the grass is a useful foil for more showy plants. It also looks distinctive planted on its own. Plant in spring, in soil-based compost. When dismantling plantings in autumn, retain vigorous clumps of the grass for planting the following spring.
See illustration page 113.

PLECTRANTHUS
Plectranthus madagascariensis 'Variegated Mintleaf'
EVERGREEN PERENNIAL   ZONE 9
The variegated foliage of this tender perennial is useful for summer displays in the container garden and it does well in partial shade. Bushy plants are covered in scalloped leaves with an irregular white edge. White and purple flowers sometimes appear in summer. 'Variegated Mintleaf' (*below*) is a scented-leaved cultivar.

Plant in late spring, using soil-based or soil-less compost. Pinch back young shoots to encourage bushy growth. Keep well watered and feed with a liquid fertilizer every two weeks, starting three to four weeks after planting. Rooted cuttings can be overwintered.
See also illustrations pages 101, 110.

Plectranthus *Plectranthus madagascariensis* 'Variegated Mintleaf'

BAMBOO
Pleioblastus variegatus
EVERGREEN SHRUB   ZONE 5
Whether grown in sun or shade, this dwarf bamboo makes dense clumps, up to 90cm (3ft) high and 45cm (18in) across, of variegated leaves. Some leaves are almost entirely dark green, others nearly white, others more balanced.
*See also page **185**.*

RED, PURPLE AND BRONZE FOLIAGE

Red foliage tints are usually associated with seasonal change, either the time when the leaves unfurl in spring or the brief period in autumn before the leaves drop. Those plants that retain the red, bronze or purple colouring of their foliage for weeks or months provide an unusual feature and make a useful contrast to other foliage in a container garden. They add depth to plantings, but need the companionship of lighter colours in foliage or flowers to relieve their sombre tendencies.

JAPANESE MAPLE

Acer palmatum
SHRUB   ZONE 5
The Japanese maple has produced a large number of cultivars with purplish, coppery or bronze foliage. One of the most richly coloured is 'Bloodgood', which can grow to 2.5m (8ft) or more. It is clothed in summer with tiers of elegant, five-lobed leaves of

rich purplish red, and in autumn the glowing red foliage is even more outstanding. The name *A. palmatum* Dissectum Atropurpureum Group covers several forms with finely divided leaves that are bronze-purple in summer turning to vivid red in autumn (*below*). These slowly form a mound about 90cm (3ft) high but spreading to 1.5m (5ft) or more.

The autumn tints of the maples must be taken into account when choosing plants for foliage colour. The seven-lobed leaves of the cultivar 'Osakazuki', a small tree under 10ft (3m) high, provide an exceptionally fiery display. *See also pages 178, 183; illustrations pages 46–7.*

BUGLE

Ajuga reptans
EVERGREEN PERENNIAL   ZONE 4
Bugle, suitable as an underplanting to shrubs, makes low rosettes of over-

Bugle *Ajuga reptans* 'Burgundy Glow'

wintering leaves and sends up 10–15cm (4–6in) spires of purplish-blue, tubular flowers in early summer. The purple foliage of *A. r.* 'Atropurpurea' has a metallic sheen; in 'Burgundy Glow' (*above*) the leaves are a mixture of wine-red, pink, bronze and cream.

Plant in autumn or spring, using a soil-based compost. Divide and replant in spring.

BURNING BUSH, SUMMER CYPRESS

Bassia scoparia f. *tricophylla* 'Childsii'
HALF-HARDY ANNUAL
The narrow pointed leaves that cover this upright plant, often still listed under *Kochia*, give burning bush a superficial resemblance to a bushy cypress. In late summer and autumn, its pale green foliage turns a rich shade of red. An attractive plant to grow in individual pots as part of a formal scheme in a sunny spot, this plant grows up to 60cm (2ft) high.

To raise from seed, sow in warmth in early to mid-spring. Harden off before planting outdoors in late spring or early summer, using a soil-based compost.

REX BEGONIA

Begonia rex
EVERGREEN PERENNIAL   ZONE 9
Many of the highly ornamental perennials derived from *B. rex* are popular indoor plants that can also be used outdoors in summer, either on their own or combined with other

Japanese maple *Acer palmatum* Dissectum Atropurpureum Group

Rex begonia *Begonia rex*

plants. Although the hairy leaves are varied in shape and markings, many have patterns of red, bronze or silver on shades of green (*above*). The pale pink flowers are less important than the decorative foliage.

Plant up in mid-spring, using a soil-based or soil-less compost, and move outdoors in late spring or early summer. Apply liquid fertilizer every two weeks.

BERGENIA
Bergenia
EVERGREEN PERENNIAL   ZONE 4

The bergenias are impressive foliage plants throughout the year and their sprays of pink or white flowers are an additional attraction in spring. Among the most appealing bergenias are those with foliage that turns rich shades of purple and red in winter. *B. cordifolia* 'Purpurea' has rounded leaves up to 75cm (30in) high that colour richly as cold intensifies. The flowers in spring are magenta. *B. purpurascens* makes a clump of narrow leaves about 45cm (18in) high, which in winter change from dark green to deep plum-red with a vivid carmine underside. The pink flowers are borne on reddish stems. 'Abendglut' ('Evening Glow') is one of numerous hybrids that colour well. Its oval, crinkled leaves form a low rosette, and in winter they are deep maroon with a brighter reverse. It grows to 30cm (12in) and has semi-double bright pink flowers in spring.
See also page 179.

ORNAMENTAL CABBAGE
Brassica oleracea Capitata Group
ANNUAL

The most vivid of the ornamental cabbages are those in which the rosettes are wholly or partly red, or purple-red. Whether grown on their own or as a contrast to those with creamy variegation, they are among the most colourful foliage plants for winter container displays.
See also page 186; illustrations pages 95, 103.

CANNA LILY
Canna
PERENNIAL   ZONE 7

Many hybrids of these handsome perennials have been raised, and in temperate regions they are grown mainly for their luxuriant foliage, which comprises paddle-like green or purple leaves (*below*). Where the climate is mild, they also carry showy flowers. Plants grow to 1.2m (4ft) high, or even taller. 'Roi Humbert' has bronze-red leaves and scarlet flowers, 'Wyoming' purple leaves and apricot-orange flowers. Like all cannas, they should be grown in a sunny, sheltered spot.

Start the rhizomes into growth in warmth during late winter or early spring, using a rich, soil-based compost to which leaf mould or other humus has been added. Transfer the growing plants into their final pots or tubs in mid-spring, but do not move these into the open until late

spring. Water generously during the growing season and feed with a liquid fertilizer every two weeks, starting two to three weeks after moving plants outdoors. Lift plants before there is any risk of frost. During winter keep the rhizomes slightly moist and store them in frost-free conditions.
See illustrations pages 21, 111.

CORDYLINE, CABBAGE TREE
Cordyline australis Purpurea Group
EVERGREEN TREE   ZONE 9

The purple-leaved forms of cordyline add the interest of rich colouring to the jagged spiky shape of the plain-leaved form. Specimens used in containers are usually no more than 90–120cm (3–4ft) high, although these slow-growing plants can eventually develop into trees that produce large sprays of white flowers.
See also page 179–80; illustration page 111.

HEUCHERA
Heuchera micrantha var. *diversifolia* 'Palace Purple'
EVERGREEN PERENNIAL   ZONE 4

This striking heuchera (*below*) is one of the most useful perennials for container planting in sun or shade. A clump of its deep purple or coppery leaves, broadly heart-shaped but boldly cut, makes an excellent background or contrast to more diffident plants. Specimens can have a height and spread of 45cm (18in), and their sprays of tiny white flowers

Purple-leaved canna lily *Canna* hybrid

Heuchera *Heuchera micrantha* var. *diversifolia* 'Palace Purple'

float gracefully above the leaves in early summer.

Plant in autumn or early to mid-spring, using soil-based or soil-less compost. Lift and divide the plants at least every other year and in between top-dress generously in spring. *See also pages 186–7; illustrations pages 16, 106–7, 121.*

Houttuynia *Houttuynia cordata* 'Chameleon'

HOUTTUYNIA

Houttuynia cordata 'Chameleon'
PERENNIAL   ZONE 6

The variegation displayed in *H. c.* 'Chameleon' (*above*) is so vivid that this perennial is best planted on its own. The green, heart-shaped leaves are splashed with intense red, bronze and yellow, making them far more eye-catching than the creamy flowers. Plants are 30cm (12in) high but spread to 45cm (18in) or more, and look best spilling over the rim of a container placed in sun or partial shade.

Plant in early to mid-spring, using a soil-based compost. Keep plants well watered during the growing season and feed with a liquid fertilizer every two weeks, starting three or four weeks after planting. Repot annually in early to mid-spring.

SACRED BAMBOO

Nandina domestica
EVERGREEN SHRUB   ZONE 7

This shrub – not a true bamboo – produces a clump of unbranched stems

to a height of 1.2–1.8m (4–6ft), well clothed with compound leaves. These are green in summer, tinged red in spring, but at their most beautiful in autumn, when they turn shades of reddish purple. White flowers in mid-summer are sometimes followed by red fruit, which lasts into winter. The sacred bamboo must have a sunny spot and shelter from cold winds.

Plant in early to mid-spring, using soil-based compost to which leaf mould or other humus has been added. Water generously during the growing season. Cut out old or weak growths after flowering, but repot only when the roots are congested. Top-dress annually in spring.

BLACK LILY TURF

Ophiopogon planiscapus 'Nigrescens'
EVERGREEN PERENNIAL   ZONE 6

The black lily turf (*below*) is one of the most distinctive of all foliage plants and makes a striking contrast to snowdrops and to grey and gold foliage. It does well in sun or partial shade.

Grassy tufts of arching leaves betray only a hint of green at the base of the clump, which is 20cm (8in) high and slowly spreads to 30cm (12in) or more. Short sprays of mauve flowers in summer are followed by black berries.

Plant in autumn or early to mid-spring, using soil-based compost to which leaf mould or other humus has been added. Top-dress with fresh mix annually in spring.

Black lily turf *Ophiopogon planiscapus* 'Nigrescens'

PELARGONIUM, GERANIUM

Pelargonium
EVERGREEN PERENNIAL   ZONE 9

Markings in shades of red and bronze add distinction to the leaves of many pelargoniums, in particular the Zonals. 'Mrs Quilter' is a good example of those with bronze foliage; above its leaves stand heads of single pink flowers. More sensational is the creamy-margined leaf of 'Dolly Varden', with its prominent red zone that merges with sage-green. The single flowers are red. Both Zonals grow to a height of about 45cm (18in).

One of the most striking of the scented-leaved pelargoniums is 'Chocolate Peppermint'. Its large three-lobed leaves have a conspicuous red-brown mark down the centre and release a powerful peppermint scent when bruised. Plants often exceed 50cm (20in) in height. *See also pages 135, 147–8, 153–4, 163, 170, 181–2, 184, 187, 194.*

PHORMIUM, NEW ZEALAND FLAX

Phormium tenax
EVERGREEN PERENNIAL   ZONE 9

Phormium is a stiffly upright plant with sword-like leaves, which is best grown in full sun. The largest of the purple-leaved cultivars can reach to more than 2.5m (8ft). More suitable for containers are several compact selections: the fan of reddish-purple leaves produced by 'Bronze Baby', for example, rarely exceeds 60cm (2ft) in height. 'Sundowner', about 90cm (3ft) high, has purple-pewter leaves with creamy margins. Both of these cultivars sometimes produce woody stems that carry dull red flowers.

Plant in spring using a soil-based compost. Top-dress or repot in autumn. *See also page 185; illustrations pages 12, 121.*

PIERIS

Pieris formosa var. *forrestii* 'Wakehurst'
EVERGREEN SHRUB   ZONE 8

The genus *Pieris* provides a number of pleasing evergreen shrubs, most of which produce attractive, lily-of-the-valley-like flowers from mid- to late spring. The young growths of some are also spectacularly coloured: one of the finest is *P. f.* var. *forrestii* 'Wakehurst', with its long-lasting red foliage, which shows off the sprays of white flowers. When growing in a container it is usually 1.8–2.5m (6–8ft) high. Several more compact hybrids, including 'Forest Flame', are similarly ornamental. Because the young foliage of all of these shrubs is vulnerable to frost damage, give plants light overhead protection when there is a risk of frost.

Plant in mid-autumn or early to mid-spring, using an ericaceous compost to which leaf mould or other humus has been added. Keep well watered during spring and summer. Little pruning is needed, but faded flowers and any weak growths should be removed. Repot only if the roots are congested. Top-dress generously in spring.

SAGE
Salvia officinalis
EVERGREEN SUB-SHRUB   ZONE 7
Sage is useful as an ornamental plant as well as being a valuable culinary herb. The purple sage (*S. o.* 'Purpurascens') is especially lovely, making a spreading bush up to 60cm (2ft) high, densely covered with greyish-purple leaves. *S.o.* 'Tricolor' (Zone 8), which has leaves that are variegated purple, pink and white, is less vigorous. All sages are best in a sunny, sheltered spot.
*See also page **197**.*

SEDUM
Sedum spathulifolium 'Purpureum'
EVERGREEN PERENNIAL   ZONE 5
The heads of yellow flowers that appear in late spring or early summer are but a short-lived attraction of this

Sedum *Sedum spathulifolium* 'Purpureum'

sedum (*below*); what sustains interest are the tight rosettes of waxy purplish leaves. *S. s.* 'Purpureum' is normally under 10cm (4in) in height but can have a spread of 25cm (10in) or more. It often spills out of troughs and sinks, where it looks good planted with other sun-loving rock-garden plants.

Plant in mid-autumn or early to mid-spring, using gritty soil-based compost. *See also page 195.*

Houseleek *Sempervivum*

HOUSELEEK
Sempervivum
EVERGREEN SUCCULENT   ZONE 5
Houseleeks bear fleshy leaves arranged in neat rosettes, often with a beautiful waxen texture and in rich shades of mahogany, bronze and red (*above*). They produce offsets freely – a single plant in a pot can create a tightly patterned colony of new plants over the whole surface. Houseleeks, which need full sun, combine successfully with small rock-garden plants in sinks and troughs.

Although the contrast of grey-green leaves and mahogany tips on the 8cm (3in) rosettes is attractive in the common houseleek (*S. tectorum*), many cultivars display even more striking colours: 'Commander Hay', for example, has rosettes 15cm (6in) or more across that are purplish red with green leaf tips. Most send up stems carrying sprays of star-like flowers in summer.

Plant between autumn and mid-spring, using a gritty soil-based compost. Repot every two to three years, or earlier if rosettes are congested, and top-dress with fresh mix in the intervening years.
See also page 195.

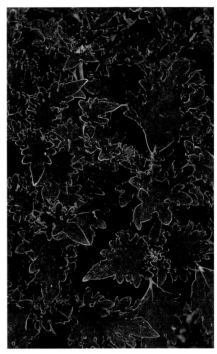

Cut-leaved coleus *Solenostemon*

COLEUS
Solenostemon
ANNUAL
The vivid foliage colouring of coleus (*above*) makes it a popular greenhouse plant, but it can also be used for summer planting outdoors. It is best grown in a well-lit but lightly shaded spot, because fierce sunlight can cause scorching. The nettle-like leaves, sometimes elaborately cut, are patterned in an astonishing variety, with mixtures of green, red, bronze, purple, yellow and white. Although coleus can be raised from overwintered cuttings, it is more frequently treated as a tender annual. Seed strains, including Wizard Mixed, give a mixture of compact, free-branching plants 30cm (12in) high. 'Scarlet Poncho' has glowing red leaves outlined in purple and pale yellow. This lax plant, about 30cm (12in) in height and spread, is a good choice for a hanging basket.

To raise from seed, sow in warmth during mid-winter in order to allow plants of good size to develop. The standard practice of pinching back growing tips to produce bushy plants is less important with compact selections. Repot as necessary before moving outdoors in late spring or early summer. Use either soil-based or soil-less potting compost and feed with liquid fertilizer every ten days. Remove flower spikes.
See illustration page 106.

GREY, SILVER AND BLUE FOLIAGE

Foliage in this colour range is especially valuable in the container garden, where light colours help to ease the congestion of flowers crowded together for maximum effect. The silvers and greys, in particular, will calm potential colour clashes and provide a sympathetic background to soft colours. Most foliage plants in grey, silver or blue are best in full sun and many need free drainage.

ARTEMISIA, WORMWOOD
Artemisia
EVERGREEN SHRUB/PERENNIAL
ZONE 5

The artemisias include some of the loveliest plants with silvery foliage. One that adapts well to life in containers is the sprawling evergreen perennial *A. stelleriana* (Zone 3). This is an excellent edging plant in full sun, making a spreading clump up to 20cm (8in) high built up of beautifully cut, white-felted leaves (*below*). More suitable for a sunny trough of rock-garden plants is the shrublet *A. schmidtiana* 'Nana'. It makes a low silvery dome, only 8cm (3in) high but up to 20cm (8in) wide, of soft, ferny leaves.

Some of the taller aromatic artemisias that are such valuable border plants in warm, sunny gardens are rather tender and in containers are best incorporated in summer plantings that thrive in full sun. Outstanding for its lacy and silvered foliage is the evergreen shrub *A. arborescens* (Zone 8), which grows to 90cm (3ft). This species is probably a parent of 'Powis Castle' (Zone 6), which makes a dense, silvery mound 60cm (2ft) high. The evergreen perennial *A. absinthium* 'Lambrook Silver' also has silver, much-divided foliage on plants up to 60cm (2ft) high.

Plant *A. stelleriana* and *A. schmidtiana* in early to mid-spring and well-grown specimens of the taller artemisias in mid- to late spring. Use a gritty, soil-based compost for all and top-dress with fresh compost in spring. Where the taller artemisias are unlikely to survive outdoors in winter, overwinter rooted cuttings under glass.
See illustration page 119.

BRACHYGLOTTIS
Brachyglottis 'Sunshine'
EVERGREEN SHRUB   ZONE 9

Masses of yellow daisy flowers make *B.* 'Sunshine' (syn. *Senecio* 'Sunshine') a conspicuous shrub in early summer, but its enduring appeal lies in the grey-green foliage and the felted whiteness of the underside of leaves, stems and the unopened flower buds (*below*). This sprawling shrub, which is 90–120cm

(3–4ft) high but often spreads more than 1.8m (6ft), needs full sun and is particularly useful in coastal gardens.

Plant in autumn or mid-spring, using soil-based potting compost. Repot only when roots become congested, but top-dress with fresh compost annually in mid-spring. Removed faded flowers and any weak and straggly growths in mid-summer.

CYPRESS
Chamaecyparis
EVERGREEN CONIFER   ZONE 5

The Lawson cypress (*C. lawsoniana*) has provided many dwarf or medium-sized cultivars in a wide range of foliage colour, including grey-green and grey-blue. A cultivar that slowly forms a dense column up to 1.8m (6ft) high is 'Ellwoodii'. Its feathery sprays of juvenile foliage are grey-green in summer but turn a metallic blue colour in winter.

The sawara cypress (*C. pisifera*) also has many dwarf and slow-growing cultivars. 'Boulevard' has soft juvenile foliage that is steel-blue in summer but takes on a purplish tinge in winter. It makes a broad-based cone that slowly attains a height of 3m (10ft) or more.

Both of these conifers can be grown in full sun or light shade, the foliage of 'Boulevard' being brightest when it gets some shade.

Plant in early to mid-autumn or mid-spring, using soil-based compost. Repot only when roots become congested but top-dress annually with fresh compost in mid-spring.

OLEASTER
Elaeagnus angustifolia
DECIDUOUS SHRUB   ZONES 3–8

The oleaster makes a spreading, loose shrub or small tree notable for the silveriness of its willow-like leaves and the honeyed fragrance of tiny flowers in late spring or early summer. The yellowish oval fruits that follow are edible. Its hybrid 'Quicksilver' is exceptional for the bleached grey of its foliage (*above right*).

In containers the oleaster is best grown on a single stem with the head lightly shaped, and specimens maintained at an overall height of 1.8–2.5m (6–8ft). Position in full sun.

Artemisia *Artemisia stelleriana*

Brachyglottis *Brachyglottis* 'Sunshine'

Oleaster *Elaeagnus* 'Quicksilver'

Plant oleaster in autumn or early to mid-spring, using a slightly gritty, soil-based compost. Insert a cane at planting time and tie shoots in. Trim plants in early to mid-summer, after flowering.

BLUE FESCUE

Festuca glauca
EVERGREEN GRASS   ZONE 4

The blue fescue, a perennial grass, makes short tufts 20cm (8in) high of fine leaves that are grey to grey-blue. The flower spikelets in summer are purplish. This fescue, which needs full sun, makes an attractive contrast in a trough of sprawling rock-garden plants.

Plant in autumn or early to mid-spring, using gritty, soil-based compost. Divide large plants in autumn.

CURRY PLANT

Helichrysum italicum
EVERGREEN SHRUB   ZONES 7–9

The powerfully aromatic foliage of several helichrysums have earned them the common name 'curry plant'. A large container of sun-loving plants could include *H. italicum*, which has needle-like silvery leaves and in summer clusters of yellow button flowers on stems that grow up to 60cm (2ft) high. *H. i.* subsp. *microphyllum*, a short, stiff plant under 8in (20cm) in height, is more suitable for a trough of rock-garden plants.

Plant in early autumn or mid- to late spring, using gritty, soil-based potting compost. Cut back in mid- to late spring to promote dense new growth. Lift and replant in fresh compost every two to three years, and in other years apply a light topdressing of fresh compost in mid-spring.
See illustration page 100.

HELICHRYSUM

Helichrysum petiolare
EVERGREEN SHRUB   ZONE 9

H. petiolare (sometimes listed as *H. petiolatum*) is a tender shrubby perennial, but because it is fast growing, producing numerous trailing stems 60–90cm (2–3ft) long in a season, it is usually treated as an annual. Few foliage plants can touch this helichrysum as a moderator between strong colours, as an intensifier of pastel shades and as a light-coloured filler that works its way elegantly through other plants. It sometimes bears straw-coloured flowers in summer which fit in with its subdued colouring. 'Variegatum' is similar with cream variegation.

Plant in late spring or early summer, using soil-based or soil-less compost. Keep well watered and apply liquid fertilizer every fortnight, beginning two to three weeks after planting. Rooted cuttings can be overwintered under glass.
See also page 184; illustrations pages 12, 39, 97, 101, 104, 108, 113, 115, 116, 127.

HOSTA

Hosta
PERENNIAL   ZONE 3

The most distinguished of all the hostas have foliage in the grey to blue range, and the largest of these make outstandingly impressive container plants when well grown.

'Krossa Regal' is one of the largest hostas, the clumps of foliage sometimes exceeding 1.2m (4ft) and topped in late summer by spikes of mauve flowers. The glaucous leaves are long stemmed and pointed. 'Snowden' also has pointed leaves that make a large grey-green mound but its flowers are white with a tinge of lilac. *H. fortunei* var. *hyacinthina* is shorter but one of the best hostas in the grey-green range, the leaves having a distinctive fine glaucous rim. It makes a clump up to 75cm (30in) high and provides a good display of mauve flowers.

In the blue-grey range *H. sieboldiana* var. *elegans* holds its place as a plant of rare distinction. The huge rounded leaves, up to 30cm (1ft) long and more than that wide, are deeply veined and wrinkled, which adds depth to the glaucous colouring. There are mauve-white flowers over a clump that stands 75cm (30in) high. 'Halcyon' (*below*) is another good blue, showing its colour best in shade. It grows to 45cm (18in) and has attractive mauve flowers.
*See also pages **184**, **187**; illustrations pages 15, 18.*

Hosta *Hosta* 'Halcyon'

JUNIPER
Juniperus
EVERGREEN CONIFER   ZONE 4
There are numerous dwarf forms of *J. communis* (Zone 3). One of the most popular is 'Compressa', which forms a narrow column up to 60cm (2ft) high of grey-green foliage with hints of blue. It is like a miniature version of the Irish juniper (*J. c.* 'Hibernica'), which is also suitable for containers but is a more uniform grey-blue and slowly attains a height of 3m (10ft).

Blue tints are found in many other junipers. 'Blaue Donau' ('Blue Danube') is a shrubby cultivar up to 1.8m (6ft) high of *J. sabina* (Zone 4). It has grey-blue, scale-like leaves on branches that can spread more than 2.5m (8ft). The range of blues is particularly remarkable in the flaky juniper (*J. squamata,* Zone 5). 'Blue Star', for example, is a compact plant up to 50cm (20in) tall and 60cm (2ft) across that has foliage of an intense steel-blue. *See also page 181.*

HONEYBUSH
Melianthus major
EVERGREEN SHRUB   ZONE 9
Although the melianthus (*below*) is rather tender, it is worth taking the trouble to grow, because it is a foliage plant of great beauty. If necessary, it can be overwintered under glass or plunged in the garden. In the open garden established plants can reach 2.5m (8ft) or more, but in containers they do not usually exceed 1.2m (4ft). There may be maroon flower spikes in late summer, but they are much less important ornamentally than the large, grey-green leaves, which are deeply divided and notched with a jagged edge.

Plant in mid- to late spring, using a soil-based potting compost. Plants that have been cut down by frost will often shoot again from the base. In mid-spring remove dead and damaged foliage and add a topdressing of fresh compost. *See illustration page 13.*

PELARGONIUM, GERANIUM
Pelargonium
EVERGREEN PERENNIAL   ZONE 9
Several of the scented-leaved pelargoniums have attractive grey-green foliage that adds to their appeal, and makes them extremely useful in summer planting schemes, where they will act as a foil to flowering plants with indifferent foliage.

The jagged three-lobed leaves of 'Grey Lady Plymouth' are a subdued grey-green and when bruised smell of roses. This handsome scented-leaved pelargonium, which grows to about 45cm (18in), has small pink flowers with purple veining. The Fragrans Group covers a range of compact, scented-leaved pelargoniums with elegant grey-green foliage that is nutmeg scented. Their small flowers are white.
*See also pages 135, 147–8, **153–4**, 163, 170, 181–2, 187, 190.*

PLECOSTACHYS
Plecostachys serpyllifolia
ANNUAL/EVERGREEN PERENNIAL   ZONE 9
This silvery foliage plant, often listed as *Helichrysum microphyllum*, looks much like a small-leaved version of *H. petiolare* and is also usually grown as an annual. The lax stems, which are 60–75cm (24–30in) long and closely covered with tiny leaves, are seen to good effect trailing from summer plantings in hanging baskets.

Plant in late spring or early summer, using soil-based or soil-less compost. Keep well watered and feed with a

Honeybush *Melianthus major*

liquid fertilizer every two weeks, starting two to three weeks after planting. Overwinter rooted cuttings under glass.
See illustrations pages 10, 112.

RAOULIA
Raoulia australis
EVERGREEN PERENNIAL   ZONE 8
While the tiny sulphur-yellow spring flowers of raoulia are easily overlooked, its grey-green leaves make a useful small ground-hugging mat that will fit neatly into the corner of a trough planted as a miniature rock garden. This species, which needs a position in full sun, is under 2.5cm (1in) in height but can have a spread of 25cm (10in) or more.

Plant in mid-spring, using gritty, soil-based compost.

WILLOW
Salix 'Boydii'
DECIDUOUS SHRUB   ZONE 8
The gnarled stems of this dwarf, slow-growing willow, in height and spread rarely exceeding 30cm (12in), help to give a trough of rock-garden plants an established look. The catkins are not conspicuous but the rounded and prominently veined leaves are downy and silver-grey.

Plant in autumn or early to mid-spring, using a gritty, soil-based compost. Top-dress with fresh compost in spring in alternate years.

COTTON LAVENDER
Santolina
EVERGREEN SHRUB   ZONE 8
Cotton lavender (*S. chamaecyparissus*, also listed as *S. incana*) makes a rounded bush with a height and spread of up to 60cm (2ft). It is densely clothed with soft feathery leaves, aromatic to the touch, which are silvery grey (*above right*). In mid-summer it is covered with yellow button flowers; in some colour schemes it is preferable to trim these off. The dwarf form *S. c.* var. *nana*, with even whiter foliage, is only 15cm (6in) high. Another cotton lavender, *S. pinnata* subsp. *neapolitana*, has nearly white foliage that is delicately feathered and makes a loose bush up to 30in (75cm) high, covered in mid-summer with lemon-yellow flowers. The dwarf cotton lavender can be used in window boxes or in troughs containing sun-loving rock-garden plants. The taller

Cotton lavender *Santolina chamaecyparissus*

cotton lavenders are best combined with other sun-loving plants in large pots or other containers.

Plant in autumn or early to mid-spring, using gritty, soil-based potting compost. Cut back hard in mid-spring to promote vigorous new growth and trim either before or immediately after flowering.

SEDUM
Sedum spathulifolium 'Cape Blanco'
EVERGREEN PERENNIAL   ZONE 5
This is similar in many respects to other forms of *S. spathulifolium*, a succulent evergreen that makes a mat of tight leaf rosettes, normally under 10cm (4in) in height and with a spread of 25cm (10in), topped in late spring or early summer by heads of yellow flowers. What distinguishes it is the silvery green of its waxy foliage.
*See also page **191**.*

COBWEB HOUSELEEK
Sempervivum arachnoideum subsp. *tomentosum*
EVERGREEN SUCCULENT   ZONE 5
This houseleek makes rosettes of red-tipped, fleshy leaves that are covered by a curious criss-cross webbing of white hairs, which give the plant a silvered look (*right*). In summer stems 15cm (6in) high bear deep pink flowers. Plants often have a spread of more than 15cm (6in), with the parent rosette spawning a ring of smaller rosettes.
*See also page **191**.*

SENECIO
Senecio
EVERGREEN SHRUB   ZONE 9
This popular component of summer bedding schemes, sometimes listed as *S. maritima* or *Cineraria maritima*, is also an adaptable foliage plant for container gardens. It is usually grown as a half-hardy annual, making a bushy plant about 30cm (12in) high in a season. There are several leaf forms, all felted and silvery grey, including the feathery 'Silver Dust' and 'White Diamond', with broader, less divided leaves. Another silvery senecio is the finely dissected *S. viravira* (also listed as *S. leucostachys*), an evergreen tender sub-shrub that can grow to more than 90cm (3ft) in a season.

To raise from seed, sow in warmth in late winter or early spring. Plant out in early summer. To achieve their most startling silvery whiteness, plants need full sun and gritty, free-draining potting compost. Rooted cuttings can be overwintered under glass.
See illustrations pages 8, 23, 100.

LAMB'S EARS, LAMB'S TONGUE
Stachys byzantina
EVERGREEN PERENNIAL   ZONE 4
The woolly grey leaves that have inspired this plant's common names make an attractive feature at the edge of a large container planted with other sun-loving plants. The species is sometimes listed as *S. lanata* or as *S. olympica*. The felted stems can grow to 45cm (18in), the flowers in the woolly spikes being pinkish mauve. 'Silver Carpet' is a more compact, non-flowering cultivar.

Plant in autumn or mid-spring, using a soil-based compost. Feed with liquid fertilizer two or three times during the summer. Divide plants every two years.

Cobweb houseleek *Sempervivum arachnoideum* subsp. *tomentosum*

195

HERBS

Herbs are among the most worthwhile plants to grow in the container garden. Many culinary herbs are compact and so easily accommodated in a small space. The fresh sprigs and richly aromatic leaves they supply over a long season can make memorable meals of the simplest dishes. In addition, many have extremely attractive foliage.

CHIVES
Allium schoenoprasum
PERENNIAL   ZONE 3
Chives form grassy clumps up to 25cm (10in) high of hollow leaves that can be cut throughout summer to give a mild onion flavour to salads and other dishes. The rounded heads of starry pink flowers are decorative (*below*) but, if plants are being grown specifically for leaf cutting, remove the flowers as soon as they develop. Grow a single clump, consisting of a cluster of three or four chive plants, in a pot or as part of a mixture of moisture-loving herbs in a window box or trough. Chives thrive in sun or partial shade.

Plant from early to mid-spring, using soil-based compost. Keep well watered and feed with liquid fertilizer every three weeks, starting three to four weeks after planting. Plants die down in winter, but those taken under cover during winter will provide leaves for cutting in spring. Lift and divide established clumps every two years.

BORAGE
Borago officinalis
ANNUAL
The nodding blue stars of borage make it one of the prettiest herbs in flower. It quickly grows to 90cm (3ft) high, its hollow stems carrying rough, hairy leaves. Because of their cucumber flavour, the young leaves – and also the sweet-tasting flowers – are sometimes added to fruit cups and salads.

Borage is easily grown from seed in full sun in soil-based or soil-less potting compost. Sow where it is to grow in mid-spring and, for a lasting supply of young leaves, continue sowing until mid-summer, thinning seedlings to 25cm (10in) apart.

SWEET BAY
Laurus nobilis
EVERGREEN SHRUB   ZONE 8
The leathery aromatic leaves of the bay provide one of the indispensable flavourings of Mediterranean cooking, and the plant itself (*below*), grown in a tub or large pot, evokes a sunny terrace. It can reach 15ft (4.5m) or more but in containers is traditionally grown as a standard with a clear stem of 90–180cm (3–6ft) or shaped, either as a cone or as a drum. These simple geometric shapes are useful for formal arrangements of containers. The flowers are inconspicuous but on female plants are followed by dark berries.

Plant from early to mid-spring, using a soil-based potting compost. Top-dress annually in mid-spring with fresh compost, and repot only when the roots become congested. To create and maintain topiary shapes, cut back in early and late summer. Use secateurs to remove whole leaves.
See illustration page 13.

MINT
Mentha
PERENNIAL   ZONE 3
Most mints are invasive in the open garden so there are good practical reasons for growing them in containers, from where they can provide a supply of freshly piquant sprigs throughout the summer. Spearmint (*M. spicata*) has prominently veined, mid-green leaves on erect stems up to 60cm (2ft) high. Apple mint (*M. suaveolens*, also listed as *M. rotundifolia*) can grow to 90cm (3ft) and has hairy, pale green leaves, while its lovely cultivar *M. s.* 'Variegata' has irregular creamy markings to the leaves. Grow these mints in sun or light shade.

Plant in early to mid-spring, using either soil-based or soil-less compost. Keep well watered throughout the growing season and feed with liquid fertilizer every two weeks, starting three to four weeks after planting. Divide and repot annually or every second year in spring. Top-dress with fresh compost in spring in alternate years. To provide fresh sprigs for cutting in early spring, keep potted plants under cover during winter.

SWEET BASIL
Ocimum basilicum
HALF-HARDY ANNUAL
The deep, clove-like flavour of sweet basil has earned this annual a high reputation as a culinary herb. Growing to about 60cm (2ft) high, it has large bright green leaves or, in the cultivar 'Purple Ruffles', shiny dark leaves that are fringed and crinkled. French or bush basil (*O. basilicum* var. *minimum*) is less strongly flavoured, but its dwarf bushes, under 20cm (8in) high and packed with small, light green leaves, make pretty and useful pot plants. All basils need a warm, sheltered spot.

To raise from seed, sow in warmth in early spring. Harden off before

Chives *Allium schoenoprasum*

Sweet bay *Laurus nobilis*

planting outdoors in late spring or early summer, using soil-based or soil-less compost. Allow the compost to become nearly dry between waterings. Feed with a liquid fertilizer every two weeks, starting three weeks after planting. Plants usually resprout after being cut back hard and will last into autumn and winter if brought under cover. *See illustration page 102.*

MARJORAM
Origanum
PERENNIAL   ZONE 4

Several marjorams are grown as culinary herbs. Wild marjoram (*O. vulgare*), which grows up to 45cm (18in) high, has mid-green leaves of rather coarse flavour. The golden-leaved cultivar *O. v.* 'Aureum' is more widely grown. Sweet marjoram (*O. majorana*, Zone 9), a bushy plant up to 2ft (60cm), has red stems carrying soft grey-green leaves and in summer mauve, pink or white flowers. All these marjorams need a sunny, open spot.

Plant marjorams in mid-spring, using a soil-based compost. Feed with a liquid fertilizer every three weeks in summer, starting two to three weeks after planting. Trim plants to keep them compact and cut back hard in early to mid-spring. Top-dress with fresh compost in spring. To grow sweet marjoram as an annual, sow in warmth in early spring and plant outdoors after hardening off in late spring.

PARSLEY
Petroselinum crispum
ANNUAL/BIENNIAL

The attractive leaves of parsley are much used for flavouring and as a garnish, and the plant is easily grown in containers. There are two main types. Those with curled leaves make a dense mound of deeply divided and crested, bright green foliage (*above right*). Plain- or broad-leaved cultivars form clumps of much-divided flat leaves. Although less ornamental, they generally have a better flavour. The foliage of both types grows to about 45cm (18in). Remove flowers promptly so that the foliage remains useful.

To raise parsley from seed, sow in decomposable pots from early to mid-spring for summer supplies, and from early to mid-summer for supplies to last from autumn to the following spring. Transplant into a larger container in

Parsley *Petroselinum crispum*

late spring or late summer, using either a soil-based or a soil-less compost. Water regularly and feed with a liquid fertilizer every two weeks, starting two to three weeks after planting. In cold areas keep pots under cover in winter.

ROSEMARY
Rosmarinus officinalis
EVERGREEN SHRUB   ZONE 8

The sweetly aromatic foliage of rosemary releases its scent when lightly touched, so it is a pleasing shrub to have in a sunny spot near a path or a garden seat. Plants can be upright or sprawling, the stems, up to 90cm (3ft) high, closely covered with narrow, deep green leaves that are felted and grey on the underside. Pale blue flowers are carried between late winter and mid-spring. The erect 'Miss Jessopp's Upright' is attractive in pots, while the laxer plants in the Prostratus Group (Zone 9) have arching or trailing stems that will hang over the container edge.

Plant singly in early to mid-spring, using a soil-based compost. Top-dress annually with fresh compost in spring. Prune hard in mid-spring. In cold areas protect in winter.

RUE
Ruta graveolens 'Jackman's Blue'
EVERGREEN SUB-SHRUB   ZONE 5

Rue is a pungently aromatic bush with bitter-tasting leaves, and the cultivar most widely grown, 'Jackman's Blue', is generally cultivated for its ornamental foliage. It goes well with other herbs

that like sunny, well-drained conditions. Making a rounded bush with a height and spread of 60–90cm (2–3ft), it bears a dense cover of divided blue-green leaves and, in early to mid-summer, clusters of yellow-green flowers.

Plant from early to mid-spring, using a soil-based compost. Feed with weak liquid fertilizer two or three times during the summer. Top-dress with fresh compost annually in spring. Cut back hard in mid-spring.

SAGE
Salvia officinalis
EVERGREEN SHRUB   ZONE 6

The grey-green foliage of sage, forming a dense mound up to 60cm (2ft) high and as much across, provides a sympathetic accompaniment to other sun-loving herbs and many ornamentals. Its broad leaves are pungently aromatic and slightly rough to the touch. The purplish summer flowers must be removed to encourage leafy growth. The purple-leaved cultivars and also the compact 'Icterina' (Zone 7), with yellow-variegated, light green leaves, can all be used for culinary purposes in the same way as the common sage.

Plant in spring, using soil-based compost. Apply a liquid fertilizer four times in summer. Trim back and top-dress with fresh compost in mid-spring. Replace plants every three years. *See also page 191.*

THYME
Thymus
EVERGREEN SHRUB   ZONE 5

The deliciously aromatic foliage of the common thyme (*T. vulgaris*) has made it an indispensable culinary herb. It is a dwarf shrub up to 20cm (8in) high but spreading so that it makes a good edging plant. The wiry stems are densely clothed with narrow, dark green leaves, and in summer the plant is covered with short spikes of mauve flowers. Several other thymes with different flavours are available, including lemon thyme (*T. × citriodorus*), which grows to 30cm (12in). All thymes are suitable for planting with other sun-loving herbs and dwarf ornamentals or singly in pots.

Plant in autumn or from early to mid-spring, using soil-based compost. Top-dress with fresh compost in spring. Trim bushes in spring and summer and replace plants every three years. *See also page 185.*

FRUIT

A large number of trees, climbers and perennials that produce fruit can be grown in containers. These are often highly ornamental as well as producing usable crops, even though yields are less than those provided by plants in the open garden. In selecting plants for containers this factor and the level of management required must be taken into account. One advantage of growing fruit in containers – particularly relevant in cool-temperate regions – is that plants can be moved under cover during cold weather. Another is that the scale of container-grown plants makes them more easily netted to prevent bird damage.

ORANGES AND LEMONS
Citrus
EVERGREEN SHRUB   ZONE 9

There is a long tradition in Europe of growing oranges and lemons (*below*) in containers, plants being placed outdoors during the summer months but moved under glass in cold weather. Although some citrus fruits tolerate a light frost if it follows a period of steadily falling temperatures, a sharp drop in temperature or a long spell of

Lemon *Citrus limon*

freezing weather is likely to prove fatal. The hardiest of the citrus fruits are tangerines and mandarins. Lemons are more tender, with the exception of the hybrid 'Meyer'.

All these citrus fruits grow up to 1.2m (4ft) high and have lustrous dark green leaves. The main season for the small clusters of creamy white, exquisitely fragrant flowers is spring, but there is often sporadic flowering at other times. Citrus trees are self-fertile so that in the right conditions a single tree will bear fruit. However, oranges and lemons are often grown simply for their ornamental value, with little expectation of fruit reaching maturity. For fruit to ripen, flowering must be followed by a period of six months or more when temperatures do not fall below 13°C (55°F), and higher temperatures are needed for their flavour to develop fully. The fruits ripen slowly, sometimes taking more than 12 months, so it is usual to see fruit and blossom on trees at the same time. When citrus trees are moved outdoors they should be placed in an open, sheltered spot.

Plants can be grown from pips, but for reliable fruiting buy grafted specimens of named cultivars. Plant in a frost-free environment in late winter or early spring, using soil-based compost. Citrus trees dislike root disturbance, yet may need to be repotted annually in winter until they have reached the required size, after which they should be top-dressed in mid-spring, using fresh compost. Water regularly in summer, but in winter keep the compost just moist. Feed with a liquid fertilizer every two weeks from late spring to late summer. Prune young trees in early spring to encourage them to develop a balanced, compact shape.

FIG
Ficus carica
DECIDUOUS TREE   ZONE 7

In sub-tropical and warm temperate regions figs, which have deep green, attractively lobed leaves, can produce two or three crops annually. In a cool-temperate climate just two crops are carried in a year, although only one usually ripens. In areas with severe winters pot-grown specimens can be

moved under cover with the onset of cold weather.

Figs are well suited to growing in containers, the restriction of their roots encouraging plants to produce fruit rather than foliage. A single plant does not need to be cross-fertilized in order to bear fruit. Bushes can be restricted to a height of about 90cm (3ft) or plants can be grown as short standards with a clear stem to a height of 90–120cm (3–4ft). Cultivars such as 'Brown Turkey', 'Brunswick' and 'White Marseilles' – with red, yellow and almost transparent flesh, respectively – are grown on their own roots.

Plant singly in mid- to late autumn or early spring, using a soil-based compost, in a container about 30cm (12in) wide and deep. There is no need to repot each year; just remove 5–8cm (2–3in) of old compost and top-dress with fresh in mid-spring. Water regularly during spring and summer and apply a liquid fertilizer every two weeks from late spring to late summer.

STRAWBERRY
Fragaria
PERENNIAL   ZONE 3

The strawberry, the most widely grown of all the soft fruits, gives quick returns and does well in containers (*above right*). Special pots and tubs for strawberries are available: the most common are terracotta pots with holes in the walls, and wooden barrels with 5cm (2in) wide holes bored in the sides at regular intervals about 25cm (10in) apart.

There are three main types of strawberry: the ordinary, luscious, large-fruited strawberries, which crop only once, in early summer; the perpetual or remontant strawberries, which are similar but crop in a succession of irregular flushes throughout summer and into autumn; and the alpine strawberries, which bear small, rather dry fruit prolifically, also in flushes throughout summer. All types can be grown in containers, but the yields from perpetual strawberries are poor in the second year and they are not much grown in this way. All strawberries are prone to virus diseases and certified virus-free stock should always be obtained.

Plant strawberries in mid- to late

Strawberry *Fragaria vesca*

summer, using soil-based potting compost to which humus, such as well-rotted garden compost, has been added. Containers with holes in the sides should be planted up at the same time as they are filled with compost. Strawberries will crop the year after they are planted. Plants need regular watering during the growing season, although excess moisture in spring will encourage foliage at the expense of fruit. Avoid wetting the fruit, and water early in the day, because lingering dampness encourages the development of grey mould (*Botrytis*). With summer-fruiting strawberries, rotate the container once the fruit appears so that it ripens evenly. Feed with weak liquid fertilizer every two weeks in summer, starting when flowers appear. Give the plants a balanced general fertilizer in the spring of subsequent years. Remove any runners. Discard plants after two or three seasons of cropping and use fresh compost for another planting. *See illustration page 61.*

APPLE

Malus domestica

DECIDUOUS TREE   ZONE 3

The apple (*right*) is the most widely grown fruit in temperate gardens, the number of cultivars, including dessert and cooking kinds, running into many hundreds. Apples can make large trees but they are rarely grown on their own roots and the rootstock on which a cultivar is grafted will determine the eventual size. The availability of dwarfing rootstocks such as M.27

makes container-growing of apples feasible – these dwarf bushes having a stem height of a mere 45–60cm (18–24in). Place container-grown apple trees in an open, sheltered spot where frost does not linger. In frost-prone areas choose late-flowering cultivars.

Cross-pollination is necessary to get a good set of fruit, so a single apple tree is unlikely to crop well. Buy trees from an established nursery so that you can get advice on the flowering period and compatibility of different cultivars.

Buy two- or three-year-old trees that already have lateral branches; the formative pruning has been started and they will begin to bear fruit in a year or two. Soak the roots of bare-rooted trees thoroughly before planting. Plant between autumn and early spring, using a soil-based compost. Keep well watered during the growing season and feed with a liquid fertilizer high in potassium every two weeks until the fruits begin to ripen. On young trees allow only two or three fruits to develop. Prune in the dormant season, initially to consolidate the open-centred framework of permanent branches. Subsequent pruning is mainly confined to cutting back laterals, to encourage the development of fruiting buds. Repot every second year and in other years top-dress with fresh compost.

PEACH, NECTARINE

Prunus persica

DECIDUOUS TREE   ZONE 5

The peach, which has fruit with a soft downy skin, and the nectarine, a harder- but smooth-skinned sport of the peach, are widely grown in warm-temperate regions. Although quite hardy, in cool temperate areas peaches and nectarines often require protection in early spring so that the pink blossom avoids being damaged by frost. They

Apple *Malus domestica* 'Ribston Pippin'

also need a warm, sheltered spot for fruit to ripen. Provided the growing conditions are suitable, single trees will bear fruit.

Genetically compact peaches are available as short standards, usually 90–120cm (3–4ft) high, which are suitable for containers. They make a dense head about 60cm (2ft) across that needs no pruning, and they start fruiting young.

Plant trees in mid- to late autumn, using soil-based compost. Trees grown in containers about 45cm (18in) or more deep will not need repotting for several years, if the top 5–8cm (2–3in) of compost is replaced with fresh compost every spring. Water regularly in the growing season and feed with a weak liquid fertilizer every three to four weeks from late spring to late summer.

GRAPE

Vitis

CLIMBER   ZONE 6

The grapevine (*V. vinifera*) has a record of cultivation extending far back into antiquity and is today one of the most widely planted of all fruits. There are many white- and black-skinned cultivars, some of dessert quality, others more suitable for making wine, that can be container grown as vigorous and ornamental climbers, but they must be pruned regularly to ensure good crops of fruit in late summer or autumn.

There are numerous variations on the pruning of grapes, but all are based on the need for a permanent framework and the controlled production of fresh lateral shoots, on which the flowers and fruit are carried. One of the most convenient ways to grow a grapevine in a container is as a standard, with a main stem 90–150cm (3–5ft) high and a head of short spurs from which fresh laterals grow each year. A pot-grown plant can be placed in a sunny, sheltered spot in the garden and, if necessary, moved under cover in winter.

To grow a grapevine as a standard, cut back a year-old vine in autumn, train up a strong stem and in the following autumn cut it back at the desired height. In the subsequent year allow a head of shoots to develop. In late autumn begin annual pruning back to fruiting spurs. Top-dress with fresh compost in late winter. Keep well watered in the growing season and feed with a liquid fertilizer every two weeks.

199

VEGETABLES

A wide range of vegetables can be grown successfully in pots, window boxes and growing bags. The selection here includes crops such as courgettes and some salad vegetables that are easy to grow in containers and give a good yield even in a small space. There are also some slightly more demanding vegetables, such as peppers, that are decorative as well as useful.

SWISS CHARD
Beta vulgaris Cicla Group
BIENNIAL
This member of the beet family, bred for its leaves and not its roots, is a versatile crop with a long season. Its bold foliage also makes it attractive in the container garden. Plants grow to about 45cm (18in) and have white stems that are wavy at the edge. Even more eye-catching is the ruby chard, which has stems and ribs of scarlet and reddish-purple leaves.

Sow in mid-spring to harvest in summer and in areas with mild winters in mid- to late summer to harvest in winter and spring. Use soil-based compost. Water well and feed with weak liquid fertilizer every two weeks once plants are 13–15cm (5–6in) high. *See illustration page 94.*

PEPPER
Capsicum
ANNUAL
The glossy and colourful fruits of sweet peppers (*C. annuum* Grossum Group), which can be used in a wide range of cooked and salad dishes, are showy as they ripen, and they make attractive pot plants (*above right*). They grow to a height of 60–90cm (2–3ft). Thriving in heat, in areas with cool summers they are often grown as greenhouse plants, but they can be planted outdoors in sunny, sheltered spots. It is often best to plant them in their final container under glass and to move them outdoors only when temperatures rise.

Chilli peppers (*C. annuum* Longum Group and *C. frutescens*), like sweet peppers, can have fruit that at maturity is green, red or yellow. The most familiar are bright red chillis, which have an explosive flavour and are sometimes curiously tapered and

Sweet pepper *Capsicum annuum* Grossum Group

twisted. These plants, which will grow 45–60cm (18–24in) high, need warmer conditions than sweet peppers but can be grown in the same way.

Sow seed in warmth during mid-spring. Thin seedlings and pot up, using soil-based or soil-less compost, until plants are in containers 20–25cm (8–10in) deep. Harden off before moving containers outdoors in early summer. Keep well watered and move into light shade in very warm weather. Feed with a liquid fertilizer high in potassium (such as a tomato fertilizer) every two weeks once fruits begin to form.

COURGETTE, ZUCCHINI
Cucurbita pepo
HALF-HARDY ANNUAL
When harvested in their immature state, marrows and squashes are known as courgettes. Bush cultivars, bred to be picked at an early stage, are good container plants for sunny, sheltered spots, growing 60cm (2ft) high and with a spread of 90cm (3ft). They quickly produce heavy crops, and are best harvested when they are 10–15cm (4–6in) long. Even the large yellow flowers can be eaten, either raw in salads or fried in batter. Provided courgettes are harvested regularly, plants will crop over many weeks. As well as cylindrical courgettes with deep green skins there are also round forms

and skin colour includes bright yellow, as well as shades of grey and green.

Sow in warmth in mid-spring and plant out after hardening off in late spring, using soil-based or soil-less compost. Once there is little risk of frost, seed can be sown directly in a tub outdoors between mid- and late spring. Sow two seeds in the centre and, if two seedlings germinate, remove the weaker. Keep the compost moist at all times and feed with liquid fertilizer every 10 days from early summer.

ROCKET
Eruca sativa
HARDY ANNUAL
The nutty and peppery flavours of rocket leaves make it a delicious salad ingredient. It can be sown thickly and cut at the seedling stage, then allowed to regrow – an operation that can be repeated three or four times. Leaves can also be picked from fast-growing plants spaced about 15cm (6in) apart or interplanted among other crops in tubs and window boxes.

Make successional sowings in either soil-based or soil-less compost, in sun or light shade, from mid- to late spring and again from mid- to late summer. Keep well watered and feed with a weak liquid fertilizer every two weeks, starting two to three weeks after sowing.

LETTUCE
Lactuca sativa
HARDY/HALF-HARDY ANNUAL
The hearting types of lettuce include the Romaine, mainly large and upright with crisp leaves ('Little Gem' is a well-flavoured, small, Romaine lettuce) and flat 'cabbage-head' lettuces, including soft-textured butterheads and crispheads of the 'Iceberg' type. Leaf lettuces do not form a heart, and there is regrowth after individual leaves are picked or the head cut.

For containers the most suitable are small cultivars of the Romaine and cabbage-head types such as 'Tom Thumb' and various leaf lettuces, of which there are several with attractive foliage. The oak-leaved kinds have deeply cut leaves, often bronzed, and the 'Lollo' lettuces, red and green, have frizzy, tightly curled leaves. A mixture, often available as packeted seed, provides a range of leaves.

Sow indoors in mid-spring and, after hardening off, transplant into outdoor planters from late spring through to mid- or late summer, using soil-based or soil-less compost. Water regularly to ensure that plants grow quickly, and apply liquid fertilizer every two weeks.

TOMATO

Lycopersicon esculentum
HALF-HARDY ANNUAL

Tomatoes (*below*) can be grown successfully outdoors in containers, even in a cool-temperate climate, but they need a warm, sheltered spot. There is a large range to choose from, varying in size and form from the 'currant' tomatoes, with strings of tiny fruit, to the giant, fleshy American beefsteak and 'Marmande' tomatoes. Besides red, there are also cultivars with fruit that is yellow, orange, pink, white and striped orange and red. Tall-growing tomatoes can be more than 1.8m (6ft) high and must be trained to supports. Bush tomatoes, with a height and spread of about 45cm (18in), are generally hardier and less trouble to grow.

To raise tomatoes from seed, sow in warmth during early or mid-spring. After hardening off, move seedlings outdoors and transplant them into their final containers, which need to be at least 20cm (8in) deep, in late spring or early summer. Use soil-based or soil-

less compost and insert a cane or provide other support for tall-growing cultivars. Water regularly and feed with tomato fertilizer every 10 days once the fruit begins to swell. Tie in tall-growing cultivars and pinch back side shoots as they develop. Two to three weeks after mid-summer remove the growing tip at three leaves beyond the topmost truss. At the onset of cold weather pick any unripened fruit, which can then be ripened indoors.

French bean *Phaseolus vulgaris* 'Royalty'

BEAN

Phaseolus
ANNUAL

These elegant twining or bush perennials are not hardy and are almost invariably grown as annuals. In summer they carry pretty sprays of flowers, usually red but also pink and white. their ornamental qualities, combined with the good crops of succulent pods from mid-summer to autumn, make them a good choice for containers. Two main kinds are grown for eating. The climbing forms of the scarlet runner (*P. coccineus*) are best planted in a large tub with a wigwam of canes up to about 1.8m (6ft) high as support. Position the canes before sowing. Scarlet runners can also be kept low by pinching out the growing point at an early stage then regularly stopping laterals to maintain compact bushy plants. In addition to the climbing cultivars, there are true dwarf scarlet runners, which grow to about 45cm (18in). The French or dwarf bean (*P. vulgaris, above*) has many cultivars,

mostly bush forms but some climbing. The bush kinds grow 30–40cm (12–16in) high and will be weighed down by heavy crops unless stiffened by a few twiggy sticks.

Sow seed of scarlet runners under glass in mid-spring for planting out in early summer, or sow directly outdoors in the container in late spring, spacing the seeds about 23cm (9in) apart. French beans are best sown where they are to grow, and thinned to 5–8cm (2–3in) apart when the first true leaves appear. For both kinds, use soil-based potting compost to which humus, such as well-rotted garden compost, has been added. Place the container in a sunny, sheltered position.

Mist flowers and foliage regularly with a fine water spray, and feed with a weak liquid fertilizer every two weeks, starting when the first flowers are produced, but avoid excessive use of fertilizers, which will encourage foliage at the expense of flowers and beans. Harvest beans while they are still young and tender.

AUBERGINE, EGGPLANT

Solanum melongena
TENDER ANNUAL

Aubergines thrive in a Mediterranean-type climate, and this is reflected in the many delicious southern European dishes in which they are an important ingredient. In cool-temperate areas they are often raised under glass but can do well outdoors provided they are grown in a sunny, sheltered spot. The bushy plants are usually 60–90cm (2–3ft) high and are easily grown in containers, as are a few more compact cultivars. Fruits start ripening in mid-summer, the typical aubergine having a lustrous, deep purple skin, although some cultivars have white skins. Most have fruits that are 20–25cm (8–10in) long and about 8cm (3in) in diameter.

Sow seed in mid- to late winter in warmth. Pinch back the growing tip of young plants so that two leading shoots develop, and remove all side shoots. Harden off in late spring and plant in containers outdoors in early summer, using soil-based or soil-less compost. Keep well watered and feed with a liquid fertilizer (a proprietary tomato fertilizer is ideal) every two weeks, starting once fruits begin to form. Allow four to six fruits per plant and let them ripen before harvesting them.

Tomato *Lycopersicon esculentum*

All the plants listed here help to extend the interest of the container garden beyond the conventional flowering display. Berrying shrubs are particularly useful in providing touches of colour during autumn and winter. Although a number do well in shade, the best crops are usually produced when the shrubs are grown in a reasonably open spot and, in the case of those that bear male and female flowers on different plants, when male and female plants are grown close together. Grasses often provide a long-lasting display, the flowers and later the seed heads adding appealing texture rather than vivid colour.

SPOTTED LAUREL

Aucuba japonica
EVERGREEN SHRUB   ZONE 7
The plain-leaved and variegated spotted laurels are handsome and useful evergreens that tolerate a wide range of conditions. In containers they grow to about 1.8m (6ft). Their berrying capacity is often overlooked, partly because the sexes are on different plants, females berrying only when there is a male nearby. The small clusters of bright scarlet berries, which develop in autumn, attain their richest colour in spring. For good crops plants need to be grown in a reasonably sunny spot.

The variegated 'Crotonifolia' is female, as is 'Longifolia', with long, glossy green leaves. *See also page 183*.

GREATER QUAKING GRASS

Briza maxima
ANNUAL
In late spring and summer this tufted grass bears clusters of heart-shaped, purplish-green spikelets on slender arching stems. Beautiful when still, they move gracefully in the lightest breeze.

Sow seed where plants are to grow from early to mid-spring, using soil-based compost. Thin seedlings to 10–15cm (4–6in) apart.

COTONEASTER

Cotoneaster
DECIDUOUS AND EVERGREEN SHRUBS
ZONE 5
The cotoneasters include some berrying shrubs that are widely grown in the open garden. One of the most compact, and a useful addition to a trough of rock-garden plants – as much for the tight growth that moulds it over the edge of a container as for its berries – is the evergreen *C. congestus* (Zone 7). Forming a mat or hummock up to 25cm (10in) high but with a spread that can exceed 60cm (2ft), its stiff, closely packed branches are covered in small, dark green leaves. Small pink flowers in early summer are followed by red berries.

Even more distinctive in habit is the deciduous *C. horizontalis* (*below*). The main stems, each with a fishbone pattern of smaller branches, form a fan 60cm (2ft) high and 1.2m (4ft) across. The branches are tightly clothed in neat, dark green leaves; in early summer there are numerous small pink flowers. This shrub is attractive in all seasons but especially in autumn, when the leaves turn red and a thick crop of berries hugs the branches. Although these are eaten by birds, they are often left until well into winter. *C. horizontalis*, which is best grown on its own or with other shrubs in a very large container, tolerates shade but berries most freely when grown in an open spot.

Plant cotoneasters in autumn or from early to mid-spring, using a soil-based compost. Top-dress with fresh mix annually in spring and repot every three to four years.

Cotoneaster *Cotoneaster horizontalis*

GAULTHERIA

Gaultheria
EVERGREEN SHRUB   ZONE 8
The gaultherias, which now include the pernettyas, are among the best of the compact berrying shrubs. They have small white flowers in early summer, with male and female flowers usually borne on different plants. For a good display of berries, female cultivars are best planted as a group with a male plant in a large container. Female cultivars of *G. mucronata* provide a good colour range, from the startling 'White Pearl', through shades of pink in 'Pink Pearl' and 'Rosea', to the stronger reds of 'Cherry Ripe' and the rich 'Mulberry Wine'. These all have a height and spread of 60–90cm (2–3 ft) in sun, and slightly more in shade. A compact male gaultheria, forming a dense hummock 30cm (12in) high and with a spread of 60cm (2ft), is 'Thymifolia'. Its presence will encourage a good set of fruit. Rather similar to the berrying cultivars of *G. mucronata* is *G. × wisleyensis* 'Wisley Pearl', which has mat dark green leaves and bears purplish-maroon berries in autumn. The berries of all the gaultherias are extremely long-lasting.

Plant in autumn or from early to mid-spring, using an ericaceous compost. Top-dress with fresh compost annually in spring, and repot only if the roots become congested. Cut back lightly in spring to keep plants neat and compact.

SQUIRREL-TAIL GRASS, SQUIRREL-TAIL BARLEY

Hordeum jubatum
ANNUAL
This relative of barley is an especially pretty, graceful grass. In early to mid-summer flower spikes up to 60cm (2ft) high arch over the short tuft of blades (*right*). The feathery heads, which give the plant its common names, open green or purplish and turn a light brown.

Sow in pots during late summer or early autumn and overwinter under glass but without heat. Plant in containers in mid-spring, using soil-based compost. Alternatively, sow from early to mid-spring in the container where the plants are to grow and thin the seedlings as necessary.

HARE'S-TAIL GRASS

Lagurus ovatus
ANNUAL

This charming grass has soft, fluffy heads that bob lightly in any breeze. These heads, produced throughout summer, are at first greenish-cream, sometimes tinged purplish-pink, and turn light brown as they age. They are carried on stems up to 50cm (20in) high above clumps of hairy, grey-green foliage that is soft to the touch. Hare's-tail grass is attractive combined with other easy annuals.

Sow in pots during late summer or early autumn and overwinter under glass but without heat. Plant in mid-spring in containers, using soil-based compost. Alternatively, sow where plants are to grow from early to mid-spring. Thin the seedlings as necessary.

FEATHERTOP

Pennisetum villosum
ANNUAL/PERENNIAL   ZONE 8

Although a true perennial in mild climates, feathertop (sometimes listed as *P. longistylum*) is best treated as an annual when grown in a container. It makes a nondescript clump during summer, but comes into its own in autumn, when numerous arching stems carry bristly 10cm (4in) spikes that are a soft creamy pink. This late surprise is a delightful bonus in a mixed planting.

Sow seed in warmth in early spring. Harden seedlings before planting out in a sunny, sheltered spot in late spring, using soil-based compost.

ROSE

Rosa 'Fru Dagmar Hastrup'
SHRUB   ZONE 3

Several roses that produce ornamental hips are too large to be conveniently accommodated in containers. However, 'Fru Dagmar Hastrup' (*right*) is relatively compact, with a height of 90cm (3ft) and a spread of up to 1.2m (4ft). Its single, fragrant, pale pink flowers, borne intermittently throughout summer, are followed by magnificent, tomato-like hips, which are often well coloured before the flowering season is over and remain ornamental for several weeks.
See also pages 136, 142, 154, 164, 170.

SKIMMIA

Skimmia japonica
EVERGREEN SHRUB   ZONE 7

With the evergreen, shade-tolerant skimmias the male and female flowers are borne on separate plants, female plants carrying large crops of conspicuous, long-lasting berries provided there is a male plant close by. The dwarf *S. j.* subsp. *reevesiana*, 45–75cm (18–30in) high with a spread of 90cm (3ft), has white spring flowers followed by crimson fruits which persist through the winter.

A good male that will ensure a set of fruit is the free-flowering cultivar 'Rubella', which is usually less than 4ft (1.2m) in both height and spread. Its buds are an attractive red-brown in winter, then the petals open white, but with a pink tinge derived from the red

stalks. Plant in autumn or mid-spring, using an ericaceous compost. Top-dress yearly in spring with fresh compost; repot only if the roots become congested.
See illustrations pages 122, 123.

Rose *Rosa* 'Fru Dagmar Hastrup'

WINTER CHERRY

Solanum capsicastrum
EVERGREEN SUB-SHRUB   ZONE 9
POISONOUS

The winter cherry (*below left*) is usually grown as an indoor pot plant. Where the weather is mild it can be used outdoors in window boxes and other containers. The copious round scarlet fruits, 1cm (½in) or more across, are set against dark green leaves on a bush 30–45cm (12–18in) high.

Buy well-shaped plants carrying plenty of fruit in late autumn or early winter. Plant outdoors, in full sun, in soil-based or soil-less compost. Pinch back the growing tips of young plants to encourage copious bushy growth.

VIBURNUM, GUELDER ROSE

Viburnum opulus 'Compactum'
SHRUB   ZONE 4

Heads of white flowers in spring, translucent red berries and maple-like leaves that colour well in autumn help to make the guelder rose a very pleasing deciduous shrub. Although the species itself grows to more than 3.7m (12ft), the cultivar 'Compactum', which is free-flowering and bears heavy crops of berries, is usually less than 1.8m (6ft) in height, and a useful plant for containers. The best crops are produced when two or three plants are grown close together in a sunny spot.

Plant in autumn or from early to mid-spring, using soil-based compost. Prune only to remove dead, damaged, and weak growth.

Squirrel-tail grass *Hordeum jubatum*

Winter cherry *Solanum capsicastrum*

USEFUL PLANTS FOR CONTAINERS

These lists are intended as an aid to the selection of plants for containers, supplementing the help provided by the arrangement according to flower and foliage colour and also season in Plants for Containers (*see pages 126–203*). A page number referring to the main entry in that section follows each plant name.

FLOWERING SHRUBS

The following list of flowering shrubs does not include ground-hugging dwarfs. Plants with E after the name are evergreen, those with E/D are of genera that include evergreen and deciduous species and hybrids.

Anisodontea E 158
Brugmansia E 146
Camellia E 156
Choisya E 131
Fuchsia 168
Gaultheria E 202
Hebe E 168–9
Hydrangea 133
Lavandula E 169
Myrtus E 135
Nerium E 163
Pieris E 129
Rhododendron E/D 156–7
Rosa 154
Rosmarinus E 197
Skimmia E 203
Viburnum 203
Yucca E 136

SHRUBS GROWN MAINLY FOR THEIR FOLIAGE

Some of the following shrubs, which do not include ground-hugging dwarfs, have interesting flowers but their chief ornamental value lies in their foliage. Plants with E after the name are evergreen, those with E/D are of genera that include evergreen and deciduous species and hybrids.

Acer 178
Aucuba E 183
Buxus E 179
Chamaecyparis E 179
Cordyline E 179–80
Elaeagnus E/D 192–3
Euonymus E/D 183
Fatshedera E 180
Fatsia E 180
Ilex E 187
Juniperus E 181
Laurus nobilis E 196
Nandina E 190
Pinus E 182

Prunus lusitanica E 182
Salvia officinalis E 170
Thuja E 182

LONG-FLOWERING PLANTS

The following are capable of flowering over a long period, in some cases even for several months. Regular dead-heading will help prolong the season.

Ageratum 173
Argyranthemum 130–31
Begonia × *tuberhybrida* 151–52
Bellis 156
Brachyscome 173–4
Browallia 174
Brugmansia 146
Calendula 146
Calluna 159
Cuphea 146
Diascia 160
Dimorphotheca 132
Erica 137
Felicia 174–5
Fuchsia 168
Heliotropium 169
Hemerocallis 'Stella de Oro' 141
Impatiens 161–2
Nerium 163
Osteospermum 135
Pelargonium 153–4
Petunia 176
Rosa (some) 154
Salvia (many) 170
Scaevola 176
Tagetes 148
Tropaeolum majus 149
Verbena 171
Viola 143–4

ORNAMENTALS WITH SCENTED FLOWERS

All of the following are fragrant but the strength of the scent is not necessarily constant and appreciation varies from individual to individual.

Brachyscome 173–4
Choisya 131
Crocus (most) *138*
Dianthus 160
Elaeagnus 192–3
Erysimum 138
Heliotropium 169
Hyacinthus 172
Iris 144
Jasminum 133
Lathyrus 162
Lavandula 169
Lilium (many) 134
Lobularia 135

Lonicera 153
Narcissus (most) 138–9
Nicotiana 135
Primula auricula 139
Reseda 136
Rosa (many) 154
Skimmia 203
Tropaeolum majus 149
Wisteria 177

ORNAMENTALS WITH AROMATIC FOLIAGE

In addition to the following plants, most herbs (*see pages 196-7*) have strongly aromatic leaves.

Artemisia 192
Chamaecyparis 179
Choisya 131
Helichrysum italicum 193
Lavandula 169
Myrtus 135
Nepeta 176
Pelargonium (Scented-leaved exceptionally aromatic) 153–4
Pinus 182
Salvia (many) *170*
Santolina 195
Thuja 182
Thymus *197*

CLIMBING PLANTS

To this list of plants can be added several vegetables, of which runner beans are the most ornamental.

Bougainvillea 152
Clematis 131–2
Cobaea 167–8
Jasminum 133
Ipomoea 175
Lapageria 162
Lathyrus 162
Lonicera 153
Rhodochiton 170
Rosa (some) 154
Tropaeolum (some) 149
Wisteria 177

TRAILING PLANTS

Those listed with an asterisk* are grown mainly for their flowers, those without mainly for their value as foliage plants. All are particularly useful in hanging baskets. Most of the plants listed as climbers (*see above*) can also be grown without supports and allowed to trail from tall containers.

Begonia × *tuberhybrida* (some)* 151–2
Bidens* 140
Convolvulus sabatius* 174

Diascia (some)* 160
Fuchsia (some)* 168
Glechoma 186
Hedera 180
Helichrysum petiolare 193
Lamium 187
Lobelia (some)* 175–6
Lotus 147
Lysimachia 185
Pelargonium (Ivy-leaved)* 153–4
Petunia (many)* 176
Plecostachys 194–5
*Scaevola** 176
Verbena (some)* 171

DWARF BULBS

In addition to the many tall or medium bulbs there are a number of small size that do well in containers. Many flower in early spring but some bloom in autumn or even in winter.

Chionodoxa 172
Crocus 138
Cyclamen 165
Fritillaria 166
Galanthus 137
Iris 144
Muscari 172
Narcissus (some) 138
Scilla 173
Tulipa (some) 150–51

ROCK-GARDEN PLANTS

The following low-growing plants are suitable for growing in troughs or sinks and look attractive combined with dwarf bulbs. Dress the surface of containers with stone chippings.

Aethionema 158
Anacyclus 130
Anthemis 130
Aquilegia (some) 167
Armeria 151
Artemisia schmidtiana 'Nana' 192
Aubrieta 166
Aurinia 138
Campanula 174
Cotoneaster congestus 202
Dianthus 160
Euphorbia myrsinites 138
Geranium (some) 161
Helianthemum 141
Lavandula (some) 169
Phlox subulata 129
Primula auricula 139
Pulsatilla 166
Raoulia 195
Salix 'Boydii' 195
Saxifraga 140
Sedum spathulifolium 191
Sempervivum 191

PLANTS FOR SMALL POOLS

Many aquatics and marginals are very vigorous but the following genera include plants suitable for small pools.

Eichhornia 174
Nymphaea (some) 142
Juncus 181
Typha 182

SHADE-TOLERANT PLANTS

All of the following plants are to some extent tolerant of shade and those marked with an asterisk* are especially so.

Acer 178
*Adiantum** 178
Ajuga 188
Alchemilla 178
*Asplenium** 179
Astilbe 158–9
*Athyrium** 179
*Aucuba** 183
Begonia × *tuberhybrida* 151–2
*Bergenia** 179
*Buxus** 179
Camellia 156
*Cyclamen** 165
*Dryopteris** 180
Fatshedera 180
Fatsia 180
Fuchsia 168
Glechoma 186
Hakonechloa 184
*Hedera** 180–81
Heuchera 189–90
*Hosta** 184
Houttuynia 190
Hydrangea 133
Impatiens 161–2
Lobelia 175–6
*Matteuccia** 181
Mimulus 147
Myosotis 173
Nicotiana 135
Osmunda 181
*Polystichum** 182
Rhododendron 156–7
Skimmia 203
Viola 143–4

SURVIVORS

Even plants that show remarkable tolerance of drought in the open garden may succumb as container specimens when not watered regularly, their restricted root run placing them at a disadvantage. The following, however, will often survive short periods of neglect.

Aethionema 158
Agapanthus 173

Anacyclus 130
Anthemis 130
Arctotis 145
Argyranthemum 130–31
Artemisia 192
Aucuba 183
Aurinia 138
Bergenia 179
Bidens 140
Brachyglottis 192
Bougainvillea 152
Calendula 146
Convolvulus sabatius 174
Cyclamen 165
Dianthus 160
Dimorphotheca 132
Elaeagnus 192–3
Euphorbia 138
Felicia 174–5
Ficus 198
Hedera 180–81
Helianthemum 141
Helichrysum 193
Heliotropium 169
Iberis 133
Lavandula 169
Lobularia 135
Melianthus 194
Lotus 147
Nepeta 176
Nerium 163
Osteospermum 135
Pinus 182
Pelargonium 153–4
Rosmarinus 197
Ruta 197
Salvia 170
Santolina 195
Scaevola 176
Sedum 191
Sempervivum 191
Senecio 195
Stachys 195
Thymus 197
Yucca 136

ORNAMENTALS EASILY RAISED FROM SEED

In addition to these plants, several vegetables, including beans and peas, are easy to grow from seed.

Calendula 146
Clarkia 159
Cosmos 132
Helianthus 141
Iberis 133
Lavatera 162
Lathyrus 162
Lobularia 135
Reseda 136
Tropaeolum 149